AUGSBURG SERMONS

SERMONS ON
EPISTLE TEXTS FROM
THE NEW LECTIONARY
AND CALENDAR

augsburg sermons

EPISTLES
SERIES A

AUGSBURG PUBLISHING HOUSE
MINNEAPOLIS, MINNESOTA

AUGSBURG SERMONS—EPISTLES—SERIES A

Copyright © 1977 Augsburg Publishing House

Library of Congress Catalog Card No. 77-72464

International Standard Book No. 0-8066-1581-8

All rights reserved. No part of this book may be used or reproduced in any manner whatsoever without written permission except in the case of brief quotations embodied in critical articles and reviews. For information address Augsburg Publishing House, 426 South Fifth Street, Minneapolis, Minnesota 55415.

Scripture quotations unless otherwise noted are from the Revised Standard Version of the Bible, copyright 1946, 1952, and 1971 by the Division of Christian Education of the National Council of Churches.

MANUFACTURED IN THE UNITED STATES OF AMERICA

Contents

Introduction   11

FIRST SUNDAY IN ADVENT
Isa. 2:1-5   Matt. 24:37-44
Knowing God's Hour — Rom. 13:11-14   Ralph Wallace   15

SECOND SUNDAY IN ADVENT
Isa. 11:1-10   Matt. 3:1-12
Expect — Rom. 15:4-13   Richard O. Hoyer   19

THIRD SUNDAY IN ADVENT
Isa. 35:1-10   Matt. 11:2-11
Be Patient — James 5:7-10   Richard A. Hodges   23

FOURTH SUNDAY IN ADVENT
Isa. 7:10-14 (15-17)   Matt. 1:18-25
Miracle of Miracles — Rom. 1:1-7   Earl E. Matson   27

THE NATIVITY OF OUR LORD — Christmas Day
Isa. 52:7-10   John 1:1-18
Cosmic Christmas — Heb. 1:1-9   Dennis V. Griffin   31

FIRST SUNDAY AFTER CHRISTMAS
Isa. 63:7-9   Matt. 2:13-15, 19-23
To Receive and to Thank —
Gal. 4:4-7   Frederick W. Kemper   35

THE EPIPHANY OF OUR LORD
Isa. 60:1-6   Matt. 2:1-12
A Messiah for All People —
Eph. 3:2-12   Louis H. Valbracht   39

THE BAPTISM OF OUR LORD — First Sunday after the Epiphany
Isa. 42:1-7   Matt. 3:13-17
The Few and the Many — Acts 10:34-38   Richard L. Trost   45

SECOND SUNDAY AFTER THE EPIPHANY
Isa. 49:1-6   John 1:29-41
A Glory to Be Shared — 1 Cor. 1:1-9   Edgar C. Rakow   48

THIRD SUNDAY AFTER THE EPIPHANY
Isa. 9:1-4   Matt. 4:12-23
Holding the Family Together —
1 Cor. 1:10-17   Raymond W. Hedberg   52

FOURTH SUNDAY AFTER THE EPIPHANY
Zeph. 2:3; 3:11-13   Matt. 5:1-12
God's Serendipity for You —
1 Cor. 1:26-31   George S. Johnson   56

THE TRANSFIGURATION OF OUR LORD —
Last Sunday after the Epiphany
Exod. 24:12, 15-18   Matt. 17:1-9
How to Lighten Your Burden —
2 Peter 1:16-19 (20-21)   George F. Lobien   60

THE FIRST SUNDAY IN LENT
Gen. 2:7-9, 15-17; 3:1-7   Matt. 4:1-11
A Word for Us Moderns —
Rom. 5:12 (13-16) 17-19   K. Glen Johnson   65

SECOND SUNDAY IN LENT
Gen. 12:1-8   John 4:5-26
God's Strange Economy —
Rom. 4:1-5, 13-17   Allan H. Sager   69

THIRD SUNDAY IN LENT
Isa. 42:14-21   John 9:1-41
From Darkness to Light — Eph. 5:8-14   David A. Preisinger   74

FOURTH SUNDAY IN LENT
Hos. 5:15—6:2   Matt. 20:17-28
The Cartography of Faith —
Rom. 8:1-10   Constance F. Parvey   78

FIFTH SUNDAY IN LENT
Ezek. 37:1-3 (4-10) 11-14   John 11:1-53
The Spirit in You — Rom. 8:11-19   E. Silas Torvend   83

SUNDAY OF THE PASSION — Palm Sunday
Isa. 50:4-9a   Matt. 21:1-11
Power—Abuse and Use — Phil. 2:5-11   Richard J. Gotsch   87

MAUNDY THURSDAY
Exod. 12:1-4   John 13:1-17
Food for Thought — 1 Cor. 11:17-32   Ronald C. Peterson   91

GOOD FRIDAY
Isa. 52:13—53:12   John 18:1—19:42
Jesus Is Our Great High Priest —
Heb. 4:14—5:10   Roger D. Pittelko   95

THE RESURRECTION OF OUR LORD — Easter Day
Acts 10:34-43   John 20:1-9
Because of the Resurrection — Col. 3:1-4   Richard Rehfeldt   98

SECOND SUNDAY OF EASTER
Acts 2:42-47   John 20:19-31
Cause for Joy! — 1 Peter 1:3-9   Merle G. Franke   103

THIRD SUNDAY OF EASTER
Acts 2:22-32   Luke 24:13-35
First the Ending, Then the Beginning —
1 Peter 1:17-21   Michael L. Sherer   107

FOURTH SUNDAY OF EASTER
Acts 2:36-41   John 10:1-10
I Sit and Look Out — 1 Peter 2:19-25   Edward M. Ralph   111

FIFTH SUNDAY OF EASTER
Acts 6:1-7   John 14:1-12
Called to Witness — 1 Peter 2:4-10   David R. Gerberding   114

SIXTH SUNDAY OF EASTER
Acts 8:5-8, 14-17   John 14:15-21
The Perfect Comeback —
1 Peter 3:15-18   Walter C. Huffman   118

THE ASCENSION OF OUR LORD
Acts 1:1-11   Luke 24:44-53
More Light from Our Ascended Lord —
Eph. 1:16-23   Henry F. Fingerlin   122

SEVENTH SUNDAY OF EASTER
Acts 1:6-14   John 17:1-11
The Passion of the Church — 1 Peter 4:13-19   Paul F. Bosch   127

THE DAY OF PENTECOST
Joel 2:28-29   John 20:19-23
The Miracle of Pentecost—Then and Now —
Acts 2:1-21   Charles H. Maahs   131

THE HOLY TRINITY — First Sunday after Pentecost
Deut. 4:32-34, 39-40   Matt. 28:16-20
Children of the Triune God —
Rom. 8:14-17   Harold F. Dicke   135

SECOND SUNDAY AFTER PENTECOST
Deut. 11:18-21, 26-28   Matt. 7:21-29
Getting Right With God —
Rom. 3:21-25a, 27-28   Charles A. Endter   139

THIRD SUNDAY AFTER PENTECOST
Hos. 6:1-6   Matt. 9:1-13
How You Can Have a Stronger Faith —
Rom. 4:18-25   Larry Christenson   144

FOURTH SUNDAY AFTER PENTECOST
Exod. 19:2-6a   Matt. 9:35—10:7
Saved for Living — Rom. 5:6-11   John H. Krahn   149

FIFTH SUNDAY AFTER PENTECOST
Jer. 20:7-13   Matt. 10:26-33
Without Parallel — Rom. 5:12-15   James E. Bennett   153

SIXTH SUNDAY AFTER PENTECOST
Jer. 28:5-9   Matt. 10:34-42
What's It Like? — Rom. 6:2b-11   Dawn M. Proux   156

SEVENTH SUNDAY AFTER PENTECOST
Zech. 9:9-10   Matt. 11:25-30
Saint and Sinner — Rom. 7:15-25a Herb Schmidt   161

EIGHTH SUNDAY AFTER PENTECOST
Isa. 55:10-11   Matt. 13:1-9 (18-22)
Living the Double Life — Rom. 8:18-23   Philip A. Jordan   166

NINTH SUNDAY AFTER PENTECOST
Isa. 44:6-8   Matt. 13:24-30 (36-43)
God Knows You! — Rom. 8:26-27   Oscar Sommerfeld 171

TENTH SUNDAY AFTER PENTECOST
1 Kings 3:5-12   Matt. 13:44-52
In Spite of Everything — Rom. 8:28-30   Ronald C. Starenko 175

ELEVENTH SUNDAY AFTER PENTECOST
Isa. 55:1-5   Matt. 14:13-21
God Is for Us — Rom. 8:35-39   Wallace E. Fisher 178

TWELFTH SUNDAY AFTER PENTECOST
1 Kings 19:9-18   Matt. 14:22-33
The Struggles in Christian Witnessing —
Rom. 9:1-5   Paul F. Reyelts 183

THIRTEENTH SUNDAY AFTER PENTECOST
Isa. 56:1, 6-8   Matt. 15:21-28
Miserere — Rom. 11:13-15, 29-32   Dale D. Hansen 188

FOURTEENTH SUNDAY AFTER PENTECOST
Exod. 6:2-8   Matt. 16:13-20
He Puts Us in Our Place — Rom. 11:33-36   Richard I. Preis 191

FIFTEENTH SUNDAY AFTER PENTECOST
Jer. 15:15-21   Matt. 16:21-26
The Transformed Life — Rom. 12:1-8   Carl R. Evenson 196

SIXTEENTH SUNDAY AFTER PENTECOST
Ezek. 33:7-9   Matt. 18:15-20
Authority and Power — Rom. 13:1-10   Edward C. May 200

SEVENTEENTH SUNDAY AFTER PENTECOST
Gen. 50:15-21   Matt. 18:21-35
Our Unity in Christ — Rom. 14:7-9   Gerald O. Pedersen 205

EIGHTEENTH SUNDAY AFTER PENTECOST
Isa. 55:6-9   Matt. 20:1-16
What a Fellowship! — Phil. 1:3-5, 19-27   Nelson W. Trout 211

NINETEENTH SUNDAY AFTER PENTECOST
Ezek. 18:25-32   Matt. 21:28-32
Your Life in Christ — Phil. 2:1-5 (6-11)   Robert Kamprath 214

TWENTIETH SUNDAY AFTER PENTECOST
Isa. 5:1-7   Matt. 21:33-43
Experience Joy and Peace — Phil. 4:4-8   Carl W. Weber 218

TWENTY-FIRST SUNDAY AFTER PENTECOST
Isa. 25:6-9   Matt. 22:1-10 (11-14)
This Is the Secret — Phil. 4:10-13, 19-20   Harald D. Grindal 223

TWENTY-SECOND SUNDAY AFTER PENTECOST
Isa. 45:1-7   Matt. 22:15-21
God Measures Our Church—1 Thess. 1:1-5a   W. A. Poovey 228

TWENTY-THIRD SUNDAY AFTER PENTECOST
Lev. 19:1-2, 15-18   Matt. 22:34-40
It's the Wound! — 1 Thess. 1:5b-10   Alan L. Solmonson 233

TWENTY-FOURTH SUNDAY AFTER PENTECOST
Zeph. 1:14-16   Matt. 25:1-13
Rapture or Resurrection? —
1 Thess. 4:13-14 (15-18)   Paul G. Hansen 237

TWENTY-FIFTH SUNDAY AFTER PENTECOST
Hos. 11:1-4, 8-9   Matt. 25:14-30
The Tension of Now — 1 Thess. 5:1-11   Robert H. Shoffner 241

TWENTY-SIXTH SUNDAY AFTER PENTECOST
Mal. 2:1-10   Matt. 23:1-12
God's New Way — 1 Thess. 2:8-13   Karl Thiele 246

LAST SUNDAY AFTER PENTECOST — Christ the King
Ezek. 34:11-16, 23-24   Matt. 25:31-46
The Kingly Rule of Christ —
1 Cor. 15:20-28   Raymond D. Christenson 251

A DAY OF THANKSGIVING
Deut. 8:1-10   Luke 17:11-19
Thanks—and No Thanks — 1 Tim. 2:1-4   Steve Swanson 253

Introduction

The Calendar and Lectionary introduced by the Inter-Lutheran Commission on Worship (ILCW) in Advent 1973 has become one of the most popular liturgical tools for contemporary worship and preaching. It is the answer to many requests in Lutheran churches for a revision of the church year and a new lectionary.

The church year calendar has been modified and modernized. The lectionary has been extensively overhauled by drawing on parallel efforts by the Protestant Episcopal, Presbyterian, and Roman Catholic churches.

The New Church Year Calendar

This new calendar is similar to all previous calendars in that Easter is still the heart of it, and the Gospel still tells the story of Jesus Christ throughout the year.

The revisions in the new calendar are these:

- The *gesima* Sundays, sometimes known as pre-Lent, are now listed as Sundays after Epiphany. The season of Epiphany is therefore lengthened, which makes possible a fuller development of Epiphany themes.

- The Sundays between Easter and Pentecost will be known as the Sundays *of Easter*, rather than *after* Easter.

- The Latin titles for the Sundays of Lent and Easter have been deleted.

- Passion Sunday has been moved from the Fifth Sunday in Lent to the Sixth Sunday (Palm Sunday).

- The Sundays in the Pentecost-Trinity season have been numbered *after Pentecost* instead of *after Trinity*.

- In color terminology, *purple* replaces *violet,* and *red* is suggested for use during Holy Week.

The New Lectionary

The new lectionary presents a three-year cycle of lessons for the church year. The texts designated for the specific year will be chosen alternatively from Series A, Series B, or Series C of this lectionary.

This lectionary follows the traditional pattern of appointing an Old Testament lesson, an Epistle, and a Gospel for each Sunday. During the Easter season, however, a reading from the Acts of the Apostles replaces the Old Testament lesson.

The Epistles of Series A

The first three volumes of *Augsburg Sermons* based on the Gospels are now available. Series A is based on Matthew; Series B on Mark; and Series C on Luke. *Augsburg Sermons,* Epistles, Series C is also available.

Beginning in Advent of 1977, Series A will again provide the texts for worship and preaching. This time, however, the Epistles will be highlighted, and therefore the present volume is offered as a year-long resource for preaching and meditation on the Epistle texts for the next church year.

This book, like its predecessors is offered in the hope that the sermons, the calendar, and the lectionary will contribute to the renewal of preaching.

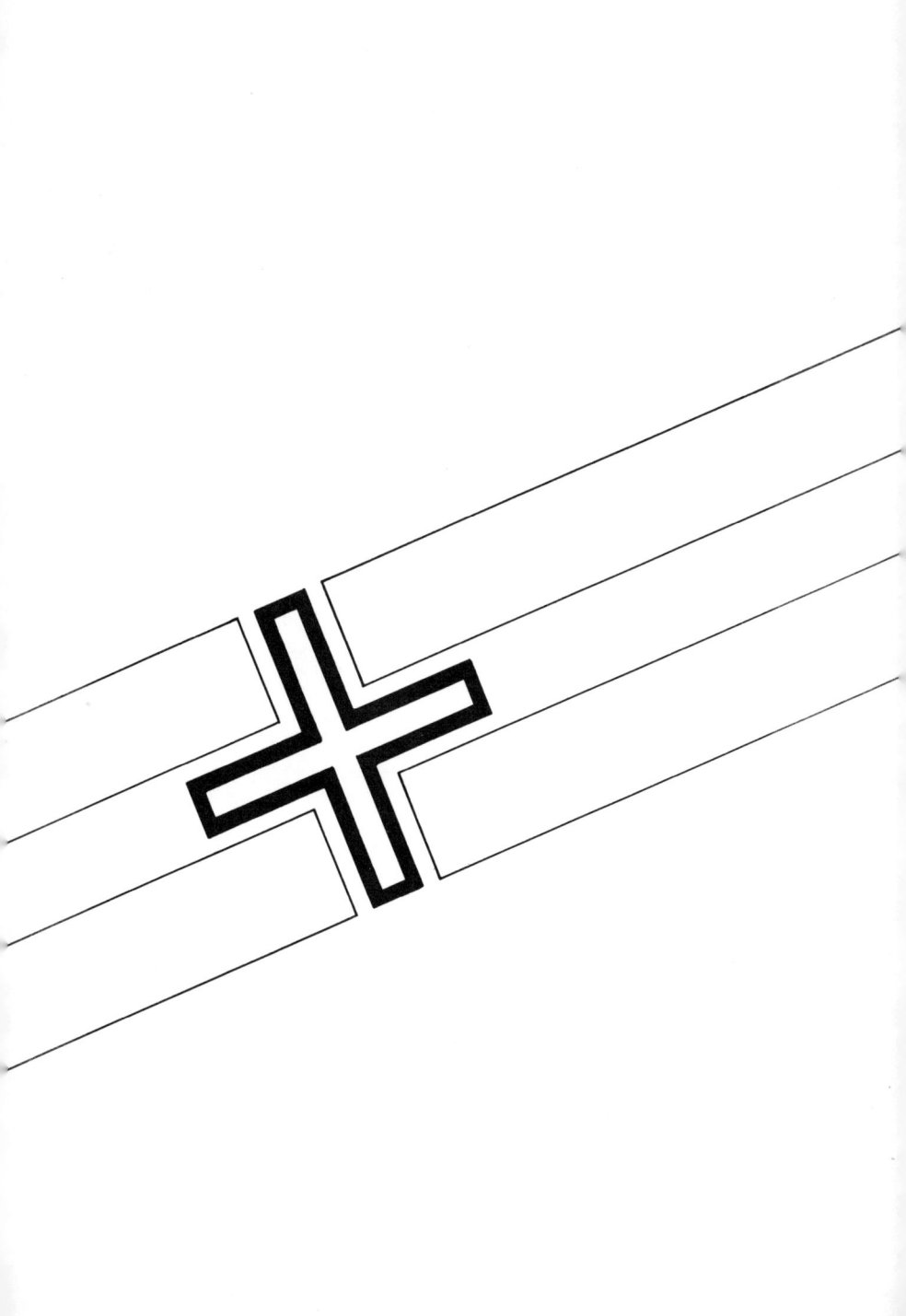

KNOWING GOD'S HOUR
First Sunday in Advent
Romans 13:11-14

There are many good personal reasons for knowing what time it is. Knowing the hour makes the difference between cereal and steak, between work and rest, between repairing a leaky faucet and making love. Knowing the hour determines whether we will be takers or givers, whether we will be spongelike offspring soaking up the resources of our parents or supportive sons and daughters who are meeting the needs of adjusting mothers and fathers. Knowing the hour even helps distinguish normalcy from abnormality. Being faddy, flippant, and frivolous is acceptable in the hour of adolescence, but those characteristics in a fifty-year-old raises eyebrows and causes concern.

There are good eschatological reasons for knowing the hour. Knowing the hour helps bring purpose and direction to the many experiences that are ours. We do make a greater effort to shove ourselves into the molds of acceptable morality if a doctor tells us that we have limited life. The awareness of our day of death and of the end of our earthly existence turns us toward greater concern for others and toward greater contributions to them.

There are good personal and eschatological reasons for knowing the hour. So five-and-ten-cent stores sell imitation watches for prekindergarten children. We put Mickey Mouse and Pluto timepieces on little arms. Inexpensive, digital computers are available for preteens. And we teach them all that it is time for a nap when the little hand is at the one and the big hand is at the three. We teach them to act differently when the twelfth month has arrived. They must be good little boys and girls.

Knowing God's Hour

If there are good personal and eschatological reasons for knowing the time, there are even better ones for knowing God's hour. Knowing God's hour gets us above merely noting the difference between cereal and steak, work and rest, plumbing and making love. Knowing God's hour gives meaning to those mundane experiences, just as knowing his hour moves us toward being givers rather than takers and toward normalcy rather than abnormality. Knowing that this is God's hour means that all meals can be his means, that labor and relaxation can be his channels, that plumbing and intimacy can be his tools for upbuilding his people. By understanding this hour to be God's, you and I can be more than faddy takers and flippant sponges. We can be God's witnesses more effectively. For we hear and believe the Apostle's saying, "For salvation is nearer to us now than when we first believed; the night is far gone, the day is at hand."

So St. Paul teaches us to tell God's time. In the Epistle for today, the First Sunday in Advent, the Apostle tells us how to recognize the hour of God. Always, at the hour of God, *the little hand is at the Law and the big hand is at the Gospel.*

The Little Hand Is at the Law

In our home we are just beginning to live through something that has become passé to many of you, though I am sure you remember the experience well. Dating is becoming the big thing in our home and the strange thing about having a date is that it applies the law. As the all-important evening draws nearer and nearer, sleep becomes more and more difficult. Wakefulness widens, alertness intensifies, rapidity of speech rises, excitement expands until it borders on insomnia and forces the super-sensitive person into an endless series of doings. If a new outfit can't be purchased, a different combination of old clothes must be discovered. The most perfect schedule for the evening must be decided; one that will preserve dignity and provide privacy. Then the person must be preened, from shining hair to painted toe. And, of course, there is that endless process of putting off and putting on. The wardrobe has to be gone through several times, with most of it strewn over bed and chair and mirror when the clock strikes the deadline. All of this wakefulness and putting off and on is made necessary by the coming of a particular person at a particular time. The advent of a date claims the teenager. It controls the youth. It demands certain behavior and forces compliance. We know what time it is when we see the little hand at the Law.

St. Paul indicates that the hour of God is recognizable in the same fashion. Whether his hour is the personal one or the eschatological one, whether his hour is his presence in the present or at the parousia, it is known when the little hand is at the Law.

As in the case of the teenaged daters, our appointment with God in Christ keeps us awake and alert. Suddenly we realize that we have been called out of sin, and signed with the cross, and sealed in Baptism. We become aware that we have been chosen and set aside as new creatures who are guaranteed a new relationship with the coming One. Our eyes are opened to the realization that we have been moved out of the realm of darkness into light, out of anonymity into being somebody, out of mediocrity into specialty. Suddenly we are aware of what we can become through the means of grace. We celebrate the Communion because the Spirit in us forces us to feel that that celebration is a part of our preparation and preservation until he comes. God's invitation to be with him compels every aspect of our being to reach out to him.

That kind of sanctification, St. Paul says, also involves a great deal of putting off. No longer will there be room in our lives for the open and shameless boisterousness of perverse peer groups that moves from beer behind the drive-in to vodka at the summer home to marijuana when the authorities are away to the bed of illicit sex. There is absolutely no getting around the demands brought by God's invitation to meet and be with him, either now or tomorrow. We are compelled to rid ourselves of that which St. Paul calls "the works of darkness." We have to take off that which Isaiah labels "our righteous deeds" that "are like a polluted garment."

Yes, God's making a date with us in Christ certainly does introduce us to the Law. We know that God's hour has arrived *when the little hand is at the Law*. A little-handed clock, though, is not precise enough. Accuracy and truth depend on knowing where the big hand is. So St. Paul adds that the hour of God is known

When the Big Hand Is at the Gospel

Return with me, for a moment, to the illustration of dating. What is it that enables a person to accept the demands of a date? What makes us willing to meet the challenges of a new companionship? Why do we want to live under the laws that a new relationship imposes on our lives? I find it amazing that insecure adolescents will crawl out on a limb again and again and risk their personal sense of worth by chancing rejection. That date may not ask them out again, ever. I am astonished that lethargic ladies and gentlemen can burn up so many hamburgers and french fries in getting ready for one evening out when they so recently did not have the energy for raking leaves and reordering rooms. I am flabbergasted by youth who want the foundation of the family and the discipline of the home, yet will revolt so violently for the freedom to stay out into the dangerous hours.

What motivates that puzzling notion in the lives of our youth? It is the prospect of a promise fulfilled. It is the chance of a creature completed. It is the possibility of a person's becoming what he or she is intended to be. There is good news in being asked out. It is the good news of maturity mastered, of goals gained, of human purpose accomplished. In our everyday living we know what time it is when we see the big hand at the good news.

Just so, St. Paul seems to balance and match the demands of God's hour with the motivation and comfort that God's hour always brings with it. Not only does he talk about a time for wakefulness and for casting off works of darkness, but also he speaks of a time of near salvation and putting on Jesus Christ.

The Apostle took a positive cue from Matthew and Mark and made it even more comforting. They said of God's coming in Christ, "And if the days had not been shortened, no human being would be saved; but for the sake of the elect those days will be shortened." He added, "For salvation is nearer to us now than when we first believed." In other words, God is doing things personally and eschatologically right now. He is sending his Spirit to build on our baptism and to confirm us through our communion and to wax us faithful through his Word. He is crashing in on us with clear witnesses throughout the world that are unsurpassed in recent history, in order that our personal salvation seems more sure and in order that the final day of salvation seems just around the corner.

The Apostle also indicates that God is getting us together in this hour, and finally tomorrow, when he refers to the present as a time for putting on Jesus Christ. Every one of God's hours is an opportunity to fall back on our baptism, back into the life and death and resurrection of Jesus Christ, and forward into new Christian adventures. Every one of God's minutes is the occasion for our having the filthy rags of unrighteousness forgiven and for being decked out in our Lord's acceptable crosswork. Every one of God's seconds holds our potential maturity in the Master. In fact, if we view time as God does in his Word, it is a process in which he is moving his creation toward its commendable completion. His hour is his effort to make our salvation more real and realized than it was a second ago. That is the good news. That is the Gospel. That is the remarkable report that God is doing for us all those things that he demands of us. And when we see the big hand at that Gospel we not only know that God's hour has arrived, but we also rejoice in it.

RALPH WALLACE
St. Paul Evangelical Lutheran Church
Columbia, South Carolina

"What Do You Expect?"

EXPECT
Second Sunday in Advent
Romans 15:4-13

In the minds of most people hoping is really nothing more than wishing. And wishing is a waste of time. Ever since we've been old enough to know that there is no Santa Claus we've known that wishes don't come true. So hoping, like wishing, we know to be futile, silly.

But our brother Paul in the Epistle this morning calls upon us to hope. Does that mean we should live in a dream world, wistfully wishing that things were not the way they really are? Is that what religion is all about? No. To hope in Bible language is not wishing at all, but confidently expecting! So when Paul today calls on us to hope in God, that means we are called to live before him in confident expectation.

We Don't Expect Much

So, what do you expect from God? Not, what do you wish would happen, but what do you confidently expect God to do? I suppose, if we're very honest, we'd have to say, "Not much, really. We *ask* him to do a lot. We pray and pray, but it's not often we get what we ask for, so we've pretty well given that up, too." We don't expect much from God. We make our own way through life, struggling and fighting to get ahead, worrying and fussing and sweating to make ends meet. And we manage, with a little help from our friends. No, we don't expect much from God. Of course when terrible emergencies strike and no one can help us, then we'll turn to God as an act of desperation. When we are terribly sick and the doctors say there's nothing more they can do, then we'll turn to God. When we are in trouble beyond any human help, then we'll pray. When we are facing death, then we'll plead for mercy. But even then I don't think we really expect God to do anything. It's more an act of desperation. Wishful thinking.

No, we don't expect much from God. And that's really pretty serious. Somebody was asked once what he did for exercise, and he said, "Oh, whenever I feel the need to exercise, I lie down until the feeling passes." And everybody laughs. But a doctor might not laugh at all and think him very foolish for so neglecting his heart. So when we are asked what we expect from God, and we say, "Nothing, really," that's not something we should take casually. To expect nothing from God is to get nothing, and if we get nothing from God we are left with only death. Our lack of hope, our failure to expect blessing from God is a sign and symptom of our sin, the tragic consequence of our common rebellion against God.

So it is the will of God for us again today that we be moved to hope! He wants us to be on tiptoe with expectation for his presence in our lives, as a child eagerly expects the coming of Christmas.

How Can We Expect?

But how can we make ourselves hope? Just as we can't bring ourselves to believe in Santa Claus again, how can we bring ourselves to have hope and expect blessing from God? Well, maybe we can't. But God can do it to us. Listen to our brother Paul: "Whatever was written in former days was written for our instruction, that by steadfastness and by the encouragement of the scriptures we might have hope." Paul found the power to hope in the Scriptures. In those sacred writings he found testimony to Jesus of Nazareth as the Messiah sent by God to redeem us from slavery to sin and death, to purify us, to make us the people of God now and throughout eternity. We find that in the Bible too. And we have it much more clearly than Paul did, because we've got the New Testament. Here is the good news. Here is the proclamation that God so loved the world that he gave his only son that whoever believes in him should not perish but have eternal life. Here is everything that makes life worth living.

But there's more than information here. There's power! We don't read the Bible the way we read a textbook, we use it the way we would a battery or a dynamo. We plug into it and it does things to us! Paul says the Bible was written so that "by steadfastness and encouragement of the scriptures we might have hope." Then he says, "May the God of steadfastness and encouragement grant you . . ." and so on. The steadfastness and encouragement that the Scriptures give is the steadfastness and encouragement of God himself! God speaks to you through the Bible. That's what we mean when we say that the Bible is inspired. God speaks to you. God comes to you. He tells you the good news of his love in Jesus Christ; and the Holy Spirit, as Paul says, "fills us with all joy and peace in believing so that . . . we may abound in hope!"

When you were a child you believed in Santa Claus because Mom and Dad created that faith in you by telling you stories about him. Thus you were filled with eager expectation for Christmas. Now you believe in Jesus your Redeemer because God himself has told you about him in the Bible and created faith in your hearts by the power of his Spirit. There's a big difference, of course. Mom and Dad were fooling you about Santa, but God is not fooling us about Jesus. Here's where we find hope. God's word makes us expect great blessing from him!

What Do We Expect?

And what do we expect? Children expect toys and playthings from Santa Claus. What do we expect from God? Listen to Paul: "For I tell you that Christ became a servant to the circumcised to show God's truthfulness, in order to confirm the promises given to the patriarchs, and in order that the Gentiles might glorify God for his mercy." Two things you may expect from him: mercy, and the keeping of his promises.

First, he gives you mercy. He forgives your sin at the cost of the sacrifice of the Lamb of God. He does not hold your sin against you. He never will. You will not get what you deserve—Christ got what you deserve. Instead you get what he deserved—glory, and a throne at the right hand of God.

Second, you may expect him to keep his promises. And those promises are awesome. The Bible is full of them.

• He promises protection: "When you pass through the waters I will be with you; and through the rivers, they shall not overwhelm you; when you walk through fire you shall not be burned, and the flame shall not consume you. For I am the LORD your God, the Holy One of Israel, your Savior" (Isa. 43:2-3).

• He promises to guide us on the twisted road through life: "And I will lead the blind in a way that they know not, in paths that they have not known I will guide them. I will turn the darkness before them into light, the rough places into level ground. These things I will do, and I will not forsake them" (Isa. 42:16).

• He even promises heaven: Jesus said, "When I go and prepare a place for you, I will come again and will take you to myself, that where I am you may be also" (John 14:3).

That's what you can expect, people of God. Not toys and playthings. Not quick and easy answers to all our petty and often unwise prayers. You cannot expect him to do things your way. But he does give you mercy, and he does keep his promises to protect, and guide, and bring you to heaven. Expect that!

How Do We Expect?

And then look what happens. Paul lets us know that people who hope are people who are steadfast. That's the opposite, you see, of being people who expect nothing, who ignore God. We are steadfast! We live with God in faith and prayer. We do not use him to satisfy our cravings; we serve him. Standing steadfast on his promises, we overcome our doubts with trust. In the words of John the Baptist this morning, people who are steadfast are people who are always repenting. Repentance is more than being sorry, it is turning to God. People who hope are people who are always turning to God and standing steadfast beside him.

Most important of all, people who hope are people who live in harmony. Paul writes: "May the God of steadfastness and encouragement grant you to live in such harmony with one another, in accord with Christ Jesus, that together you may with one voice glorify the God and Father of our Lord Jesus Christ. Welcome one another, therefore, as Christ has welcomed you, for the glory of God." "Live in harmony," he says, "Welcome one another." That means more than be hospitable. The word Paul uses here means "take to oneself." Accept one another. Be one together. "As Christ has welcomed (or accepted) you!" Christ does not withhold his acceptance of you until you meet his standards. He takes you as you are, and forgives you, and by the power of his love transforms you. We who hope find power to accept one another that way. We have our faults. We have prickly personalities. We are often crass and boorish and hurt one another's feelings and sensibilities. We are often downright ugly or mean or lazy or dishonest. Nevertheless, we who hope accept, and forgive, and love one another into wholeness.

A brother and sister I know used to fight with each other an awful lot when they were little children. It was pretty mean and ugly sometimes. But on Christmas eve they would sit side by side and even arm in arm before the Christmas tree in rapt attention as father began to give out the gifts. It can be that way with us. With our minds and hearts focused in eager expectation on the Christ and on what he gives to us, we cannot be distracted into fights and squabbles, into meanness and cruelty. People who hope accept each other and live in harmony. That's what the Bible said in the First Lesson this morning: "The wolf shall dwell with the lamb, and the leopard shall lie down with the kid, and the calf and the lion and the fatling together, and a little child shall lead them. They shall not hurt or destroy in all my holy mountain; for the earth shall be full of the knowledge of the Lord, as the waters cover the sea." As, good peope, isn't that something to hope for, something to look forward to with eager expectation? And it can begin right now, for people who live in harmony with one another.

People of God, no more for us the glum despair, the gloomy scramble through life as people who have to make their own way, who expect nothing from God. We have seen the Christ in the manger of the Holy Scriptures, and with "all joy and peace in believing, we abound in hope!"

RICHARD O. HOYER
The Lutheran Church of the Redeemer
Philadelphia, Pennsylvania

BE PATIENT

Third Sunday in Advent

James 5:7-10

How many times have we been admonished to be patient? How many times have we admonished someone else to be patient? It happens many times in the course of a month at our house. I'm sure it also happens many times at your house. Children come in from playing, they are hungry, they want to eat right now "or else they will die." But mother says, "Be patient, dinner will be ready in a few minutes." We are all experiencing a lot of impatience during this season of Advent. Gifts appear under the tree and everyone, children and adults, wonders what they contain. We shake them and listen for a telltale rattle. We weigh them in our hands and try to guess what is hidden inside. We apply the "feel" test to see if that will yield the answer. In and through all of this we are admonished to be patient because Christmas will soon be here. Christmas goodies are being baked and we would like "one little taste." Candy and nuts are bought and we sneak a few "just to see if they are any good."

The other day I stopped by my daughter's classroom. The third graders had just constructed a gingerbread house. They had decorated it with all kinds of candies on the top and the sides. They had built a candy fence around it. With eyes dancing, she said, "We get to eat it on the last day of school!" To which the teacher replied with a smile, "It probably won't last that long."

Impatience—it is found among all ages, in all situations. Young people are told to be patient with their sexual desires, minorities are told to be patient as they wait for a share of the American dream, the world's poor are admonished to be patient in their quest of justice.

The Difficulties of Patience

Advent is a time when the Scriptures speak to us about patient waiting, about expectation of that which is to come. It is a good concept but something always seems to get lost in the translation.

"Be patient therefore brethren until the coming of the Lord" James tells us. Advent is a time when we can let the Scriptures speak to us about patient waiting, about heightened expectation concerning the one who is to come. Our impatience at this time is only one small sign of the greater impatience we have in all areas of our existence. We seem always to be in a rush to get ahead of ourselves. The "trim-the-tree" department opens in the middle of September on the spot where the "back-to-school" shop stood only a day or two before.

Patience is a great virtue but many times we have trouble practicing it. Our wants and our desires, indeed our greed, is skillfully exploited by commercial interests. And so, we begin to want what we never wanted before, and need what we never needed before. We become impatient to get a hold of all those good things of life. We are admonished to grab all that we can because we only live once. The wonders of modern technology make us long for instant everything. We want instant communication, instant gratification, and I even find myself becoming impatient when that "have it my way" burger seems to take longer than its allotted 30 seconds or whatever its gestation is supposed to be. And I begin to ask myself, "Hey, what's the problem, why am I so impatient?"

I sense this impatience in many areas of life. I hear it as a nagging question of those undergoing physical illness and pain. They wonder why the doctors can't find out what the problem is, why can't they find out what's wrong? Once they establish what the cause is, there is heightened anxiety when no cure can be found. We have been led to believe that there is a pill for every ache and pain we experience. We want instant, long-lasting relief. I hear it behind the emotional pain that people experience when there are tensions between husband and wife. "Why can't we get this thing straightened out?" they ask. It is a problem that has been building over a period of months, maybe even years, but we want it set right overnight. I find that more often than not the basic question people are asking is, "Why doesn't God do something?—Why doesn't he make me well? Why doesn't he take care of my husband's drinking problem? Why doesn't he make my wife less of a nag?" We become very impatient when the solution is not instantly at hand.

The Four Ps of Patience

Patience is a great virtue but a hard one to practice. There are four Ps that I would like to call to your attention regarding patience: it is personal, it perseveres, it is perceptive, and it preserves.

How easy it is to tell others to be patient. "Don't worry, everything will work out, don't get uptight." How many times have we used that kind of language? And then the least little thing upsets our schedule and we become impatient. We must first of all hear the word of patience for ourselves before we admonish others with it. When we have known it for our own lives then we are in a position to share it in a meaningful way with others. Until we have known physical or emotional pain, we ought to be careful in telling others to be patient.

Once we have personally experienced the need for patience, we know also that patience perseveres. Take the example of the prophets, James tells his readers. They were proclaiming the word of God to a hard-hearted people and so they knew injustice, they knew pain, both physical and emotional. But they persevered because they knew that the God of justice would ultimately work out his will within the world. Job knew patience and so he knew that he could rely on the sure word of the Lord. We all know people who persevere in the times of pain and suffering because they trust in the word of the Lord. They believe that Christ's justice will ultimately work itself out in their lives.

Patience is also perceptive. It reads the signs of hope and life that God gives to us. It knows the signs of love and forgiveness that God gives to his people and that he invites us to share with one another. Those signs say that God is still with his people, that he has not forgotten them nor abandoned them. The water of Holy Baptism, the bread and the wine of the Eucharist are signs of his presence and his love. Patience that is true Christian patience is perceptive and knows those signs and acknowledges them.

Finally, patience preserves us and keeps us from being given over to despair. It preserves us and sustains us in those times of darkness and trial. It preserves us in those times when there seems to be no sign of hope, when there seems to be no possibilities, no way out. What I'm really talking about is a patience that is related to faith. It is not a blind stumbling in the darkness, but a quiet confidence that comes because we have perceived the signs and know his presence. We are preserved by his grace, and are given opportunities to live out that grace in our lives.

Christ as Our Example and Source of Patience

The example of patience is certainly none other than our Lord Jesus Christ, "God of God, Light of Light, Very God of very God, Begotten, not made, Being of one substance with the Father, By whom all things were made." Those are the great words of the Nicene Creed. But he was not impatient, he did not come in his full glory, but grew silently in the womb of the blessed virgin Mary. He did not leap over infancy and childhood and adolescence, but knew, I am sure, the pain, the hope, and the joy of those periods of life. He was patient with his disciples. So often they seemed not to know his will, they seemed often to somehow miss the point. Peter, that impatient, impetuous individual, claimed he was willing to go to any length to stand up for his Lord. Christ was patient with Peter and with the rest of his disciples when they could not watch with him even one hour. He was patient as he bore the cross to Golgotha's hill. He was patient as he lay in death's grasp in the tomb. He is patient with us. He is our example.

Sometimes we may feel like John the Baptist in the Gospel text for today. We ask, "Are you the Christ or should we look for another? Have we put our faith in you in vain, should we somehow, in this time and place be looking for some other hope, some other sign, some other way out?" Isaiah had a different vision. He had a vision for the people who were impatient. They were in Babylon, carried away from their beloved Jerusalem, not knowing when they would return and they became impatient. But Isaiah had a picture of the wilderness turning into a land that was glad, the desert rejoicing and blossoming forth, a highway upon which the people of God would go back to their home. That was the vision that Isaiah had for an impatient people.

That's a good vision for us, too, in times of trial and temptation; a good vision in times of darkness and despair, when we know not where we are going, and maybe even wondering where we have come from. The patience of the Lord will also come to us and renew us. Maybe then we can be like Snoopy in the Peanuts cartoon, where he is out dancing on the hillside, and Lucy, standing in the background is crying out, "Floods, Fire and Famine! Doom, Defeat and Despair!" But Snoopy just dances on. Finally with a look of despair on her own face, she says,

"I guess it's no use. Nothing seems to disturb him!" To know Christ is to know both the example of and the source of patience that will see us through doom, defeat, and despair. To have been baptized into him, to have eaten the meal of his presence is to be linked to a source of hope and joy that will never run dry. May God grant you such a relationship.

RICHARD A. HODGES
Lutheran Church of Peace
St. Paul, Minnesota

MIRACLE OF MIRACLES
Fourth Sunday in Advent
Romans 1:1-7

Have you ever had a deeply moving experience that you really can't describe and consequently have been unable to share with someone else? Many significant happenings often defy description or definition. How do you describe the red glow of a sunset or the beauty of a snow-capped mountain peak reflected in a clear blue lake? How do you define a deep feeling of love that you have for some person? There are times when I am experiencing some beautiful moment, some deeply meaningful time, that I wish I were more artistic than I am. I wish I could capture the moment and put it in a poem or on a canvas to preserve it and make it available for recall or for sharing.

Yet how thrilled we are that there are creative people who can capture the big moments and significant feelings, and who make them available to us through their artistic genius. I can feel exhilarated about the beauty of my mountain surroundings—the majestic splendor of the peaks, the clean fresh mountain air, the sweet-smelling forests and tumbling streams and rivers—and I'm happy that persons like John Denver have put such feelings into simple songs that I can share and enjoy.

Certainly this is why the Psalms continue to be so devotionally meaningful to us. These great expressions of praise and thanksgiving, the marvelous words of faith and commitment, describe the deep feelings we have about God, the inward churnings that are longing to be expressed. We read the Psalms and suddenly our own praise is spilling out. Our inner feelings are being expressed. We are praising God. We are thanking God. We are reaffirming our faith and commitment. We are worshiping God using the ancient words that define the praise that wants to burst forth from us and is doing so now through the Psalms.

In our text, Paul, in just a few short phrases, sums up his feelings and understandings about Jesus and about his place in Christ's church. And during this time of getting ready for the celebration of Christ's birth it is good to bring these truths into focus. What Paul is saying pretty well describes our feelings about the Christ and about our place in his family. As we are contemplating Christmas and all that this season means in terms of our own customs and cultures, we are naturally focusing our attention on the miracle of the ages—God himself coming to the world in human form—becoming flesh of our flesh. We are aware, too, that here in this place, gathered in this body called the church, we are touched by a beautiful truth that God himself calls us to share with the world. We can identify with the words of Paul. They can express our feelings about the Christ and about the festive mood which permeates our lives during these days of celebration.

The Miracle of Christ

Historically the church has consistently affirmed the fullness of Christ's divinity and the fulness of his humanity. In this man from Nazareth, Jesus the son of Mary, God himself was present reconciling the world unto himself. In him God and man meet. Paul defines both the humanity and the divinity of Christ. He talks about Jesus Christ "who was descended from David according to the flesh and designated Son of God in power according to the Spirit of holiness by his resurrection from the dead."

At the center of our faith is a person—God's man for the world—Jesus Christ. In him time and eternity, heaven and earth, meet. As we contemplate the man from Nazareth, we see in him a real human being, a person just like us with feelings and emotions and experiences of God that are like ours. And in him we meet God.

On the wall in our living room hangs a print of Christ on the cross done in contemporary style. It was a gift to our family from the artist, a former colleague. It's a beautiful piece of art and it means even more to us because we know the artist. We know the one whose personal genius is invested in the work. Something of the artist is with us through his work. This is a season for the gift giving and receiving, and you know that the best kind of gift is one that has something of the giver wrapped up in it. How thrilled we are with the gifts our children make for us in school! A lot of love goes into those gifts. The hands and hearts of our children are in them. So it is with God's gift to us, the gift of Jesus Christ. He is God's investment of himself in the work of the world's salvation.

In Jesus Christ, God himself comes to the real world, to *our* real world. He chooses to make himself known to people like you and me. He is not an abstract entity known only in complicated philosophical formulas or mystical feelings. He is not an otherworldly God at all, but is very much a this-worldly. He is a God of the flesh—a God who shares the human experience—a God who shares your life with you—a God who can be known even by little children.

And the real beauty of the story of God's incarnation is its simplicity. What is more down to earth than a barn with its usual odors, and in this setting the sudden cry of a new-born child? So utterly common is this scene, yet it is the arena of God's presence in the world! This is the miracle of Christ. He is God in the flesh—God close to us—God who knows all about the human experience, its joys and sorrows, its good times and bad—God who shares every moment of life with us—God who stands with us—God who knows what real living is all about. It's no wonder Paul rejoices about Jesus Christ who is of the flesh and also designated Son of God. We can understand his exuberance, his explosion of joy, as he begins his letter to the church at Rome.

The Miracle of the Church

Paul is also rejoicing over the gift of the church. He expresses a deep affection for the Christians in Rome who, like him, are "called to belong to Jesus Christ." He calls them saints. They, too, are set apart and belong to Jesus Christ for a specific purpose. Paul obviously feels a very deep affection for these Christians in Rome—a closeness created no doubt by their common faith, their shared loyalty and mission, the fact that they, like him, received "grace and apostleship to bring about the obedience of faith for the sake of (Christ's) name among all the nations."

You can understand Paul's feelings. Close relationships are important to you. Persons who share deep things with you— beliefs, attitudes and life-styles—are important to you. You feel close to people who share your concerns in life, who are interested in the same things that interest you. You rejoice in the bonds that unite you with other people—in the closeness you feel toward persons whose lives enrich yours and with whom you can share something of the person you are.

To be alone or to feel alone must be one of the most painful experiences imaginable. And I'm sure you know what that's like too, because you've spent some time in the empty pit of loneliness. You were alone with your feelings, misunderstood, sometimes rejected. You may have been surrounded by masses of people, but you were a stranger. All around you were bodies, but nobody who really cared about you at all.

Unfortunately this describes so much of what life is like today in many places. Relationships between people often go no deeper than "I care about you because you can do something for me." So we manipulate other people and are manipulated by them. We use other people and are often used by them. And that's as far as it goes sometimes. That's all there is to people encountering people, and in that ball park people are lonely.

But the church as I have known it and experienced it is not like that. I rejoice in the life and ministry of the church, this community of people where caring goes much deeper. Day after day I see so much evidence among Christ's people of love being fleshed out and lived out in our relationships with each other and with persons who are not part of our fellowship. In the church I seem to be constantly in touch with persons who care about me and who rejoice that I care about them.

During this season of the year we see a lot of caring actions happening and this is good. The cards that bring holiday greetings and express good wishes are deeply appreciated. During this season there is a genuine caring about lonely people. Society in general doesn't like the idea of a person being alone or a child going without a gift at Christmas. It's good to see and experience the good that's happening all around us during these Advent days. But far too often the concern that is being expressed during these days is here for only a season. When the holidays are over we're all tired out, ready to be done with the festivities for another year. There are still hungry people and ill-clad children, and not far from where you live. But after Christmas their struggles are often overlooked. The season to be jolly is over and it's back to business as usual.

In the church, however, I am constantly in touch with a caring community, people who are genuinely concerned about others and not just for a season, but week after week and month after month over the years. As we continue to encounter the miracle of Christ in Word and Sacrament, love grows in our midst. Our affection for each other and for the world Christ calls us to serve becomes more intense. We love and care for each other. And together we know the deep joy of reaching out in love to hungry people, to people who suffer. We have all experienced the peace that comes to us when we care for someone else—the peace of seeing some person's life enriched and uplifted—the joy of experiencing the restoration of some broken relationship.

Yes, I feel deeply affectionate toward people in Christ's family and good about the family life we share. I can understand the warmth of Paul's greeting to the church in Rome and you can too. I know how in this congregation the pastoral ministry is appreciated—not only the one which goes from pastor to congregation, but also the love and caring that you share with me and with each other.

During this season of rejoicing we are reminded of the joy that fills our life together in the church, not only for a season but for always. Our life together is centered in the Christ, Immanuel, God with us. We praise God for the miracle of Christ, the Christ who binds us together in love and is creating the miracle of the church. I'm feeling good today about Jesus Christ and about the growing love that we share. The opening words of Paul's letter make sense to me. They describe feelings I have as I think about the Good News that God shouts to the world— the Good News of love fleshed out in a Person—and persons.

EARL E. MATSON
Bethany Lutheran Church
Colorado Springs, Colorado

COSMIC CHRISTMAS

The Nativity of Our Lord — Christmas Day
Hebrews 1:1-9

Manger, shepherds, lowly mother, hillside village, shining star, wise men from afar. Tiny baby, cattle lowing, sheep resting, little family gathered in the midnight air. Lovely carols, warm feelings, gentle notions, love and peace and giving presents. Christmas cookies, colored lights, grandma's coming, fancy ribbons, excited children. This, and a long, long list to which each of you could add, is Christmas. The tenderest, the warmest, the most sentimental time of the whole year. This, and much, much more, is Christmas.

Who would change one bit of it? Certainly not I. To be sure, we know it can be overly sentimental. We know that some of it is crassly commercial, some blatantly secular. But now, on this day, all those thoughts are brushed away. And that which remains is soft, and warm, and tender, and good, and loving. This is Christmas.

This is a time when all of us agree with G. K. Chesterton: "Grow up, but keep your childishness, forget the pedant's creeds and strictures, and don't believe in anything that can't be told in colored pictures." And 100 million pictures, printed on cards, have been sent again from home to home, telling once more the story. Color it warm, color it good and loving, color it full of peace and of joy, for this is Christmas. This is the time for which children have waited, for which adults have prepared, and which we all rejoice to see again.

The Cosmic Christ

As Christians, we affirm all of this and more. We can say, "May your Christmas be the best and the happiest ever!" But then, into the midst of this wonderful sentiment, good feelings, joyous spirit, we would be so presumptuous as to say one word more. As Christians we need to hear and to believe that Christmas is more than a manger and more than a baby. Christmas is more than sweet carols and warm thoughts; it is about one who reflects the very glory of God and bears the stamp of his nature. Christmas is more than bright ribbons and good food and gathered family; it is about one who reflects the glory of God, and who upholds the universe by the power of his word. Christmas is the incarnate word of God breaking with boldness into human life!

By all means, enjoy your gifts, both given and received. With your feast and fellowship know the warmness of family and of home. But never forget: the day comes to us because of one who is the eternal word, one who is the cosmic Christ, one who came to make purification for sin.

> The feet of the humblest may walk in the fields,
>   where the feet of the holiest have trod.
> This, this is the marvel to mortals revealed,
>   When the silvery trumpets of Christmas have pealed,
> That mankind are the children of God. (Phillips Brooks)

Bold, straightforward, with power we proclaim: Christmas is cosmic! What happened on that night involves the meaning of the whole universe. To be sure it is about a boy, a fully human boy,

> A boy who was born in Bethlehem,
> who knew the haunts of Galilee,
> He wandered on Mount Lebanon
> and learned to love each forest tree.

It is about a baby, and a mother, and tender loving things. But even more, it is about the power and the might of Almighty God, for Christmas is cosmic. It is about that one who in many and various ways was spoken to his children, trying to win them back, to return them to their rightful destiny as his sons and daughters. And finally he has spoken to them, through a Son, a clear, persuasive, complete Word, Jesus Christ.

Confronted by the Word

This Christmas, that Word confronts each of us with a choice. Who wants to make decisions on Christmas? But there is a choice: it's going to be God's way, or it's going to be our way; it's going to be Christ, or it's going to be chaos.

It's so much easier simply to enjoy all of the trimmings, all the sweet sentimental things, even some of the things that are pagan in origin (like your Christmas tree, or that mistletoe, or the plum pudding). Why spoil all of this with talk of cosmic Christmas, with ultimate questions of God, life, death, sin, grace, and forgiveness? We wouldn't for a moment spoil any of it. But in the name of that God who has spoken in these days through his Son, the Word must be said. The one who has come reflects the glory of God and the very stamp of his nature.

What is that glory? Not some heavenly pomp and ceremony, not ostentation and display. Too often in our minds the glory of God reflects what we might consider to be glorious in our world. Power, and empire, wealth and wisdom, and popular acclaim. Not these. For the glory of God does not reflect the ideas that we might consider to be glorious. The power that made the universe, the eternal Word that is spoken, that first-born Son brought forth and laid in a manger, surprised the world. For he came to give himself, to walk among the common people, to touch their sin-filled, disease-warped lives, to have children sit on his lap, to have men and women weep at his feet; to take a towel and a basin and, like a slave, wash the feet of his followers. And then in one final stroke of glory, to die, nailed to a wooden cross. Through this one, through this Word, that glory is set loose in our world.

You can still see it, if you will but look and observe, for it is a glory that is reflected in the eyes of every man, woman, and child who knows what it is to be redeemed, to be free, to be forgiven. It is a glory reflected in the life of every person who has been given strength to endure suffering, or pain, or sorrow.

It is a glory that is reflected in every home represented here today, where father and mother and child know the spiritual resources that are needed to live as a family in our world. And it is a glory that is shared every time two or three gather to unite their hearts in prayer under the power of God's grace. That is the Word. It reflects the very nature of God: that he is love. Not awesome power, not explosive, forceful, destructive. Not the clap of thunder, the roar of wind, the pounding of the surf, but the still, small voice of God coming into the world as a helpless infant, to touch your life with a cosmic dimension, a cosmic Christmas.

Sharing the Mystery

We know what we share is a mystery. It is beyond our comprehension. God has spoken and, to be sure, some refuse to listen. There are always those who will not allow God to be God in their lives. They have the right to make that awesome choice. When we are honest, we know that spirit of uncertainty touches the lives of all of us. We live in a skeptical age, and skepticism has weakened the Christian conviction of many. The long tradition of Christian faith has been dulled in the lives of not a few. I suppose there are even some, perhaps some here this day, who would be embarrassed to be found in church at any other time than Christmas or Easter. Someone might think they took the message seriously! We do. We take it seriously.

Let Christmas mean to every individual exactly what one wants it to mean. Let us not diminish the joy and the peace and the happiness that anyone can derive from it. Let even the skeptic be touched by the soft sentiment of the babe and the manger, and let God's gift for him be at least that moment of thoughtfulness, and caring, and giving and love.

But let there be this Word as well. And let none of us be captive to the illusion that any man or woman is competent to work out one's own destiny with no thought of God. Let Christmas be this much: a cosmic Word, an eternal Word, a life that bears the very stamp of the nature of the power that stands behind the universe. The Word that became flesh to dwell among us, full of grace and truth. Let there be lovely carols, sweet songs and sentiment. Well and good, but let us remember it is cosmic Christmas that is the foundation of our faith. It is beyond our comprehension, beyond our understanding, fables and foolishness to some but it is the very light of the world to those who believe.

A skeptical age may have its say, but for us there can be no mistake. It is cosmic Christmas, Christ the eternal Word made flesh, that has brought all of us to this time and place. "The voice," as Isaac Watts has said, "that rolls the stars along, speaks all the promises." He is the one whose thoughts are higher than our thoughts as the heavens are higher than the earth (Isa. 55:9). He is the one by whom all things exist and from whom we derive our existence. It is he who heals the broken hearted, and also counts the number of stars and calls them by name (Ps. 147:3-4). It's all of this and much more that stands behind the manger, and the shepherds, and the young mother, and the tender infant. And for this we who number ourselves among God's faithful children can sing for joy on this day: "Glory to God in the highest, and on earth peace among men with whom he is pleased."

DENNIS V. GRIFFIN
First Lutheran Church
Sioux Falls, South Dakota

TO RECEIVE AND TO THANK
First Sunday after Christmas
Galatians 4:4-7

Note: Some parts of this sermon must be printed in the service bulletin to allow the congregation to participate.

In Christ, dear friends:

It is a good thing that Christmas does not depend on the number or the quality of gifts one gives or receives. For many people the gift exchange may be the measure of a successful Christmas, but there are countless thousands for whom there are no gifts or whose only gift is another person's charity. Yet there is no such thing as a giftless Christmas, for Christmas is the celebration of God's gift of Jesus Christ to us and of the profound and exciting ramifications of Jesus Christ in our lives. When the gift list is reviewed and the time for writing of thank you notes arrives, send the first loud note of gratitude to God. In fact, why don't we make this Lord's Day morning our time to speak our Christmas thanks to him?

God's Gift List

St. Paul didn't have Christmas in mind when he wrote the words of our text to the Galatians, but it is difficult to read them again without hearing God's kind of Christmas running through every line. Divine gifts heap divine gifts until we are staggered by their accumulation. Words almost fail for gratitude. The list reads like this. Christmas gifts from God: (one) Incarnation of the Son of God; (two) Redemption, rescue; (three) Adoption; (four) the Spirit; (five) Inheritance!

Would you mind if we held each gift to look at it again for just a moment before we send our thanks to the throne room?

One: The Incarnation

You have to stretch your imagination to appreciate the Incarnation of the Son of God. In what must have been the most awe-packed moment in the history of creation, the very Son of God laid aside his Son's prerogatives—power, glory, omniscience, omnipresence—to be stored against his return from earth. He was going on a mission. The mission was to seek and save mankind from its plunge toward hell. The Son would not be ministered to for his mission was to minister. He would redeem mankind by substituting hmself for all humanity under the terrifying wrath of God. So the Son of God became God's Anointed, God's Christ, and through his entrance into our world by way of human birth became one of us that he might be our substitute. Handle the gift of the Incarnation of Christ with love. It is an absolutely priceless gift.

Two: Redemption

Mankind was under the Law imposed upon it by God. The Law is a vicious taskmaster. It is a prison house from which there is no escape. Every person under the Law is a person on death row, waiting the death row penalty. It doesn't matter how you say it, "The wages of sin is death," or "The soul that sins shall die," the end of the Law is always and irrevocably death and hell. Mankind is in slavery to the Law, bound and beaten by it, but now this second gift from the heart of the Father. Christ came to redeem, to rescue us. He opened the cell doors and the cell block barriers and the great barred gates of the prison walls for us. He moved into the prison house in our stead. The great wall gates closed behind him; the cell block barrier slid shut behind him; the cell bars clanged behind him as he entered our death row cell. And of a morning Caiaphas and Herod and Pilate set their signatures to the death warrant . . . and . . . and the

Father granted no reprieve to his only Son. But in the process we who were concluded under sin were set free. Handle freedom with love. It cannot be price-tagged. Yet, use the gift, for its patina, like a precious pearl, keeps lustrous only by use.

Three: Adoption

Look at this next gift. It is the adoption paper that makes you a child of God. The Father was there waiting at the prison gates. In the same moment that you elected to come out of the prison house of the Law, or to put it another way, in the same instant that you offered your redeemed life to God, he took you into his family. No longer a slave now. No longer a prisoner. The Substitute has made daughterhood and sonship possible in the family of the heavenly Father. Here is another way that Paul has of saying that freedom in and with Christ and under God the Father is the alternative that Christ offers to slavery and prison, to bondage and to death. Guard the papers, hold the faith, that move you into the family of the Most High. They are an incomparable gift.

Four: The Spirit

Next is the gift of the Spirit sent by the Father into your hearts that cries "Abba, Father," on your behalf. What a blessing and a gift that Spirit is. Life is full of temptations and frustrations. The devil is never quiet; our flesh gives us little peace; the old Law still screams at us; death never lets us alone, and all the while the Spirit sent us by the Father is crying, "Abba, Father" and the Father hears. There is no uncertainty. The Scripture has made a promise and the promises of the Father stand sure. He hears! Treasure this gift for "owning" it will see you through life's worst vexations and troubling doubts.

Five: Inheritance

The Law is over and done with; the Spirit and Christ are in your heart. You are no more a servant, no more a prisoner, no more a slave to the Law. You are a child and heir of God through Christ. As if the promises for this life were not enough, St. Paul adds the promises of the future. The inheritance of God—is it the mansions Christ went ahead to prepare for us? The heritage from God—is it a special place in glory somewhere near the throne? This we can be certain about, if the heritage is from God, it is inheritance much to be desired. Take God's promise. Tuck it away in a safe place in your heart. Then one day, when all things are accomplished, God will make good his promises. You, the heir, will come into your own in his kingdom of glory.

Thank You, Lord

Let no one say there are no presents at Christmas, for God has given us lavish gifts. For certain death he has given us eternal glory; for slavery he has given us freedom; from the dominion of Satan he has called us to his dominion. It is time to say our thanks. Would you be willing just here and now to turn St. Paul's Christmas list into a prayer and pray it with me? You will find it printed in your service bulletin. Let us pray together:

> For sending forth your Son
> > to be born of a woman,
> > to be born under the Law,
> > to redeem us from the Law,
> > > accept our gratitude.
> For our adoption into your family,
> for the Spirit of the Son
> > who cries to you on our behalf,
> for our elevation from slavery
> > to be your sons and daughters, and
> for our promised inheritance,
> > accept our thanks and praise, "O Abba, Father,"
> > > through Jesus Christ our Lord. Amen.

Thank You Again, Lord

In the Epistle to the Galatians Paul's great burden is that we recognize our freedom from the Law and all its dread consequences. Before the Epistle is finished he will reiterate that "For freedom Christ has set us free" (5:1) and he will sound a solemn warning to remind his readers that freedom is not license. "Do not use your freedom as an opportunity for the flesh," (5:13) he admonishes. We are free only in Christ, and with Christ, and for Christ. Paul says very little about the privileges of freedom to the Galatians. Use your freedom in love "to be servants to one another" (5:13). Well, we are servants after all! But we are in bondage now to Christ who freed and frees us. It is Christ himself who has laid the command to love on us.

Now the text has come full circle and the recurring motif of the Christian faith can be restated. St. John says it most clearly, "As the Father has loved Me, so have I loved you" (John 9:15).

This glorious Sunday after Christmas the motif can be restated, perhaps something like this: As the Father has given us gifts of such magnificent proportions, let us freely share such gifts, such love, such talents and time as we have, each with the other and with the whole family of man. Our adoption as sons and daughters of God through Christ gives us the privilege of the house. Our Father in his love takes time for us. He makes himself consistently available to us. But being sons and daughters imposes the need for obedience upon us. It becomes our joy in life to do the Father's will. This text, coming just at Christmas time (or truly, at any time), is a strong motivation to the Christian life of love and giving. God's Christmas impels us to the highest of Christian selflessness.

Join me once more, this time with the prayer that we each grow in our commitment to all the opportunities of self-giving that so continuously confront us.

> I believe that God sent forth his Son,
>   born of a woman,
>   born under the Law,
>   to redeem me from the Law's curse
>   that I might be adopted into the family of God.
> And because I am a child of God
>   the Spirit of his Son is in my heart
>   crying, "Abba, Father."
> Through God I am no longer a slave to the law, but a member
>   of God's family;
>   and as a member of the family, I am an heir of
>   eternal life.
> Therefore, I will love my neighbor as myself. Amen.

FREDERICK W. KEMPER
Calvary Lutheran Church
Silver Spring, Maryland

A MESSIAH FOR ALL PEOPLE
The Epiphany of Our Lord
Ephesians 3:2-12

Several years ago, a young woman strayed into our church. At nineteen years of age, she had been a prostitute, had borne an illegitimate child, been married and divorced, and was well on her way to alcoholism. She wanted, and desperately needed, the help of the Gospel of Jesus Christ. She needed a Savior.

She had a beautiful singing voice, and I suggested that she begin her relationship with our congregation by joining the choir. After the first rehearsal and the first service at which this woman sang with the choir, I heard one of the elderly members of the choir say to a friend of hers: "And there she sat, right in the choir, along with the rest of us, just like she belonged there." What a tragedy!

Another time, in another city, I heard a neighboring church referred to by one of its members as a "very exclusive church." What a horrible contradiction! How could that organization, whatever it was, be a part of the church of Jesus Christ and be "exclusive?"

In another case, a church member told me one time about a family of prospective members whose names I had received from someone in the congregation. Those prospects happened to be the neighbors of the member who gave his estimate. He said to me: "Quite confidentially, Pastor, I don't think you would want them as members of our church. They just are not our kind of people."

And so it has gone, the terrible *exclusiveness* of part of the church of Jesus Christ, negating the message of the Gospel, which was meant for all people, the understanding of which first came about through the dynamic, untiring efforts of the Apostle Paul, who almost singlehandedly carried that Gospel outside of the Jewish culture where some people, including St. Peter himself, sought to confine it.

The Twelfth Day

We like to sing about the "Twelve Days of Christmas." We go through the whole song to the twelfth day of Christmas. But I venture to say that if I were to ask you what *is* the twelfth day of Christmas, there would be probably half of you that wouldn't know. Usually, even though we sing about the twelve days of Christmas, we never make it. By that time, our trees are down, the decorations are all packed in their usual places for another year, the children are back in school, and the January White Sales have begun.

What is the twelfth day of Christmas? It is January 6th, the Epiphany of our Lord. Epiphany was the first Christmas, the most ancient celebration of Christmas in Christendom, and a lot more valid, incidentally, than December 25th. We put the festival of the birth of Christ on that date so that we could compete with the pagan festival of Saturnalia. Epiphany was the great celebration. That word coming from the two Greek words *epi* and *phaino*, means "to show forth." The glory of Christ was shown forth, for this is the day that we observe the visit of the Magi or the Wise Men to the child Jesus, and notice that I said "child," not "infant."

I am sure that you are well aware by this time that contrary to much of our Christmas art and imagery and Christmas cards, and even our crèche out in front of the church, that the Magi did *not* arrive at the same time as the shepherds at the stable in Bethlehem. They arrived between one and two years after the birth of Christ. Mary and Joseph and the young Jesus was not living in a stable at that time. The Gospel clearly states that they were living in a home. And it doesn't call Jesus an "infant," it calls him a "young child."

The Magi

We sing "We three kings of Orient are." But there are three things wrong with that song. In the first place, they weren't kings. In the second place, they weren't from what we consider the Orient. And, in the third place, there weren't three of them. And yet, we sing that song as one of our Epiphany hymns.

Actually, these men came, not from what we call the Orient, but from the area of ancient Babylon, the Tigris-Euphrates valley. They were men who were much more respected than kings, because, in those days in the Middle East, kings were a dime a dozen. These were the representatives of the school of the Magi. They were the astronomers, the astrologers, the scientists, the physicians, the prophets, the religious seers of their day. At the height of their fame and influence, they were honored far above kings, because kings were not particularly notable for being wise men. Kings don't travel somewhere to worship other kings. They usually are going out to kill them.

But here is the Epiphany, the "showing forth" of the glory of Christ. Here is the miracle of joy.

Here was a marvelous manifestation in the heavens—a star so new, so brilliant, so unusual that it stirred the school of the Magi into immediate contemplation and study, and finally action. What did the Magi see? What kind of a star? Is it still in the heavens? Why did nobody else see it? Remember, they were Zoroastrians. They were astrologers, the chief astrologers of their day. They were the ones who believed—the way some people foolishly believe today—that the movement of the stars had something to do with the behavior of people here upon earth. And so, through calculations of astronomers and historians, we have determined that Christ was born, not in the year 1, but because of many changes and mistakes in our calendar, He was born in the year 6 or 7 B.C.

Now in the 17th Century, the astronomer Kepler found that something *did* occur in the year 7 B.C. that only occurred once in every 805 years in the solar system. And so, obviously, the Magi could have known nothing about that. In 7 B.C., in the winter, there occurred a very close grouping—actually a juxtaposition—of the three planets Mars, Jupiter and Saturn, as they were viewed from the earth. They became, literally, one light in the sky, more brilliant, obviously, than anything else in the sky at that time. That grouping occurred under the sign of the Zodiac, Pisces, in the winter. Some of you have noted that in my regular clerical garb I sometimes wear a medallion with the figure of Pisces on it. That is not because I'm an astrologer or believe in astrology. It is a Christian symbol. It symbolizes the coming of Christ, the glory of Christ, and it was the first symbol of the early church, not just because I was born in that period of the year. The sign of the fish!

This portion of the sky in which this juxtaposition occurred was known as the House of the Hebrews. And so, it was perfectly readable to the Magi as they studied the stars as though planets came together in that grouping that had never before occurred in their experience, and it occurred in the House of the Hebrews. It was obvious that something important was happening to the Jews. And since they knew that the Jews expected the coming of a great king, it was obvious to them that he had apparently come. And so, they eventually started out on their caravan, and it was about sixteen months later, in the spring of 6 B.C., that something happened that only happens once every one hundred twenty-five years in the solar system. The planets of Jupiter and Saturn came together, and to the Wise Men looking at it from Jerusalem, it appeared right over Bethlehem. So it is explained why the Wise Men knew that Jesus was in Bethlehem.

The Irony of Epiphany

This marvelous manifestation happened, and yet the shepherds of Bethlehem didn't see it. You know, we send out Christmas cards showing the shepherds out in the fields and the star shining above them. Well, that's O.K., if you want to put the star in, but don't show the shepherds looking at it, because they didn't see it. The priests and Levites didn't see it. The Romans didn't see it. Herod didn't see it. And here was the sad beginning of the fulfillment of the prophecy: "He came unto his own, and his own received him not."

Here is the irony of God's revelation of himself to us. The first to fall down and worship Jesus Christ as a divine king were not the ones who were supposedly waiting and watching for him, but the despised, the hated, the pagans, the heathen. They fell down and worshiped him. They came, as they told Herod, for the expressed purpose of worshiping him.

Everyone else was so preoccupied with the pettiness of life that they didn't notice the coming of Christ. They were too busy even to notice that the King of kings had come. But that is typical, even in our day.

Back in the early 1950s, the world was all involved in what we called the cold war. Oh, we were fighting a nasty little war over in Korea, but that wasn't really important. What was important was the cold war, in which the world was choosing up sides over the barbed wire of the Berlin wall. Everyone was wondering about the balance of terror between the Communist countries and the so-called Free World. Everyone was concerned about the arms race, the atomic race, the missile race. Everyone wondered when World War III would begin, and how. The old, moldy, empty minds among the military and political leaders on *both* sides in the cold war thought of nothing else except the inevitability of a final, tragic confrontation between these two opposing sides, and so we were feverishly preparing for that.

Notice that a generation of babies was being born throughout the world at that time, and those babies are now young adults or students. Today in every part of the world, those young adults are soundly rejecting the tired, old, stupid clichés of the tired, old, stupid, statesmen and militarists of the world. They no longer accept the inevitability of war. They no longer believe the scare warnings of the militarists. Thousands of them refused to take part in our war in Vietnam. They are well on their way to rejecting forever war as an instrument of international relationships. Yes, in the 1950s everybody was looking at the arms race. No one noticed that God was bringing to life a generation which might take a good look at all of this and get rid of both piles of that bloody junk their fathers had paid for!

Twenty years ago, the church was in its heyday. The heyday was popularity, and the church was feverishly building up the establishment. One denomination competed with another for numbers, wealth, power and prestige. The church moved to the suburbs to attract the more affluent. Left behind were the plaguing problems of the inner city—the poverty, the hunger, the unemployment. Left behind was the question of racial equality in the churches. The parishes sought refuge in the lily-white suburbs and neighborhoods where they deal with such problems by ignoring them. They didn't know that at the time they were raising their statistics of "success" in their own eyes, they were also raising a generation of young people who would reject this kind of "Establishment" church in all of its glory and strength and wealth. We were raising youth, both white and black and brown and yellow and red, who would ask: "But what is the church doing to carry out the mandates of the Gospel of Jesus Christ about these problems that we face today? How relevant is this organization? What was the church doing to meet the real problems of the day? Does Christianity mean anything?" They are still asking that.

It's Up to Us

And so, history repeats itself. We are the people of God. We worship every week in his temple. We read the Scriptures. We know all about the promises about the Second Coming of Christ. And yet, we are so preoccupied with our own little projects that when Christ comes in Spirit in revolutionary power in our culture, we don't even recognize him. In fact, we even resent and resist the upsetting influence the Gospel has when it interjects itself into our social and national and international lives. It threatens our position as the self-righteous policemen for the rest of the world.

Here, then, was the irony of the coming of the Magi. The ones to whom the Messiah was promised were too busy worrying about the preservation of the kingdom to know that the king had come. They saw no star. They experienced no light. But, lo, Jesus was born in Bethlehem, and there came pagans, Gentiles, heathen, from the East who said: "We have seen his star and have come to worship." What about you? Have you seen the star?

No, we don't preach every Sunday that Christ is coming soon, that we know this by private knowledge or study of the Scriptures. That's nonsense! There's not a word in Scripture that tells us anything about when Christ is coming, and there will be no one, the Scripture tells us, who knows the day or hour of his coming.

No, we don't know *when* he is coming, but we know he *is* coming, not alone to the Jews, or to the Americans, or to the civilized white people of the Western Hemisphere, but as a Messiah, a Savior for the *whole world!* As it says in blazing words in the

Gospel: "For God so loved *the world* that he gave his only begotten Son."

LOUIS H. VALBRACHT
St. John's Lutheran Church
Des Moines, Iowa

THE FEW AND THE MANY

The Baptism of Our Lord—First Sunday after the Epiphany

Acts 10:34-38

The Holy Scriptures are special in that they proclaim a God who is in love with all people of all nations. No one is excluded from his grace or from his justice. As Peter says, "Truly I perceive that God shows no partiality." This has been true since the very beginning.

It is unique that as the book of Genesis describes the origins of the human race, all people descend from one man and one woman. The Hebrew people whom God chooses to be his covenant servants are descended from Adam and Eve, as are also their archenemies: the Egyptians, the Moabites and the Cananites. According to Genesis, God is one and the human race is also one. In the writings of the other world religions, the people who mediate revelation from their gods are frequently depicted as being descended from their gods. They are genetically extraordinary; they are inherently superior to other human beings. Not so the Hebrews. Their origins as a people are not different from any other nation. What distinguishes the Israelites is God's call to servanthood and their response of faith or unfaith.

This invitation of God and our response (or lack of response) is also what distinguishes us as Christians. Obviously, not all people of all nations have come to faith. Not all want to be included in the embrace of his everlasting arms. Not all fear him and do what is right. Those who respond affirmatively are few. Abraham was one person for God in a great sea of unbelief. Elijah hid himself from the wrath of an unbelieving king and complained to God that of all Abraham's children, he alone was faithful. The Apostles were but a few who knew the true light among the many who walked in darkness. Martin Luther remarked that the number of the faithful is like a molehill compared with a mountain.

The Rule of the Lord

But the God of Scripture claims sovereignty over the many, not just the few who love him and believe in him. All of creation and all human beings of his creation are subject to his rule. "The earth is the Lord's and . . . those who dwell therein" (Psa. 24). In today's Old Testament lection God is identified as the creator of all and the source of life for all human beings. Jesus said, "Go therefore and make disciples of all nations" (Matt. 28). Isaiah's prophetic vision of the "nations who shall flow to the house of the Lord and many peoples shall come" (Isa. 2) reinforces this claim of God's universal sovereignty. Jonah's mission to the heathen of Nineveh speaks of God's presumption to be the Lord of all. He is concerned for the many and he is concerned for the few.

That is the message of the cross. Jesus Christ died for the many and for the few. "This cup is the New Testament in my blood shed for you and for many for the remission of sins." "God so loved the world . . ." and Titus 2:11, "God our Savior has appeared for the salvation of all people."

The Gospel is the message of this inclusive love which omits no one. Jesus paid the debt of Mary's sin and the sin of Simon Peter and the sin of Judas Iscariot. He paid our debt and that of other transgressors of our day. "Behold the lamb of God who takes away the sin of the world." By means of the cross God extends his arms to embrace our whole fallen race; no one is excluded. From the cross, God the Son rules in love for the salvation of all people. The crucified Christ is the Lord of all.

St. Peter preaches this Gospel here in Acts 10 to Cornelius and his friends and kinsmen who are gathered in his house (none of whom is a member of the covenant people). "Jesus Christ is Lord of all!" declares Peter. He is not the Shepherd of just the few; he is the good shepherd who leaves the ninety and nine and goes off in search of the one lost sheep. He holds himself accountable for the whole human race. "Truly God shows no partiality."

The Word of the Lord

Therefore the Word of the Lord is good news for the nations. The few and the many long to hear it, because the benefits it declares are meant for all. No one is excluded. Rather, the Gospel is inclusive.

This is the reason for believers' confidence. And this is why Peter could confidently witness to Cornelius that he—a heathen of Rome—and his kinsmen were definitely included in Christ's gracious work. Even Peter, who had denied his Lord at a moment of high drama, was not excluded because of what he had done. Praise be to God for this amazing grace! My salvation does not depend on my faithfulness or on my decision for Christ, but on Christ's faithfulness and his decision for me. I am saved by faith alone, not by faithfulness.

This makes the word of the Lord good news from the Lord and good news about the Lord. It breathes confidence into doubting hearts. How can I question whether or not that death on the cross was for me when I hear the report: "Jesus Christ is Lord of all!" Or, listen to Peter's own words from Acts 10, "God shows no partiality."

The Work of the Lord

What a pleasant task the apostle has, to share such a love-filled message. The Jesus of whom he witnesses was busy all his ministry "doing good and healing all who were oppressed by the devil." Jesus was anointed at his baptism by the Holy Spirit for this ministry to the many. We at our baptisms were anointed by the Holy Spirit for ministry to the many. The baptism command itself is inseparably attached to the commission for ministry to the many: "Go therefore and make disciples of all nations, baptizing them. . . ." The few of Israel who regarded themselves as especially pious and loyal to the Lord were also included within his ministry. He ministered to them and also to all the others. He came for the few and he came for the many—he came for all. "Come to me all who labor and are heavy laden, and I will give you rest" (Matt. 11:28) is his gracious invitation which reaches out and gathers you all into his church.

Together with Peter, the Lord of the church has commissioned us in baptism to share in this pleasant task, this apostolic work. A witness to the lordship of Jesus is a testimony of our own personal confidence that in spite of our fumbling, bumbling churchmanship, we, too, are included in his gracious work and Jesus is our Lord. Moreover, we feel that even though we are just a few who dare to speak out and pass on to others what is so special to us, that in no way compromises the good news that is meant for the many. There is room for all . . . in my Father's house . . . and just remember this: He shows no partiality . . . Jesus Christ is Lord of all!

RICHARD L. TROST
Zion Lutheran Church
Iowa City, Iowa

A GLORY TO BE SHARED
Second Sunday after the Epiphany
1 Corinthians 1:1-9

All glory be to God! More particularly, the emphasis of this Epiphany season is: All glory be to Christ! Truly there is abundant reason to give glory unto the Lord. Think of the magnetism of his person—he drew all men unto him. He is the master teacher as men reacted, "Never man spake like this man." The majesty of his very person attracted attention and called for commendation. And then add to all this the marvel and wonder of his works. He is verily the Lord of compassion, the mighty helper, the understanding and merciful Redeemer. Jesus is worthy of the praise and plaudits of men.

But what does all of this mean to us? We like to be praised, too. We are human. We like to be well spoken of. Like a child we raise our head and straighten our shoulders when we are well spoken of by a friend, an associate, a co-worker. There is not a single one of us who does not like a pat on the back, a word of praise. However, we often fail to get it even when we rightly deserve it. Just think how often we are slow to praise, reluctant to give due credit to our fellowman. Many are the kind and noble deeds and the helping and understanding words that go unrecognized. But where men may fail, God does not. The readings for this Sunday of the Epiphany season and especially our text in the epistle lesson tell us that through God and his grace we have: *A Glory to Be Shared.*

The God of all grace who has given us his only begotten Son has

Called Us to Be Saints

The apostle Paul addresses the members of the congregation at Corinth, and this applies to us also who are members of a Christian congregation, "those sanctified in Christ Jesus, called to be saints together with all those who in every place call on the name of our Lord Jesus Christ." What a name to be called! Who are these Corinthians, yes, who are we, that we can be called saints? The congregation at Corinth was not made up of such special people. In fact, they were quite ordinary. When we read on in this letter we find that these Christians were split up in factions, the various groups acclaiming Paul, or Apollos, or Peter setting themselves up as better than the other. There was bickering and squabbling going on among them. These differences became so strong at times that they were ready to fight about their difference and even took matters to court, suing one another and bringing charges against their neighbors. Their moral standards were lax and Paul found it necessary to admonish and correct them. Lust and pride and envy and jealousy reared their ugly heads in their midst. We ask ourselves if Paul was projected into the twentieth century American scene. The problems he had to deal with among these Christians and the situations that had developed in their congregation are still a part of the way of life for many in our own day and time. People then and now, are sinful and express and show the effect of sin in their lives.

And still Paul can say, "You are called to be saints." Yes, he can say, and not just be doing some wishful thinking, because Christ shares the glory of his holiness with us. It is because we are what we are, sinners all, that the Father sent his only begotten Son into the world that he might take upon himself our very nature and bear the burden and the penalty of our sin. Jesus lived his sinless life and no one could find fault in him. In his suffering and death Christ paid the penalty for sin that we ought to have paid so that we might be set free from our guilt and be counted worthy to stand in the presence of our holy and just Father in heaven. Christ shares with us the glory of his righteousness. Now all who call on the name of the Lord Jesus Christ, accepting him in true faith as their Savior, can be called saints. The Christ who came to this earth as God's beloved Son shares this sonship with us by faith so that we, too, can be called the sons and daughters of God.

Proclaimers of the Good News

Paul reminds these Corinthians that as they received this high calling in Christ Jesus they must also share in a glorious responsibility. "In every way you were enriched in him with all speech and all knowledge—even as the testimony to Christ was confirmed among you." The apostle had preached and taught among them Christ and him crucified. This is the Gospel they had heard and believed and in which they stood. The whole mission and work of Christ had been to share this message of life and salvation. The proclamation of this great good news was continued through the preaching of the apostles and is to be made known still today through those who have come to know and accept Jesus as Lord and Savior.

What a message to share! We, too, have come to know and believe in Christ as our Savior. In him we have forgiveness, life and salvation. As God has given us the treasurers of his grace, he calls upon us to share this good news with others. The spread of God's kingdom comes through the witness of God's people through their proclamation of his Gospel. This is our privilege. This is our glorious opportunity to share the glory that is ours in Christ.

Equipped to Serve

The fulfillment of this calling to be witnesses for Christ is not always easy. But Paul reminds us that God supplies our need and has equipped us to serve: "In every way you were enriched in Christ," and "You are not lacking in any spiritual gift." When God calls us into his fellowship and makes us co-workers with him, he also equips us for that calling. When Christ was sent into the world on his mission of preaching and teaching, John the Baptist tells us in the Gospel lesson that Jesus was baptized with the Holy Ghost. The heavenly Father supplied Jesus with those gifts necessary for him to perform his task.

And God still pours out his Holy Spirit on us today. God is not stingy in providing us with the gifts needed to do his work. In every way he enriches us so that "we are not lacking in any spiritual gift." We are partakers with Christ in those gifts needed to fulfill our calling. This does not mean that each one of us has every gift. The Lord supplies everyone with what he needs according to God's loving will. All of us together as the people of God are supplied with that fullness of gifts which enables us to do the work of the Lord. We share in the blessings of those gifts which glorify God so that we can continue the mission of Christ among all people and make known in life and in word the glory of God's love. Truly, we share in a wonderful and privileged calling in proclaiming the good news of the Gospel.

Assured of Success

This life in Christ is assured of a glorious end even though there are times when the glory is dimmed and the clouds gather round. This was true even with the glory manifested by Christ in his life. We recall the times when he was rejected, when he was cast out. And remember the spurning and rejection directed at this Jesus in the last hours of his life. This was also true of the life of the Apostle Paul. In the eleventh chapter of his second letter to this same congregation at Corinth, Paul gives a summary of his trials and tribulations. So do not be surprised when the glory of being a Christian is dimmed in our lives and we wonder if there is any glory at all. We have the blessed assurance that these dark moments shall not prevail, for "our Lord Jesus Christ will sustain you to the end, guiltless in the day of our Lord Jesus Christ. God is faithful."

When sin keeps popping up in our lives, when the powers of darkness seem to attack again and again, then we share in the glory of Christ's victory over evil and the devil, for the Lord sustains us guiltless in the day of the Lord. His forgiveness does not fail us. Our God is a faithful God who keeps his promises. He will pardon, cleanse, relieve. When we become weary in the battle for God and his kingdom, when fears and doubts grip us and would fill us with discouragement and despair, then the all-powerful Lord will sustain us. His guiding providence will be at work in our lives to direct all things to our good. His power is equal to, yes, greater than any need and problem we may be confronted with in our lives.

In Christ we have the faith that overcomes the world. Christ set his face steadfastly to go to Jerusalem, to capture and trial and death, assured of the victory of God's will and God's plan for the world's redemption. We share in this same glory of victory in our calling as God's own and workers in his kingdom. We lift up our heads even in the darkest hour and see the sun of God's love and power. We see the light of victory in the conquering Christ even in the grimmest situations. We can radiate the glory of the victory over all that is ours in Christ.

Measuring Up

Mindful of our calling as saints of God, recalling our commission as workers together with our Lord in his church, we need to ask ourselves: How do we measure up to the place the Lord has given us? What kind of a reflection of the glory of Christ is seen in our lives? The Lord Jesus came forth from the Father to show forth his glory. And God was seen in Christ. Now Jesus gives us the high and holy privilege of sharing his glory with others. We are his witnesses. The glory of Christ shines also in the world today through us. He shares with us the calling of being little Christs. Share it, show it forth, let that glory shine in your life.

EDGAR C. RAKOW
Zion Lutheran Church
Belleville, Illinois

HOLDING THE FAMILY TOGETHER
Third Sunday after the Epiphany
1 Corinthians 1:10-17

Is Christ divided? This question, raised by Paul as he dealt with the disturbing disunity in the church at Corinth, places before us today the central issue for the family of God. Orthodox, Roman Catholic, and Protestant churches alike must acknowledge the invisible bond that unites all Christians and pray that the unity we have in Christ may be expressed in the way we live and work together.

No one familiar with the New Testament can escape the conclusion that God intends that those who are drawn to him by faith and live within his grace shall live in unity with each other. Jesus understood that his disciples would have problems with this, and in his heart-to-heart talk with them the night before he died, he declared, "By this all men will know that you are my disciples, if you have love for one another." When that memorable evening in the upper room concluded with his prayer of intercession, he laid before the Father the plea that "they may be one" even as he and the Father were one. Unity of mind and purpose, living in love and harmony, oneness in Christ, are God's intentions for his family. Our love for each other identifies us as disciples of Jesus.

It is over against all of this that we must face up to the divisions within the household of faith and see them, not just as inevitable consequences of history, but also as signs of human frailty and sinfulness, as signs of the attempts to reduce the greatness and grandeur of God and his limitless compassion for the whole human family to the measure of small minds and timid hearts.

"Is Christ divided?", Paul asks, and we respond quickly, "Of course not." But a second question comes bearing down on us, "Why then is his church divided?", and we are left uncomfortable and ill at ease. There is something here which is not right, and we know it.

A Divided World

This is not just a matter of concern to us within the church. It is of great importance to the entire human family, for the source of its healing is impaired. From the very beginning the story of man has been scarred by conflict and division. Although peoples of all races and nations share a common origin and draw their existence from a common source, they compete with each other for place and power, and human blood has been spilled all over the landscape. People everywhere have similar needs and share common hopes and aspirations, yet they live in fear that others will do them in. Separated from God in the attempt to make it on their own, they end up being separated from each other. So the human story is marked by strife and conflict, by hatred and prejudice, and by all the inhuman things people do to each other. If you feel a bit detached from all of this, mark how conflict and division can tear a family apart, how neighbors can act in unneighborly ways, how crime in alarming proportions has rendered our streets unsafe. The fundamental human problem is not just in some distant place; it is at our doorstep, it is even in our own hearts.

It is to such a world that God has moved to turn things around. Isaiah caught a glimpse of it when he wrote, "The people who walked in darkness have seen a great light." Matthew saw these words fulfilled as Jesus began his ministry. The core of his message was, "Repent, for the kingdom of heaven is at hand." Change your mind, for the reign of God is knocking at your door. A new kingdom has arrived. A new way of living together is here. God is creating a new people, the society of the twice-born, a fellowship in which people find peace with God and peace with each other.

After this announcement, Jesus' first order of business was to select his disciples—the people with whom he would live and work until they were prepared to bring to the world the good news of what God is doing. This is the beginning of the church, the people called out from the world into this new society that they may go back into the world to make known by word and deed the power of Jesus Christ to bring healing to the nations. Love and peace are not ideals hung high in the sky, but are the actual experience of those to whom God offers the gracious gift of his kingdom. Into the society of man, torn and fragmented, a new society has been placed. It is a light shining in the darkness because he who is the light of the world lives and moves within it. It is a city set on a hill that cannot be hid.

The Church at Corinth

We can understand then why Paul was so troubled as he wrote to the church at Corinth. Word had come to him that this fragile church, barely on its feet, was torn by dissension. The people were not getting along together. They were dividing into competing groups, based on which apostle had led them to faith. One group identified with Paul, another Apollos, another Peter, and another—as if to say a plague on all your houses—claimed they belonged to Christ. Instead of rejoicing in their oneness in Christ, they were splitting off into separate groups, each one uncertain about the integrity of the other.

Paul could see that the future of that congregation, set within the turbulent environment of bustling Corinth, was threatened. "I appeal to you, brethren, by the name of our Lord Jesus Christ, that all of you agree and that there be no dissensions among you, but that you be united in the same mind and the same judgment." Paul was not just offering some sound advice, but was calling upon the authority of Christ himself to set things right. It was immaterial who baptized them; the overriding truth was that they had come into a new kingdom of love and grace, and this determined that they should live in peace and harmony with each other.

It may seem to us that these people were hung up on unimportant matters, and that is just the point! Time and time again the unity of the church has been threatened by turning minor matters into major issues. We all have our hidden agendas, those self-protecting motives that drive us to make big issues out of small ones. Our priorities can easily become confused so that we lose sight of the fact that it is Christ that we serve and not ourselves.

We all see things with our own eyes; we test every event by our own experience, but the central reality that brings us together is Christ. He it is who reveals God the Father to us and brings us to the forgiveness of sins. It is his continued presence through the Holy Spirit who creates faith and gives form and shape to our life in Christ. To live in his kingdom does not mean that we surrender our uniqueness. We each come as we are, with our gifts and talents, with our distinctive powers. It is our sins which are taken away, not the splendid investment of powers and possibilities which God has made in us. In the broad expanse of God's love there is room for varieties of experience and expresson, but all of them find their source and draw their power from Jesus Christ.

Holding the Family Together

Is Christ divided? That question leaps out of our biblical text to challenge our satisfaction with the way things are in the household of faith, and to keep us moving toward fuller expressions of the unity we have in Christ.

How can we speak the reconciling word to a fragmented world if we ourselves are not reconciled to each other? How can we bring healing to the gaping wounds of the human family if we ourselves are not healed? How can we share the warmth of God's love to lonely people, if we feel isolated and alone and retreat from each other? How can we speak of the victory of Christ over all the forces of evil in the world, if we ourselves are defeated by the subtle evils that creep into our own lives?

We cannot speak of love to the world if we ourselves act in unloving ways. Nor can we press upon others the demands of justice if we are unfair to each other. Nothing less than the credibility of the church, is at stake, and this is why Paul was constrained to speak so forthrightly to the people of Corinth. The kingdom of love and grace is not a pious theory hovering on some distant horizon, but is the life-transforming experience of those who have found their place within it. If, indeed, we are the people of God, set in this place at this time, we will be drawn by the power of the Holy Spirit to reach out to each other. We will not be hung up by minor matters but will see that the things that unite us are far greater than the things that might keep us apart. It is Christ who holds the family together, and the closer we are drawn to him, the closer we are drawn to each other.

In a world anxiously searching for peace, in a world where people urgently need to help each other, God is calling his church, united in love and purpose, to lead the way! And you and I, thank God, through the gift of our baptism, share in the new society of his kingdom. Strengthened and shaped by faith, nourished in the Holy Supper, we live within his grace and love. Out of these unlimited resources, in the places where we live and work, we can do our part to make the dream of unity and peace come true.

RAYMOND W. HEDBERG
Arlington Hills Lutheran Church
St. Paul, Minnesota

GOD'S SERENDIPITY FOR YOU

Fourth Sunday after the Epiphany

1 Corinthians 1:26-31

Serendipity is one of those "in" words among many Christians these days. I am uncomfortable when a group of people use jargon that excludes some who don't know the language, so I want to begin with a definition of terms. Serendipity is a term used to refer to a pleasant, unexpected event or experience; a surprise experience or insight when God's love comes to you. To put it very simply, serendipity is a *surprise experience of God's grace,* one you didn't plan on ahead of time or work for. You can't predict serendipity.

Serendipity Is Grace

At our men's breakfast last Wednesday one of you mentioned how every Christmas you hear the same story. The Virgin Mary —the manger—the shepherds—the Wise Men—the star over Bethlehem. The story doesn't change, but each Christmas we experience something new and something different in that same story. There is no new twist to the story today. The carols are the same. But I am confident that there is serendipity for you— a new and unexpected experience of God's love.

You may miss it if your heart is closed or cold. You may ignore it if your life is too cluttered with other things. You may reject it if you prefer to live in your own closed shell or you may even fight it as Herod did, knowing that there is a conflict between what I want and what God wants to do in this world. Yes, as with every Christmas, some of us will miss it. Some of us will ignore it. Some of us will reject it. Some of us fight it. But some will follow the star. They will not be distracted by the Herods who want to take advantage of the event for personal gain and attention, but will follow the star to Bethlehem. And without a lot of explanation or fanfare they will fall down and worship the child, having found in him God's serendipity, God's surprise visitation, a new experience of God's unexpected presence.

Serendipity Is Surprise

Paul was well aware of serendipitous nature of God's love. That's why he wrote to the Corinthians saying, "God chose what is foolish in the world to shame the wise. He has chosen what is weak to shame the strong." Nowhere do you see this more dramatically acted out than at Christmas. The wise and the strong referred to here are those who think they have everything figured out in life. They have all the answers. There are those who live as though they don't need God. They don't need faith. They don't need the fellowship of the church. They don't need people. The wise and strong that Paul refers to are those who live as owners rather than debtors. How easy it is to become oblivious to the "giftness" of life and lose sight of the meaning of the beatitudes when Jesus said:

> "Blessed are the poor in spirit for theirs is the kingdom of heaven.
> Blessed are the meek for they shall inherit the earth."

God is full of surprises. He has chosen the foolishness of becoming one of us, "being born in the likeness of sinful flesh." The Christmas Story reminds us that God has come to pitch his tent alongside ours. He has become one of us. That in itself is so contrary to our wisdom that it blows our minds to think about it.

Few of us have caught on to what this means for the church's mission in the world today. What does it mean for us to become one with those we are sent to help? Too often when we come in the flesh we come as the superior ones, the rich ones, the ones with all the answers. God has come in the flesh. He has come in weakness. I don't understand all this, yet it has helped me to appreciate his presence and his love.

He still comes in the flesh. He is present in people today. He is especially present in people who are hurting. "For I was thirsty and you gave me drink; I was in prison and you visited me; I was hungry and you fed me." Yes, he has chosen foolishness . . . weakness to bring about his creative presence in our midst.

The Christmas story is full of foolishness—full of weakness. It is full of surprise. Born in a barn with animals and manure . . . God's chosen one. Born of a virgin, perhaps a 15-year-old Jewish girl of no wealth or status. Born in Bethlehem . . . a small, two-bit town of no importance. The first to hear about it were the peasant farmers . . . the shepherds putting in their graveyard shift on the hillsides outside Bethlehem. That's as foolish as Jesus coming to California and the first people to hear and see him were the Mexican farm workers in the lettuce fields. Why the shepherds? Why the foreigners from those pagan eastern countries? God has chosen the foolish, the weak. God is full of surprises. He does not always play according to our rules. He does not always fit into our system. He pops up and makes his presence known in the most unusual places and circumstances.

Often we are as surprised and fearful as the shepherds were or as Herod was.

Last summer, while on vacation, I read the book *Born Again*. Who would have guessed that the hatchet man in a corrupt administration would have come to know Christ. Again I was reminded that God is full of surprises. I also read Mark Hatfield's book *Between a Rock and a Hard Place*. That was serendipity for me. God came to me through that book and said, "don't give up, George. There are Christians in politics who believe in justice, who are working to correct oppression. There are signs of hope in the system."

Serendipity Is "Foolishness"

There is another serendipity in the Christmas narrative that has come to my attention this year. It appears in the magnificat, the Song of Mary, a song of praise, which she uttered after she became aware that she was pregnant and to be the mother of God's servant. You will find it in the first chapter of Luke. Mary talks of God's goodness, God's action in history. She tells how God exalts those of low degree. "He fills the hungry with good things, but the rich he will send empty away." These words of Mary speak of social revolution at the core of the Gospel.

According to Mary, the birth of Jesus would mean good news for the poor, the hungry, but the rich would be sent away empty. Now my problem is, how am I to read this since I am among the rich in the world? Where is there any good news for me in the Christmas story if Jesus came to identify with the poor . . . the forgotten . . . the powerless? I live in America where we have accumulated most of the wealth and riches of the world. I live among the 6 percent of the world's population that is consuming 40 percent of the earth's resources. As God looks down upon his creation this night I have no doubt that I am among the rich. And the Bible says God's coming in the flesh will mean the rich will be sent away empty.

Talk about foolishness. Anybody with any smarts knows that if you are going to accomplish anything in this world, you need to make your appeal to those with means, with money. People with money are able to make things happen. Get to know the right people. Right? But God has chosen foolishness in the world to shame the wise. The words of Mary about the coming of Jesus are not only foolish sounding, they are disturbing . . . revolutionary. Some of God's surprises don't appeal to me, or go in my favor.

Of course, one way I can get off the hook is to spiritualize this passage and say it means spiritually poor. That's an easy out. Or I can say he meant only the very rich, like the millionaires. But integrity with the scriptures will not allow me to take either escape hatch. One of God's serendipities is that he does seem to identify with hurting people of this world . . . with the poor and oppressed. The rest of the Gospel narrative bears this out. This is one aspect of the Gospel that is becoming more and more disturbingly clear to me. I am learning that if I want to follow Jesus, I will find him among the poor and oppressed. This does not mean that he loves me any less because I am among the rich. But it does tell me something about what my priorities will become if I take Jesus seriously. You will not find him in the inn: You will find him in the manger of a barn. "God has chosen what is weak to shame the strong."

Serendipity Is Insight

Could it be that God's serendipity, God's surprise for us this Christmas is the insight that enough is enough . . .
- that in a more simple life-style I will experience God's love?
- that the foolishness of "small is beautiful" is putting to shame the covetousness of more and bigger?
- that through greater interdependence with other peoples and with creation I find healing and health?
- that God is saying something very profound and clear through the world hunger crises?

God is full of surprises. At first glance, it looks like foolishness or weakness, but within and underneath the hay and swaddling clothes we find the very presence of God, and something happens to us.

Who would have guessed it? That a Saturday trip to an orphanage in Tijuana would change a person's whole attitude toward life? Some who went to Tijuana only saw dirty faces and bumpy roads. But there is someone sitting here who experienced God's presence at that orphanage more clearly than they had ever experienced sitting in a sanctuary.

Who would have guessed it? A young mother was driving home from the doctor's office having just learned that surgery was necessary . . . immediately. It might be malignant. Then in the mailbox she found a card from those in her small group saying, "We love you. God cares, so do we." It felt like God was putting his arms around her at that moment.

Who would have guessed it? A storm off the coast of Mexico

caused an amateur sailor to leave his sailboat and hitchhike several hundred miles through Mexico, where he encountered poverty as he had never seen it before. What looked like nothing but disaster helped someone to learn to be thankful for life and what simple living is all about. God's surprise appearances are often hidden beneath pain and suffering and crisis.

Who would have guessed it? Panic pantry . . . the practice of bringing a can or two of food on the first of the month. What good does it do? Listen to a letter received this week. It is addressed to you.

Dear friends:

I want to thank you for bringing joy into my life. The food and money you shared was deeply appreciated. You will never know how hopeless it seemed.

My son has been in three different prisons. My one daughter is on drugs and has two children but no husband. My life has been one disappointment after another. Most days it looks so hopeless.

But when I needed some help, you people were so willing to share. Please tell your people that God's love came to me and my family through your generosity. Thank you and God bless you.

God has many surprises for you. I don't know how or when or where they will happen, but you will find serendipity. And then God's love will warm your heart and shake you loose from your drowsiness and indifference, and open your eyes to the real reason for your existence. The manger, the cross, the empty tomb are all part of the foolishness of God. To the eye of faith that foolishness becomes the power of God that brings life out of death and despair.

GEORGE S. JOHNSON
Christ Lutheran Church
Long Beach, California

HOW TO LIGHTEN YOUR BURDEN

The Transfiguration of Our Lord—Last Sunday after the Epiphany
2 Peter 1:16-19 (20-21)

One of the more novel Christmas gifts I received was this sturdy, disposable flashlight. I have used it in my automobile to read maps after dark. It has helped me find house numbers and see the names on street signs. My little green flashlight is a handy gadget.

On Wednesday morning of last week, I awoke at quarter of five. An uneasy feeling came over me. The house seemed particularly chilly. I rolled over and tried to fall back to sleep but could not. So I got up to put my mind at ease that everything was all right. Then I discovered that we had no electricity. There was a good reason for the unusual chill, besides the lowering of our thermostat. I groped about in the dark, walked down the stairs and into my study where this flashlight was lying on the desk. How relieved I was to find light with which to check the fuse boxes of our home. My flashlight even helped me find the telephone number of my friendly electric utility company. I appreciate light the most when I am trying to escape the darkness.

The Transfiguration Vision

It was a dark hour for Jesus when God sent light for a special purpose. Near the end of his earthly life, Christ spoke openly with his disciples about his suffering, death and resurrection (Matt. 16:21ff.). Peter thought such a destiny was unfit for the one he acknowledged to be the Messiah—God's promised person sent to redeem and restore the people of Israel. Both before and after his transfiguration Jesus spoke of how he would be tortured, killed, and raised again on the third day (Matt. 17:22ff.). The inevitability of Christ's suffering and death provided the dark framework within which the transfiguration vision occurred.

Four men braved the exertion of trudging up a high mountain. Perhaps their faces were still flushed, their veins and arteries beating full of blood, their breath coming hard, when one of them began to glow. He grew brighter, not with the brightness of a person freshly bathed. The brightness of his face was like the painful glare of the white hot sun. His clothing became as brilliant as light itself. Strange visitors appeared on the scene—Moses and Elijah. After they disappeared, Peter was talking about building memorial booths, when the sky above them thundered with the voice of God, "This is my beloved Son, with whom I am well pleased; listen to him."

That did it. The three fell over with fright. Jesus touched them. Feeling his presence, they had the courage to look up. The four were alone. Jesus might have said, "How'd you like that? That was really something, wasn't it?" Instead, he spoke quietly, "Tell no one the vision, until the Son of man is raised from the dead." (Matt. 17:9).

"Save the light for the darkness," Christ seemed to say. "The time will come when you stand naked and alone in the midst of a dark day. Then the light of this moment will lighten your burden. You will be able to witness to me. Impoverished by worldly standards, your life will be abundant—because we shared this moment together."

Christ didn't say all of that. But if you read the meaning of the transfiguration experience from the life of Peter, you understand that that is what the event meant to him.

The Transfiguration for Peter and John

Propelled by the Pentecost miracle, through their locked doors and into the streets of Jerusalem, Peter and John spoke boldly to all who would listen, saying that the same Jesus who was crucified was now risen and powerfully ascended. Thousands responded to their stirring spirit-filled speech. Perhaps the day after Pentecost, the two approached the temple at the hour of prayer, where a man lame from the time of his birth begged from them. Boldly the pair promised to free him from his beggary. What joy and wonder happened as the lame man walked and praised God for the unexpected gift. Everything was going well.

Then someone turned the lights out as the priests, the captain of the temple and the Sadducees vented their jealous anger against Peter and John. Both were arrested and thrown into a stinking jail overnight. In the morning the magistrates demanded as a condition of their release that they cease preaching a risen Jesus Christ. It was a dark hour—a time of testing that proved the two disciples had more than the light of success to sustain their ministry. They would not go away quietly, but instead replied, "Whether it is right in the sight of God to listen to you rather than to God, you must judge; for we cannot but speak of what we have seen and heard" (Acts 4:19-20).

Peter and John had heard the Word! Peter and John had seen the light! Each said it their own way. For John it was: "The word was God . . . and the Word became flesh." "In him was life, and the life was the light of men. The light shines in the darkness and the darkness has not overcome it." John the Baptist came to bear witness to the light. Jesus said, "I am the light of the world."

Like rays of light that pierce through dense fog, Peter in the text for today spoke to people plagued by false prophets, tempted to immoral living, and mocked by those who said there was no life after death.

Peter found light for the darkness of doubt on the mountain of transfiguration. The light he saw there in the face of Jesus, and the enlightenment he received from the words of God which pounded against his eardrums, authenticated the claim of Christ that the entire Old Testament was filled full of new meaning in his life, his death, his rising again. That Old Testament became like a guiding light to Peter, on the basis of his personal experience when Christ was transfigured.

The Transfiguration and You

The testimony of Peter and the witness of John are more than first person accounts of what it was like in the good old days. If that's all there is, then we came to this moment for naught. The Holy Spirit given to Peter and John on Pentecost is still active and powerful, working through their witness.

Look what has been happening throughout history when the glory of God is revealed to his people. Our Old Testament lesson for today speaks of a time when Moses, like Peter and John, was called up into a mountain. In the day of Moses, the people of Israel were commanded not to touch the base of that mountain lest they become consumed by God's glory. According to the book of Exodus, the glory of God descended on Mount Sinai and covered it for six days. The appearance of the glory of the Lord was like a devouring fire (Exod. 24:12, 15-18).

What a difference between that scene and the good news that the glory of the Lord shone round about the shepherds outside the town of Bethlehem. Listen to the song of Simeon as he sings a ballad about a baby born as "a light for revelation to the Gentiles, and for glory to the people of Israel" (Luke 2:32). The words on top of transfiguration mountain are, "Rise, and have no fear" (Matt. 17:7). "There is light and power for successful living in all the murky, confusing mess of daily life as you encounter it," Peter is saying. It's true. There is! God has come into our life to enable us to make a change. God did not only transfigure Jesus. When we discover the glory of God in the person of Jesus Christ, God transfigures *us*.

Maybe we don't shine and sparkle like the sun. Perhaps no one has yet offered to build a monument to our life. It may be that only on rare occasions has our life been so dynamically lived that those around us have heard the voice of God while in our presence, "This is my beloved son or daughter." But it is not sacrilege to say that that is precisely who we are.

When you were baptized into Jesus Christ, you put Christ on —life, death, burial, resurrection—the whole works including transfiguration. You became a son or daughter of God through baptism. You are no longer a weakling, unable to bear up under the burden of sin. You've been transfigured—changed! The Scriptures speak clearly on the subject. "We were buried therefore with him by baptism into death, so that as Christ was raised from the dead by the glory of the Father, we, too, might walk in newness of life (Rom. 6:4).

The glory of the Father raised Jesus and made it possible for us to resist sin. Sin can no longer overcome us when we recognize what spiritual strength we have in Jesus Christ. Has the burden of your sin made you a spiritual cripple? In the name of Jesus Christ I say to you, "Get up. Your sin is forgiven." Walk around and praise God for removing sin's burden.

Like the light of my flashlight, which may be used for many different purposes, so the glory of God and the light of the transfiguration experience may have a different application in the life of each one of us. With Peter we may appreciate it as an event which helped to authenticate the message of the Old Testament. With Peter, James and John, we may find it a power for purposeful living during those days when the presence of Christ seems far removed. With our Savior, we may find in it a witness to our own membership in the family of God—a strengthening experience for the time of tragedy. It undoubtedly helped Christ to take up his cross.

Choose any or all of these meanings. How fortunate we are to live at a time when God reveals himself with the greatest possible intimacy. Christ in our flesh! Eating his body and drinking his blood! Being the body of Christ in our world! Knowing that Christ is with us always! Who can grasp the wonder of it all? That God should be so accessible and we are not consumed by his presence but instead are empowered by his love is a miracle beyond understanding.

If Christ took our greatest burden upon himself—our sin— will he not lift all our other burdens? He will! God cared enough to give a special preparatory experience to the inner circle of disciples that when life looked the bleakest, they would have strength for the day. When darkness descends upon your living, look to the light. In the Scriptures you will find a clear witness to the power of God. In the lives of the saints who lived before you and who live with you, you will find the light of God's love intended for your life. When you see, believe—and pass the light on to others.

GEORGE F. LOBIEN
The Lutheran Church of St. Andrew
Silver Spring, Maryland

A WORD FOR US MODERNS
First Sunday in Lent
Romans 5:12 (13-16) 17-19

This is the First Sunday in Lent. Approximately 1250 years ago Gregory II, in order to obtain uniform practices in the church, declared that Ash Wednesday, the beginning of Lent, was to be observed 40 days before Easter. The history of Lent goes farther back than that however. In the early church, eight days of fasting and preparation were observed prior to the Easter festival.

This year again, tied as we are to the Christians of many centuries, we begin a season of preparation which will reach its climax when we behold the death and resurrection of Christ on the Easter weekend. We will again center our thoughts on his trial, suffering, and words from the cross. We will, at the climax, sit in amazement when we hear the fourth word from the cross, "My God, why have you forsaken me?" It is almost an unbearable word; we cannot comprehend it. There is a story told about a man who had thought for a long time about that word from the cross. He finally arose with the cry, "God forsaken by God," who can say anything about that?

We can do very little more than he. What we can do is limited to this: we can try to listen obediently and to appreciate the revelation even though that very revelation does not permit our comprehension. In so doing we at least are following the command that was laid down for us, "This is my beloved son with whom I am well pleased; listen to him."

An Incomprehensible Word

It is fitting that as we begin the Lenten season, we are faced with a similar incomprehensible revelation. Sandwiched in between the story of the temptation of Adam and the temptation of Jesus, we have these almost unbearable words of St. Paul, "Sin came into the world through one man and death through sin, and so death spread to all men because all men sinned—because of one man's trespass, death reigned through that one man—one man's trespass led to condemnation for all men."

These words of Paul are particularly incomprehensible to us today. After all, we know so much more than Paul. Why should we listen to him? Hampered as he obviously was by a limited view of the world, why should we consider seriously what he has to say. There are even some who suggest that Paul spoiled what Jesus had to say.

Paul is particularly offensive to us moderns because he says that death came into the world by the sin of one man. Now how can that be? Is not death an end to life? Is not death as natural as life? We moderns deny that death is anything other than a natural process. After all, we are finite and it is only natural that we should die.

Paul's teaching about sin is also incomprehensible to us. How can death possibly come from sin, for is not sin natural to man? Do we not all have our hang-ups, and are not all who have more serious hang-ups ill? Are we not finite and therefore subject to failure? Is this not natural? It appears to us that Paul is somewhat limited in his view of reality in his rather naive presentation and identification of sin and death. We moderns, how we prattle along.

What has it done for us—our superior view of reality, our vast knowledge of the world, our sophisticated technology, and our immodest wisdom? In our modern era we have made sin and death so natural and so unrelated that they can occur without protest. Death is permissible because death is natural. To use death in order to achieve our political and economic ends is permissible. The death of 20 million peasants was for Stalin a natural and desirable means to achieve his end, as were the 6 million Jews for Hitler. We used to complain about the Jesuit philosophy that the end justifies the means. We no longer complain about it, we utilize it fully.

One of the words that Paul uses in our text for sin is the word disobedience. He compares the disobedience of Adam to the obedience of Christ. It is significant that the word disobedience indicates not only an overstepping or violation of the law but prior to that an unwillingness to hear. We see that in the two temptation accounts. Bonhoeffer in his little book *Temptation* states that "innocence means clinging to the word of God with pure undivided hearts." The tempter must therefore utilize the name of God and expound on the word of God—Has God really said this? Have you really understood God rightly? The disobedience of the first Adam was the unwillingness to hear what God said and cling to it. The obedience of the Son, in his temptation, lay precisely in his undivided loyalty to what God said.

Incomprehensible though this word of Paul may be to us today, we have no alternative but to listen carefully even though it may contradict what we think. Revelation always casts aside what people think.

Paul's View of Sin

Paul has a very serious view of sin as did our Lord. Jesus said that out of the heart of man proceeds all forms of iniquity. Paul almost gives sin a personality. He describes it as a living thing. As you read through this chapter and the other chapters of Romans, you discover its nature and its power. It is something from the outside that came into the world and seriously affected the whole condition of mankind. Sin is a power which Paul says reigns and rules and dominates. In Galatians he says that everything is subject to it. He further states that we are all enslaved to it, that we have been sold into its services. But sin is a generous master; it pays wages to those that serve it—and the wages are death.

In one sense, it is entirely permissible to identify sin with Satan. In Romans 5:12 one can almost substitute the word Satan for sin without losing any of the force or meaning. There is an interesting comparison that is drawn in the gospel of John. In the 9th chapter, a man is spoken of as being born in sin. In the 8th chapter Jesus tells his hard-hearted opponents that they will die in their sin. Sin seems to be very definitely set in contrast to and opposed to truth. When Jesus says you will die in your sin, he is saying you will die in your falsehood. In another place he says that Satan is the father of lies, the father of that which is untrue.

Scripture portrays people as slaves—the alternatives that it presents is slavery to sin or slavery to God. Paul says by one man this living, powerful taskmaster entered into the world and became the dominant reality in everyone's life. By one man's disobedience, all were made sinners—it affected his total personhood, his relationship with God—it brought death.

Pelagius Lives On

Poor Bishop Pelagius, I say poor, because he is not a popular figure in the history of the church. Yet he did us a favor, he did bring to the fore this matter of sin and grace. Pelagius, you see, taught that Adam's sin had not really affected mankind, that we were born in a state of moral indifference, without virtue or vice but capable of both. He also said that by an act of our will we can develop in virtue and thus be saved. There was in Pelagius's view not that much need for real grace and salvation by Christ because we can by the strength of our will do what was right. This is the sort of naturalism that we still face in the modern world. It has its affect on us—we need often to turn to this statement of Paul, to this revelation of God, and face the reality of the power of sin that resides in us. In so doing, we preserve the Christological principle, that is, only by the obedience of one man, Jesus Christ, are we made righteous.

Pelagious is still with us, only he comes in more subtle forms. The last century, on the North American continent, has seen the development of a whole host of holiness sects, all dedicated to eradicating sin. In more recent years, we have witnessed the charismatic renewal, some with enthusiasm, others with some alarm.

Listen to what Frederick Bruner says in *A Theology of the Holy Spirit:* "It is the Pentecostal conviction that when Christians remove all known sin the Holy Spirit can dwell in their hearts even though there may still be unconscious or unknown (and hence, apparently, unculpable) sin. In any case, as far as the candidate knows he must be without sin, for it is impossible for the Pentecostal to contemplate sin and the Holy Spirit coinhabiting the Christian's heart."

Paul says that it is entirely possible, in fact, it is a reality, for sin and the Holy Spirit to coinhabit the heart of the Christian. Our Lord has won the battle by his obedience, by his suffering, by his death. He his destroyed the power of the evil one. He has destroyed the power of sin and death, and through his act and by his grace we are declared righteous and justified. Nevertheless, sin is still present with all its potential power for destruction. It still couches at the door.

The Lord's word to Cain is still relevant, "If you do well, will you not be accepted? And if you do not do well, sin is couching at the door; its desire is for you, but you must master it." Sin is still couching at the door in the heart of every one of us and its desire is still for each of us. The good news is that it has been mastered and that with Christ as Lord, by his grace and by the power of the Spirit, we too can be triumphant.

It is no easy task. Our Lord's 40 days in the wilderness demonstrated that. He who knew no sin came in the likeness of sinful flesh in order to save us. By the grace of that one man Jesus, the free gift not only abounds for many, but brings justification. By the grace of God and by the grace of that one man Jesus, the free gift of righteousness reigns in our life now. Though by one man's disobedience, we became disobedient, so by another man's obedience are we now called righteous.

We must cling to the word of God. That is what our Lord did, that is how he saved us, that is how he will preserve us. If sin's desire is for us, God's desire for us is greater, just as his free gift is greater than the effect of Adam's sin.

K. GLEN JOHNSON
President, Camrose Lutheran College
Camrose, Alberta

GOD'S STRANGE ECONOMY
Second Sunday in Lent
Romans 4:1-5, 13-17

God would never make it through the Harvard Business School. A strange economy marks his grace. You and I have been schooled to think in terms of the American dream. Progress, expansion, development, production, growth, bigness, the breaking of barriers, the pushing back of frontiers, the refusal to admit limits, the sense of power and success, the path of achievement and merit—these are the principles which govern our thinking. These are the values we reinforce. Think of how our speech gets punctuated with sayings like: Be strong. Stand on your own feet. Work your way up. Be self-reliant.

Haven't we been taught that America has become a great nation by dint of courageous self-reliance and hard work? The American frontier spirit of self-reliance has shaped our lives and value systems. Our capitalistic philosophy of earn-what-you-get still pays good dividends in our work-a-day world. That message gets so massaged into us that there is little wonder that our religion gets contaminated by it as well. A major spiritual hazard goes with generalizing a capitalistic merit mentality into all areas of life. Do-it-yourselfism may be OK economics, but it makes for a lousy religion and it's heretical Christianity.

In today's epistle, St. Paul helps us to think through this troublesome tendency to prefer merit to mercy and to say to God, "But Lord, I'd rather do it myself."

(Read Text)

Abraham. Now there's a hero for you. Israel's first great patriarch. The father of the faithful. Ask any person who has been even moderately faithful in Sunday school, and he'll recall some of the memorable stories about Abraham.

Some may even be able to quote that great call passage in Genesis 12: "Go from your country and your kindred and your father's house to the land that I will show you. And I will make of you a great nation, and I will bless you, and make your name great, so that you will be a blessing." Abraham believed and obeyed.

"What a beautifully obedient faith," you say. "What courage to leave home, family, and country and to journey by faith." And indeed, how remarkable. In response to the promise of land and seed, Abraham set out for a land not his own, with a wife who was barren.

Once when Abraham was camped at Shechem, the Lord appeared to him and renewed the promise: "To your descendants I will give this land" (Gen. 12:7). But what did Abraham see as he looked out upon the land? A flourishing Canaanite stronghold. Only by an act of faith could Abraham acknowledge the Lord's ownership of the land and promised intentions to transfer its title from the Canaanites to Abraham and his descendants.

And what of the promise that from Abraham's loins would come a "great nation"—as innumerable as the "dust of the earth" (13:16)? Abraham was given the promise: "Your own son shall be your heir" (15:4). Abraham accepted that promise in silent faith and looked for the son of promise.

You remember how that trust was tested after Isaac was born. Abraham was called by God to sacrifice his only beloved son on one of the mountains in the land of Moriah. Abraham responded in perfect obedience. To Isaac's probing question about a sacrificial animal, he returned an answer calculated to inspire in his son a like measure of faith: "God will provide himself the lamb . . . , my son" (22:8). In this excruciating test, father and son exhibit a splendid faith, each in the other and both in God.

Two Themes Predominate

Two themes stand out in the biblical accounts of Abraham: God's promise of innumerable seed and the land of Canaan, and Abraham's faithful response. We, like the ones to whom Paul was writing, are apt to overplay the latter at the expense of the former. We say: "Wasn't Abraham a great man? Isn't his obedience commendable? Didn't he beautifully model faithfulness?

No wonder God loved him and declared him to be righteous! Wouldn't such meritorious living deserve such a reward?"

Paul is emphatic in challenging such thinking. In the kingdom of God there are no self-made men. The rule of merit and reward has to give way to the rule of faith. Paul denies both that Abraham had anything to boast of before God and that his justification was by works. Paul is not denying either the fact of Abraham's good works or his right to pre-eminence among men on account of them, but is asserting that his favor with God was on a different basis—the basis of faith. Abraham might rightfully expect honor from other people, but that is a different matter from having something to boast about before God.

Perhaps it would be easier to credit God's mercy above Abraham's merit if we were not so selective in our remembrance of the biblical record. Perhaps our need for heroes is so great that we block out the negatives. Abraham was not without sin. One illustration will do.

An Imperfect Faithfulness

In spite of God's promise that Abraham would have a son of his own, Sarah remained barren. Despairing of bearing a child herself and no longer able to believe that God would accomplish his word, she proposed that Abraham go in to her maid Hagar, reasoning: "It may be that I shall obtain children by her" (Gen. 16:2). Abraham who showed commendable faith on other occasions fell far short here. By acceding to Sarah's plan, Abraham too demonstrated a grave lack of trust in that he doubted the Lord's power and took the matter into his own hands. Therefore, Ishmael could not be the promised child, and the fulfillment was further delayed until the birth of Isaac. It was not a question of Hagar's servant status, for according to the prevailing custom her child would legally be considered Sarah's own. It was, rather, that God's rich blessing stored up for Abraham and Sarah could not be carried through a child begotten in such faithless impatience.

"Now we know that whatever the law says it speaks to those who are under the law, so that every mouth may be stopped, and the whole world may be held accountable to God" (Rom. 3:19). Human sin is one and indivisible. All have sinned and fall short of the glory of God. And there is one radical way of dealing with it, which is the same for Jews and Gentiles, for those who are as faithfully obedient as Abraham or those who seem to have no conscience whatsoever.

If you think you will be declared righteous because you read your Bible, contribute liberally and gladly to worthy causes, do a good turn regularly, and haven't imbibed in many of the sins of the world—if you think those good marks are going to qualify you before God, you're living under a grave misapprehension of what the Bible declares. St. Paul is ruling out justification on the basis of merit.

Luther tried it for years. He was a model monk. For a considerable time he lived an awesomely austere life, cloistered from the evils of the world, incessantly in prayer, subjugating his body and mind to things of God. But he found no peace. There were always yet more sins to confess. Something deep within him told him that no matter how hard he had tried, he had not always obeyed everything, and so he was under a curse—a curse which drove him near to despair, until he rediscovered by his study of Romans that God in his love has provided an alternate plan—a plan under which, instead of you doing it, God does it for you—the basis of a religion of mercy rather than of merit— the basis for becoming descendants of Abraham by faith.

Only Two Religions

Ever since the dawn of time, there have been basically two intermingled kinds of religion. One is a religion of *mercy*, and the other, a religion of *merit*. Those who hold to merit rely on personal effort and achievement. They think they can somehow buy, earn, or finagle their way into the kingdom of God. Those who hold to mercy stand on God's unmerited grace and favor. Christians profess that God in Jesus Christ gives salvation as his free gift.

But oh, how difficult to teach and learn that distinction so that it shapes and claims the entirety of our beings. Mercy and grace sound so strange to the modern ear. Our experiences for the most part seem to lie in the areas of merit, reward, and self-achievement. The teacher says: "Don't thank me; you earned your grade." The boss says: "You deserved the raise." The scoutmaster says: "You demonstrated the skill; here's your merit badge." If you want to be successful, we are told, you must pay the price in terms of boundless energy, fine tuned judgment, and a strong personal commitment to achieve. In a competitive world, those who make the best efforts normally achieve the best rewards.

Recently, Kemmons Wilson, founder and chairman of Holiday Inns, Inc., put it this way: "No man can be successful working just a 40-hour week—not unless he's absolutely brilliant, and most people are not brilliant. It's like the old saying, 'The harder I work, the luckier I get.' "

That's the thinking that bombards our lives six days a week. Little wonder then that we may hear on Sunday from a youth about to be confirmed that he certainly hopes to get to heaven because he sure is working hard to live a Christian life. Or even more distressing, we may hear from some charter church member about the moral life he's lived, the Golden Rule philosophy he's tried to abide by—implying, you see, that he's all but earned an eternal reward of righteousness and that, at worst, he may need a little of God's grace to make up the difference somehow, somewhere—but really not all that much, because, God knows, he's tried hard enough.

That kind of talk should grieve us all because it's based in a merit mentality. And it's still all too prevalent in American churches. Our lessons today aid us in focusing on what we may call America's foremost spiritual dilemma: how to keep a grace-oriented religion alive in a capitalistic earn-what-you-get environment.

Tracing God's Strange Economy

What a strange economy marks God's grace. And it has ever been so. The initial creative investment of the Eternal was without precedent. Even at the deflated prices of those early days, who could compute the cost of a world? Can't you hear a conservative angel challenge: "Lord, do you mean we are going to schedule a sunrise and sunset for each day?"

And the expense of upkeep! God couldn't get good help. The live-in couple he brought to Eden were rebellious and scheming. And as time passed, an ecological problem of human attitude became monumental. The Lord finally washed down the world with a flood. Still, people whined for more self-determination, finer comforts, better leaders, protection against their enemies. Can you conceive of the emotional expenditures in being God when you're heading up such a company?

None of this, however, approaches his most remarkable venture. When God suggested he might leave the home office, he must have heard from his angelic comptroller: "You're not going to become involved personally in that earthly mess, are you? Better to dismiss the whole enterprise as a bad deal. Cut your losses. Take a tax write-off."

Nevertheless, he came. Some say it was just throwing good life after bad. Others say there's an extravagance to God's grace.

They have found in him relief from the enslavement of a merit mentality. Yet strangely they have found themselves bound to this One who came as gift.

Yes, there's a strange economy to God's grace. Thank God!

ALLAN H. SAGER
Lutheran Theological Seminary
Columbus, Ohio

FROM DARKNESS TO LIGHT
Third Sunday in Lent
Ephesians 5:8-14

A Parable

Manuelo was a young man who lived in a remote mountain village. You could reach that village only after hiking on a narrow footpath for several hours. It was a place where the homes and customs had not changed for hundreds of years. But Manuelo was lucky: he had a chance to visit a big modern city. And everything he saw there was wonderful! He wanted to bring some of that wonder back to his village, something that would surprise and please his hillside neighbors. What should it be? It would have to be small and easy to carry, and it would have to be cheap, because Manuelo didn't have much money. So he went into a hardware store and bought a big paper sack full of electric light bulbs. And he bought sockets for those bulbs, with switches on them so he could turn the lights off and on. And he bought wires for hanging everything up in the trees of his home village.

Then Manuelo happily traveled back to his home in the mountains, bursting with his happy secret. That same afternoon he began making ready his surprise. Everyone asked, "What are you doing?" as they watched him hanging round glass bulbs from the ceiling of his porch, and from the fruit trees in his yard and in his neighbors' yards. But he just smiled at their questions and said mysteriously, "Wait until it's dark—you'll see." And finally when it was dark enough, Manuelo began to turn the switches for his light bulbs—but nothing happened! Poor Manuelo! Nobody had told him about electricity. He didn't know that light bulbs are useless glass and wire unless they are connected to a source of electric power.

And that's how it is with us—if we are to be lights in the world, we'll have to hook up to the power source: Jesus Christ, the Light of the world. And that connection with Christ is what we call our faith. St. Paul is speaking to people like us when he says, "Once you were darkness, but now you are light in the Lord: walk as children of light." He is telling us that through our faith in Christ we are moving from darkness to light. He is talking about our journey from darkness to light.

Danger

On this journey from darkness to light, there's danger: the danger of being found out, the danger of getting the skeletons in our closet exposed, the danger that we'll be seen as we really are, the danger that the wrong and nasty things in our lives may be revealed. At the very least, this could be embarrassing—at the most, it could be incriminating.

Remember, for example, the Watergate scandal. All of its architects are now disgraced and out of office; many have been sentenced and jailed. Their deeds have been "exposed by the light" as the "works of darkness." Or, think of the domestic surveillance activities of the CIA—the tapping of phones, the interception of mail. When that was brought to light, it caused a number of people extreme discomfort and embarrassment, as well as loss of position. Then there has been the exposure of corruption in the politics of certain states and counties, bringing some of the high and mighty folk down with heavy fines and jail sentences. Now the only way all this corruption and secret finagling and illegal activity could be stopped was by bringing it out into the open, into the light of day.

And that's the danger for us too, as we daily move from darkness to light—we just may not come out of it looking clean and smelling sweet. We too, in our personal lives and attitudes, have to expose to the light what's dark and bad, what's harmful and hateful. In this process, many a street angel is exposed and seen to be a house devil!

Risk

But this is the risk we take on this journey from darkness to light, when we realize that now we're light in the Lord, and we start walking as children of light. We have to take off our masks, we have to open ourselves up to one another, we have to start confessing our faults one to another. There's no use for me to pretend to be something or somebody I'm really not; there's no use for me to play the role of the virtuous and all-knowing Herr Pastor who never does anything wrong and speaks only in biblical words!

But speaking for myself, let me tell you that is a risk I'm overjoyed to take. More and more as I grow in faith along with you, I want to open myself up to you more and more and be *myself*—not some super picture pastor that I used to think people expected me to be! How about you? Do you find yourself willing and eager to take that risk too, as you play out your "role"—as manager, or boss, or teacher, or parent, or deacon, or student leader? Or, your "role" as worker, student, son, daughter, or member? Let's walk together in the light as children of light, taking that risk of being open and honest with one another—loving and forgiving one another as God in Christ forgives us!

The people of Alcoholics Anonymous have discovered something of this walking in the light, and the risk of it, and they willingly take that risk. At AA meetings, anyone who gets up to speak always begins by saying, "My name is Eric B., and I am an alcoholic." They begin by exposing themselves to the light, by making a confession of their uttter helplessness to overcome the problem of alcoholism by themselves. And as we see and hear them going through that painful process, we are reminded of the Christian process of conversion and repentance; we are confessing to our Lord that we are helpless in our darkness, we need the power of God's Holy Spirit that comes to us through our faith-relationship with Jesus Christ.

Growth

But only when we finally open ourselves up to the dangers and risks of exposure, only when we take this journey from darkness to light, is growth really possible. That's when we finally begin to *see*—and you've got to have the lights on for that! You will know what I mean, if you have ever tried to find your way through an unfamiliar room in the darkness—or even a familiar room. You bark your shins, you stumble against the furniture; nothing seems to be in the right place. The only way to correct the situation is to turn on the light—then you can make progress through the room.

And so when we walk in the light of Jesus Christ, he can bring correction, healing, and growth into our lives. When the light of Christ shows us the wrong direction in our lives, then we can turn and change and grow, following Christ and imitating him.

Learn from the plants: In my office there are two small potted plants sitting in the window. They always turn their leaves toward the window, toward the light. Sometimes I play a game with my plants: I turn them around so their leaves are facing into the room. But slowly, gradually, in a day or two, they always manage to turn themselves back to the window, back to the light.

More and more as we walk in the light, the power, the understanding, the love, and the life-style of Christ become more and more our power, our understanding, our love, and our life-style.

Opportunity

As you grow and grow in that light of Christ—it's a lifelong process—that light of Christ brings things into proper proportion, into a right relationship—it brings you new opportunity to really live as God's person! You'll find that you see your husband or wife in a new light, or your son and daughter, or your father and mother. Try this now, if you haven't already: In your mind, right now, look at those people in your life that I just mentioned—have you opened yourself up, have you really walked in the light with them, have you really tried to love and understand them? Do it—you can, because you are light in the Lord! And try it on the person at work, or at school, who's hard to get along with; try it at the next church meeting you attend—grasp the opportunity for a new relationship with the person you often thought got in your way, or wasted time at the meeting. Try it when you drive your car, especially in the frustrations of rush-hour traffic—try it in your attitude and actions toward the drivers around you. Try it in all your contacts with people through the day—grasp the opportunity to walk in the light.

Walking in the Light

This text was probably addressed especially to newly baptized Christians, people who had recently taken the journey from darkness to light. Paul wants to make them aware of the danger and the risk, as well as the growth and the opportunity that may be in store for them.

Workers in some of the mission fields today, both in our own country and abroad, can understand Paul's point very well. I remember some of my friends in Hawaii—for there especially were newly baptized people who were very conscious of their new life and new birth as they were beginning their new life-style of walking in the light. They well knew of the *danger*—for some, it could mean being disowned by parents; in fact, many Christians would decide to postpone their baptism until their parents died. And they knew the *risk*—losing friends, perhaps, or the close associations with family members and other relatives. But they also realized the potential for *growth* and *opportunity*—they appreciated more than some of us, perhaps, that Christianity is the religion of grace, that Jesus Christ is the Lord who forgives, who doesn't hold your past against you, no matter how dark it may be.

So it was part of my own growth and opportunity in those good years to see and understand that the first part of this verse, "Now you are light in the Lord," could be just a slogan or formula, could even become blasphemy, unless or until it is translated into this: "Walk as children of light." At the same time, I know it's a lifelong process, it doesn't happen overnight. Indeed, you never totally "arrive" on this earth; you're always "becoming," always growing. Little lights are going on from day to day, from year to year—as together we walk as children of light.

DAVID A. PREISINGER
First Trinity Lutheran Church
Washington, D.C.

THE CARTOGRAPHY OF FAITH
Fourth Sunday in Lent
Romans 8:1-10

If there is any time in the cycle of the Christian life that we ought to feel as though we are on the straight path, it is during Lent. As the Sundays build up from Palm Sunday to Easter, we become increasingly aware of the profound contradiction of life: of suffering and rebirth; of crucifixion and resurrection; of our Lord mocked and scourged and crucified and raised again on the third day. Focused on the sure and certain path of our Lord, we look forward to the events of Holy Week. Out of the confusion and conflicts of our life, our Lord's death and resurrection emerges as a clear and powerful drama by which to reassess our own life journey. His story becomes incorporated in our story, and it brings us abruptly to the fundamentals of our faith and shows us the contradictions in the short-term preoccupations of our daily existence. During Lent, the light of the life of Christ exposes the darkness of our own lives with his life, illuminating our lives with mercy and love.

A Sense of Direction

But today I am not reminded so much of the example of the Lenten sojourner on the way in faith, which is the theme of our

Gospel. Rather, I am challenged again by St. Paul's words describing not what it means to be on the path, to be found, or as in the story of our Gospel for today, to argue about the privilege of sitting next to Jesus—but I am reminded of what it means to be lost; to lose one's bearings, one's orientation in life and one's sense of direction. Our Epistle for today speaks to the heart of this familiar and frequent modern malaise.

Paul, addressing the Romans, sets the law of the Spirit in tension with the law of the flesh. He presents us, his listeners, with two choices on life's way: to live according to the flesh, or to live according to the Spirit. In Paul's terms, to live according to the law of the flesh means to live according to the law of blood relationships, past conventions and material benefits. It means to fall victim to our egoistic needs for power and self-fulfillment. By contrast, to live according to the law of the Spirit means to live in freedom from these obligations of the flesh. It means to live within a power that breaks through the barriers of the flesh and our material comforts; that moves, inspires, and builds up a human community not yet envisaged, but necessary to ensure life. On the basis of his long experience with the life of faith—enduring its hardships and knowing its ecstasy—the mature Paul lets his listeners know that there is a choice that needs to be made between these two ways of living and that from this decision follow weighty and divergent consequences: one way guarantees death, the other assures new life.

Now, what is the first thought that comes to our mind in making such a choice? Is it not the question of our goal? What is our goal? What do we want to accomplish in life by our choices? What will we accomplish by our choices? These are the questions we struggle with. So the context of our questions is not merely one of a choice between flesh and spirit, but there is a very practical decision at stake. What are the consequences of our choice? Where will it lead us?

A few evenings ago it was dark and raining, and together with a friend we were trying to find our way to an unfamiliar part of the city to call on another person. We knew the address, we had a clear understanding of our destination and we had the directions of how to get there. However, as we were driving along and talking we suddenly realized that something was wrong. We had either gone too far, or not far enough. We couldn't decide which side of the crucial intersection we were on where we needed to make a turn. Finally, in the rain, we stopped a pedestrian and asked him the location of our crossroads. Fortunately, unlike us, he was oriented to the area and could tell us that we had overshot our intersection by nearly a mile. With his careful words, he indicated the way back.

We had indeed been lost, and our resources were not enough to get us back on the way to our destination. But once this person who knew the area pointed us in the right way, the rest followed, and within ten minutes we were at the right address.

Knowing Your Goal

What, you may ask, has this to do with St. Paul and the epistle to the Romans, especially our sentence for today, "but if Christ is in you, although your bodies are dead because of sin, your spirits are alive because of righteousness"? It is the same problem of being lost on a rainy night; the goal and the way are what are at issue. For what is being said is that *if* you know your goal, and *if* you know the way, then the rest follows. "If Christ is in you"—if that is the goal of your life and if that is also your direction along the way—then in spite of the fact that your body is absolutely dead because of sin, worthless in helping you find your way, your spirit is alive because it knows both the goal and the way. It is the needle on the compass, steadily giving direction in spite of the tumultuous seas or the dark unclarity of the night.

In other words, once we get the goal and the way clear, the consequences of our choice of travel begin to unfold. In our family journeys, I was sometimes the navigator and there is something of that same miracle in being the navigator when you are on a long car trip. You decide where you want to go. Then you figure out the route you want to take, and then the miracle begins. The map—the tiny drawing on a piece of paper—takes you on the way to your destination. Though this is a very simple action, it is something that is always a source of wonder. It is this cartography of travel that provides a way for us to understand the cartography of faith.

Take Up Your Map and Walk

Perhaps the classic statement of this cartography of faith is Galatians 5:25, "If you live by the Spirit, let us walk by the Spirit." "If we live" is the map. It points the way. "Let us walk by the Spirit," let us get our feet moving, the car started, the energy empowered, let us be on the way to our destination. Always in Paul, the pointing of the way is conjoined with the admonition to move. We don't just *live* by the Spirit, we must also *walk* by the Spirit. What good is the finest map if it is never used? We can dream of the places we would like to go, but the fundamental transformation of the dream takes hold only when we actually begin the journey. When we take up our map and walk. When we walk by the Spirit.

This indicative of "if we live"—this pointing the way—is as natural to "let us walk in" as a sign on a roadway. When a "sharp curve" is indicated, you can be certain that a sharp curve is ahead. The sign and the reality are conjoined, just as the living and the walking are conjoined in the thought of St. Paul.

Now what does this choice and its implications say to us about the Christian faith? It says first of all that our life choices do make a difference to ourselves, to others, to God, to the future. Second, that at the moment we make the choice we cannot see all the implications. And third, it says that we can easily get off course, but the orientation is there if the goal and the way is clearly in focus. The inner compass, the law of the Spirit in St. Paul's terms, can be trusted.

Difficult Decisions

Today, during the great national and international debate on nuclear power and public policy, we find ourselves facing national decisions that will have consequences not only for our own lifetime, but for three or four or perhaps five centuries to come. Unlike the compass which is a fairly benign technology, introduced in western navigation about five hundred years ago from the Chinese, the technology of nuclear energy creates the ever present danger of radioactive materials getting out of control and of building up residual radioactivity, the full consequences of which are beyond our imagination. Now, all of this is being done on the justification that decreasing energy means more unemployment and recession. But have we looked at the consequences of such a short term justification in terms of the long range implications of generating more and more radioactive material, and the necessity of tighter and tighter controls on our society, and more policing in order to make sure that there are "no accidents"?

As you can see, the question posed by the nuclear energy debate is ultimately not a technical one, but a moral and religious one: How do we live, how do we want to shape our society in order to pass it on to future generations? What responsibilities do we have today for future generations? Are the benefits of full employment now worth the dangers which come with generating more and more radioactive materials? What is our moral responsibility toward the people of the future, towards some guarantee that they might live in freedom and in an ecologically safe environment?

In history, this debate over nuclear energy may turn out to be the great and decisive debate of our century. Is our response to it to ignore it, to turn our back and buy a new washer-dryer so that our own personal needs of the flesh are lighter? Can we afford to be like the ostrich, to bury our little head in the sand while the main bulk of the body, of humanity, is exposed?

I feel myself lost, disoriented in this debate. I don't know which side of the intersection I'm on. What I am sure of is that this is a question as big as that which St. Paul poses for us today: Which do we choose—to live according to the law of the flesh or to live according to the law of the Spirit? I also am aware from the life of Jesus, in our gospel for today, that to live according to the law of the Spirit is much more demanding than to live according to the law of the flesh. The personal risks are much higher. The life of the law of the Spirit is a built-in struggle against the life of the law of the flesh. And in terms of the contemporary debate on nuclear energy I also see that it is mainly, but not entirely, the vested interests (the Scribes and the Pharisees of the energy world) that argue the hardest for more dependence on nuclear energy as a coal and oil substitute. So regardless of my personal tastes, I am obliged to listen carefully to the opposition. The long term implications are just too serious. We cannot "live today for tomorrow we may die." We want to be accountable to the *life,* not the death, of the future.

Now, St. Paul has posed a question relevant for our time, and we know that God gives us the privilege to struggle with it: "If Christ is in you, although your bodies are dead because of sin, your spirits are alive because of righteousness." Let these be words of comfort to us as we get lost and disoriented along the way. And lest we despair in the choices before us, let us listen to this same pointing of the way, this same trusting indicative, from the words of the prophet Hosea over 2500 years ago:

> Let us know, let us press on to know the Lord;
> his going forth is sure as the dawn;
> he will come to us as the showers,
> as the spring rains that water the earth.

In all the uncertainty of the decisions of the dark night, we can trust that God is there behind the darkness, generating the dawn. In all the barrenness and drought of the desert in the winter, God is at work generating the spring rains that will come. As we struggle against the law of the flesh and face mighty personal and public decisions, it is this confidence and hope which is the substance of the law of the Spirit. In the midst of death it generates life.

CONSTANCE F. PARVEY
University Lutheran Church
Cambridge, Massachusetts

THE SPIRIT IN YOU
Fifth Sunday in Lent
Romans 8:11-19

What makes you go? What is the push behind your life? What is it that influences your thinking, your decisions, your actions, your words . . . your life? What motivates you?

When a suspect in a crime is arrested, one of the things the authorities seek to establish is the motive. Unless the evidence is conclusive against the suspect and they find no motive, he may be released. The motive is important. We are concerned about people's motives. We often look behind the deed to ask, "Why did they do it?" Following World War II, many of us were shocked when after the United States had given aid and relief to many depressed countries abroad, we were met with signs saying, "Yankee, go home!" What had happened is that some of these countries became aware that there were strings attached to our aid. They felt the pressure to be supportive of the West and to oppose Communism. They were objecting to our motives.

Jesus was concerned about motives. He said, "For out of the abundance of the heart the mouth speaks" (Matt. 12:34). Thousands of studies and much research has been done to discover the what and how of motivating people. Popular books have been written on the subject which divulge the secrets engaged in motivating the consumer to buy.

We deal with this constantly in the church. How do we motivate people to serve in order to carry on the ministry of Christ? What is it that will motivate people in a time when great demands are made on their resources, time, talents, and money to give the ministry of Christ's church a higher priority in their life? The church has only one answer to this question and it's found in the

Gospel. This Gospel message is clearly stated in our second lesson from Romans. Here Paul says, "For all who are led of the Spirit of God are sons of God." The message we find here is that we are God's people. This good news is the sole motivation for living and serving and acting as God's people in this world.

How Can We Know That We Are God's People?

It is the Spirit of God who leads us to know this. Paul says, ". . . when we cry, 'Abba! Father!'", it is the Spirit himself bearing witness with our spirit that we are the children of God." Now who is it that calls God, "Father"? Do you? There are millions of people in this world who believe in a god, but do not call him "Father." On the other hand, there are millions who would call God, "Father," if they only knew him. How then does it happen that you call God, "Father?" Again Paul tells us, "It is the Spirit of God bearing witness with our spirit, that we are the children of God." Paul is saying that no one can call God, "Father," and no one can call Jesus, "Lord," except by the Holy Spirit. In other words he is saying that our natural spirit would never call God, "Father." Our spirit will never give us the assurance that we are God's children.

We could never figure this out with our own spirit. Our reasoning would never come to such a conclusion about God. Why? Because our spirit conceives of God as our enemy. To our natural mind, God is unreasonable and against us. It is the nature of our spirit to look upon God as the law giver who makes demands on us that we cannot attain. He sits over us as judge and vents his wrath and displeasure on us for not measuring up. He is the one who stands in our way and forbids what we want. I had a young man tell me one day, while discussing some problems in his life, "I wish God would get out of my way. I wish he would stop bothering me." This is the way our spirit looks at God. He gets in the way. Our spirit would never lead us to call God, "Father." It is God's Spirit who enables us to do this. It is the same all powerful Spirit of God loosed among the dry bones of the prophet Ezekiel's vision that brings life, revives and renews that which is dead. This is the Spirit that enables us to call God, "Father." It is God joining his Spirit with our spirit that gives new life.

How Does God Reveal the Holy Spirit to You?

God is made known to you through the Spirit in Baptism, at which time God places his seal upon you and claims you as his child. The Holy Spirit speaks to you through the Scriptures by holding Jesus before you, so that you can see through his life and his death that God has forgiven you, loves and accepts you. The Holy Spirit reveals the Father to you through the life and teachings of Jesus, who taught you to call God, "Father." This same Jesus taught you to believe that God will always be your Father, even though you turn your back in him and no longer trust in him. Is not this the message of the prodigal son which Jesus related? The Father waits for his prodigal to come home. There are earthly fathers like this. They stand by their sons and daughters no matter what they do or fail to do. But there are also earthly fathers who disown their sons and daughters when they fail to live up to their expectations, who in time of trouble desert their children. But it is not so with your heavenly Father. He always remains. So when you cry, "Father, Father," it is the power of this indwelling Spirit of God bearing witness with your spirit that you are God's child.

The Blessings of Being God's Child

Once we know that we are God's children, then all manner of blessings are made known to us. Martin Luther in his commentary on Romans, entitles this passage we have as our text, "The blessings of God's children." And indeed these blessings are clearly stated.

1. *Free from the spirit of slavery and fear*

It is this Spirit, the Spirit of sonship, which frees us from the spirit of slavery and fear. No longer need we fear not measuring up to God's demands. There are no demands to measure up to now. We are already his by the presence of his Spirit within us. We are free from slavery and bondage of the law which says you must do this and that to please God. These demands are no longer applicable. We are his. There are no standards to meet. Now we have a new motivation for our lives. It is no longer the law with its heavy demands, but it is the Spirit of God who dwells in us. This Spirit which bears witness that we are children of God because of something he did for us, motivates our lives. It is nothing which we have or have not done, it is that which has been done within us through the power of his Spirit.

2. *No longer in debt to the flesh*

We are no longer in bondage, or in debt to the flesh. Because of the Spirit of God who dwells in us, we can live after the Spirit. We can die to greed, selfish desires, pride, and ego. Now we realize that we are not what we make ourselves, we are what God has made us by His Spirit. We are children of grace. Now obedience becomes the free inclination and desire to live as children of the Father. Now it is not the law with its demands which motivates us, but the love of the Father. And love cannot be commanded. The moment it is, it is no longer love. Love is a gift of the Spirit and it is this Spirit creating love out of our awaresess of this new relationship that motivates us. And what a relationship this is with the Father.

3. *An heir of the Father*

This is no temporary foster-parent relationship. We are true children of the Father. We have become heirs, in fact we are joint heirs with God's own son, Jesus Christ. This is no secondary relationship. We are as much a child of the Father as his own Son. His blessings are our blessings. But children not only inherit blessings, they also inherit responsibilities.

4. *The responsibilities of being a child of the Father*

One of the responsibilities we inherit along with Christ, is the responsibility to bring this world back to God. So Paul says, we are "fellow heirs with Christ, provided we suffer with him in order that we may also be glorified with him." We know there is much suffering in this world, but the suffering Paul speaks of here is the suffering we do in order to bring this world back to God. We know the suffering Christ endured in order to make it possible for this world to be brought back to God. But what about our suffering? I think we know little of true suffering, but we know, too, that it is taking place. It's behind the iron curtain and among our black brothers and sisters in Africa. We have heard stories of how our fellow Lutherans in East Germany must choose between the rite of confirmation and affiliation with the body of Christ or the opportunities for education and good jobs. They know what it is to suffer for Christ. It is not that we don't have opportunities right here in our own country and throughout the world to further the cause of Christ is we are willing to suffer for it.

When we consider the injustices, the inequities and the systems which still perpetuate the suffering in our society, a grave responsibility falls upon the children of God to show the compassion and love of Christ. The world is suffering and we must suffer with it. It may cost us jobs, security and popularity. I recall attending a seminar in the middle sixties. A black man, a seminary professor of another denomination, was called in to speak to us. After his talk, he was asked the usual question being asked those days, "What can we do to help black people gain equal rights?" He shocked some of us by his answer. He said, "There is nothing you can do." The group wasn't satisfied and continued to press him for something they might do, and he persisted for some time, "There is nothing you can do." Then he finally said, "Once you can show me your scars, then I will tell you what you can do." Once we have suffered as his black sisters and brothers had suffered, then he could tell us what to do. Many of us have not come to this place of suffering in order to bring the compassion and love of Christ to people in our world. But why not? As God's children, we have no need to fear suffering. We can endure suffering, because first of all, the Spirit of God bears witness that God is our Father, will always be standing by us and will never forsake us in suffering. He will not let us be tested beyond our strength. We need not fear suffering for it cannot rob us of life. The life I possess is the life of the eternal Spirit of God. "For the Spirit of him who raised Jesus from the dead dwells in us, and he who raised Jesus from the dead will give life to our mortal bodies."

Now we have an eternal perspective of life. Suffering is only for a time. And the sufferings of the present time, Paul says, "are not worth comparing with the glory to be revealed to us." This is the glory of God's own Son with whom we are joint heirs. While we are a part of this dying world of decay and destruction, we are more. We are beyond it. By the power of God's Spirit who raised Jesus from the dead, and who dwells in us, we are eternal. Suffering is seen differently when we see it in the light of God's eternal perspective and while abiding in the hands of a loving, heavenly Father. It is this Spirit which moves in our life now. It is this Spirit, who makes all things new and is now the driving force that motivates us. Nothing else. "For as many as are led by the Spirit of God, they are the sons of God." "If you die with me, you shall also be raised with me!" "It is the Spirit that gives Life!"

E. SILAS TORVEND
Emmanuel Lutheran Church
North Hollywood, California

POWER — ABUSE AND USE

Sunday of the Passion—Palm Sunday
Philippians 2:5-11

Have this mind among yourselves, which you have in Christ Jesus, who, though he was in the form of God, did not count equality with God a thing to be grasped, but emptied himself, taking the form of a servant, being born in the likeness of men. And being found in human form he humbled himself and became obedient unto death, even death on a cross. Therefore God has highly exalted him and bestowed on him the name which is above every name, that at the name of Jesus every knee should bow, in heaven and on earth and under the earth, and every tongue confess that Jesus Christ is Lord.

When we first read these words of St. Paul, we may think that they have very little to do with power, certainly not with power as we understand and operate with it in the world. We live in an age that is very conscious of power and is particularly skilled in the use of power against others. One of the definitions of violence is the use of power against others. The widespread influence that violence against others has in our culture is of deep concern to many. That people have always acted that way does not lessen the concern. In fact, from the beginning of creation people have tried to play God, to take power and appropriate it to themselves. Perhaps at no other time in history is the use of power so much the center of our concern as it is today.

Violence and Power

It certainly is reflected in the media. A state superintendent of education said recently, "Quite frankly we are losing the battle in education to television." He admitted there was no way in which the educational system could compete effectively with the attractiveness of multimillion-dollar programming. He quoted some interesting statistics: the average young person in America today, by the time that person reaches 17, will have been in school 11,000 hours, will bave watched 15,000 hours of television, and witnessed 10,000 murders on television. Stanley Kubrick, a very successful movie producer, has written about the power of film and television. He says that the medium of the movie is like dreaming. The difference is that we can control the dream. Much of the communication that occurs through this medium is on a subconscious level. The response that people have to these forms of communication then is often acted out on a subconscious level. If that is the case, then the important question is, "What is the value system and style of life that is reflected in the media of our generation?" By looking at the answer to that question we will discover what lies at the root of the value system of people themselves.

Another study by a sociologist pointed out that the average

person watches three hours of television a day and that one-third of the acts of violence that are shown on television are performed by violence professionals. These are people who use violence as a tool to achieve power and profit. In so doing they illustrate Darwin's notion of the survival of the fittest. In that context of survival, power becomes a tool in man's hands for achieving his goal. Tied in with that is the recognition that immediate gratification of our needs is high on our priority list. If we put all of this together, what is the myth that pervades much of our society? It is "Get what you want by whatever power you have."

That is a frightening thought. This is not a matter of our sitting down with our children and in a logical way saying, "I want to teach you how to use the power you have to satisfy your immediate needs and get what you want now." Any parent would shudder at the prospect of doing that. But the question that we are faced with is whether or not in almost a subconscious way we are conditioning one another and accepting that conditioning through a variety of subtle means that surround us. We are learning that life-style from heroes who are made out of phosphorous dots on a dancing screen. For us the enemy of Christianity may not be the state persecuting Christians and throwing them into prison because they believe in Jesus Christ. Nevertheless, there may be just as serious a cancer eating away at what we believe to be important simply because of the value system of the society in which we live and the uncritical and unguarded way in which we absorb it.

Christ and the Use of Power

If this diagnosis is true, then we have to recognize that the value system of our culture is the exact opposite of the Christian faith. That faith is expressed and incarnate in Jesus Christ. That is what our text proclaims today. It is very significant that Paul uses the term "grasp" in this text. He is pointing out that Jesus, the eternal Son of God, had unlimited power. He was equal with God but he avoided the temptation to grasp that power for himself. And instead, says Paul, "he emptied himself." The form he took in this creation was that of a slave, the powerless one. He took upon himself our common likeness and became obedient unto death, even death on the cross.

If our value system says power is the name of the game and that power is to be used to gratify our own needs, then by that standard Jesus Christ was a total failure, a washout, a reject.

The very direction in which his whole life went was toward emptying himself. He emptied himself finally of his very life. And yet, says Paul, in the very mystery of that life, in the self-giving of the Son of God in the flesh, on the cross, God has turned the whole universe around. He has opened up for man a new way to live. Paul says, "Have this mind among yourselves, which is yours in Christ Jesus." Notice that the use of power in Jesus Christ is not the renunciation of power, but it is the channeling of power, the channeling of his total self *for others*. And in the shape of that life and the pattern of his self-giving love, we are confronted with the very heart and message of what God is all about and of what life is meant to be.

Our Use of Power

It is important that St. Paul speaks about having the mind of Christ *among* ourselves. This is not something that you and I can do alone.

During this past week most of us have watched at least three hours of television. The message that we have been absorbing, conscious or unconsciously is, "Get what you want through the use of your power." It has been more entertaining than a sermon. The danger, of course, is that the message of our culture drowns out the message of the Gospel. That means that we dare not hang all of our life in Christ upon a sermon. It is not enough to say, "I have taken in what I need because I was in church this week. It will take more than a sermon or a church service. We need daily to be shaped in the image of the mind of Christ among ourselves.

Now what does that mean? Take the time to look at the television guide. Do some screening and some censoring. Fill the hours with experiences of the Gospel. Taste the real world of people. Revive and protect the endangered species of the family. Let real people relate to each other in real situations. Learn in our relationships what the style of the Christian life is all about. Let our households become an experiment and an adventure in living the mind of Christ. Reach into the world around in service and witness. Finally every one of us has to take full responsibility for the decisions and the actions of our lives. Letting the mind of Christ happen is an issue that is a matter of life and death.

What is at stake here is our relationship to God. When we grasp power for ourselves and use it to gratify our needs, we are back in the Garden of Eden again, taking the fruit and trying to play God. The Gospel which is Jesus Christ calls us daily to live in his image. May our witness and living reinforce each other to be the people of God.

RICHARD J. GOTSCH
Grace Lutheran Church
Northbrook, Illinois

FOOD FOR THOUGHT
Maundy Thursday
1 Corinthians 11:17-32

Our text for today is a familiar one from the pen of Paul, written especially to the Church in Corinth and in general, to all who name the name of Jesus Christ.

Verses 17-22 set the stage for the words of our Lord which have become the introduction and interpretation of these spiritual moments when the Eucharist is celebrated in all its glory.

What started out as a traditional, common, well-loved meal, a good time together, ends up to become the beginning of something new. The beginning of a renewal potential with the capability of transforming, releasing, unchaining and setting free. A meal, a love-feast, whose intent was to be one of unifying, affirming, building up, bringing together, but which in the context of abuse becomes everything except that. Instead, dissension, polarization, superiority, arrogance, class distinction, becomes the prevailing spirit of a well-intended mealtime together. An experience quite common today in every home, on every street, in every city—Corinth, Jerusalem, Minneapolis, Plains, Washington, New York, New Orleans—your city, my city.

The relevancy of these opening verses are as contemporary as one allows them to be. Into this setting of human behavior and yet, in spite of it, our Lord make a final appearance.

Just prior to Ash Wednesday for a period of ten days, the privilege was mine to retrace the places and events of our Lord in the Holy Land of Israel and of Paul, in Greece.

Entering the old city of Jerusalem via the Sheep's Gate and twisting in and out of the masses of people, autos, carts and animals, I made my way to an old barren, cold, two-story building with an iron fire escape leading up to the second floor.

I climbed those steps and entered an almost vacant room except for a small group of tourists. I paused as I heard those resounding, penetrating and familiar words as I have never heard them before:

> *Our Lord Jesus Christ, on the night on which he was being delivered up, took bread, and, after he had given thanks, he broke it and said, "This is my body which is for you; this do that you may remember me." In the same way, after the meal, he took the cup and said, "This cup is the new covenant and it cost me my blood. Do this as often as you drink it, so that you will remember me."*

An unexplainable reality, clasped my imagination and emotions as these "words of institution" echo in the hollow chambers of this room and as the voices of the ecumenical and universal family burst into singing:

> *Break thou the bread of life, dear Lord to me.*

Yes, an "unforgettable" experience which human words cannot adequately translate but one which leads me to ask again and again and again:

1. What if Jesus Christ had canceled that supper? Would the course of events as we know them have changed?
2. What made the death of Christ any different from other deaths we are acquainted with?

The answers to such questions come less quickly for me, than do the questions themselves.

The Supper

It has been suggested, in reference to the first question, that most likely the events of Good Friday and Easter would have taken place and therefore, God's plan of redemption and salvation would have been accomplished.

But had the meal been canceled, the real losers would have been you and me. We would not have had the needed assurance of the presence of our Lord in the eucharistic meal. The words "This is my body" and "This is my blood" would have been subject to an interpretation which would have been exclusively human.

Had Christ called off the dinner, in which he made the final Passover meal sacramental, you and I may have never known fully the link between Holy Baptism and Holy Communion.

That in Holy Baptism we establish our relationship with Jesus

Christ and that in Holy Communion we participate in the act of restoration, renewing our relationship, again and again.

For this reason alone, Christ did not cancel the dinner. Tonight, Maundy Thursday, we join with scores of Christians world-wide as we raise our voices in thanksgiving.

The Death of Christ

A second question follows, "Was the death of Christ really any different than the death of others, whom we have known and loved and admired?"

If you are anything like me, every time a death occurs, I tend to seek a purpose—to find a reason, an explanation. My immediate human response leads me to utter in the midst of my bewilderment, mystery, despair and perhaps even anger—why Lord—why?

We live in a time when murder, suicide, executions, assassinations no longer really shock or disturb—no longer do they gain the front-page attention that they once did. These happenings seem to be old hat and are all wrapped up in the now famous cliche, "The whole world is crazy and it is going to hell in a hand cart."

In the final analysis, the difference between the death of Christ and the death of others lies in the fact that Jesus said, "I see death coming and I accept it for your sake." This, in fact, is the gift of all gifts.

It has been said so beautifully, that "Christ did not go on a lecture tour to discuss his pending death or to debate the subject. Instead, he gave a dinner, invited his closest friends, and at this meal something special happened. He took some bread and broke it and he gave it to each one present; then he took a single cup of wine and passed it to all. What is special? The fact that he shared the bread and the wine. Each time we participate in the sacramental meal, we share his way of dying but also we share the calling to live out his promise of unity, symbolized by one loaf and one cup. By his death, Jesus put dignity into the role of "servant" and into the privilege of doing something for someone else for the right reason." This is what Jesus meant when he said "I have come not to be served, but to serve." Every time we participate in the sacrament as one of God's children, it is one more opportunity to respond positively to the call of our Lord. We go out into his vineyard in service. We are called to translate a forgiveness experienced into a forgiveness shared.

Every time we participate in the sacrament we are assured of his presence and this becomes the example that we are to duplicate in our daily contact with people.

In Holy Communion we have the promise that Christ accepts us, that he heals us, and that he sends us back into business as usual with wholeness and a new beginning. Each time we participate in this sacrament we are made aware of the fact that although we are all different, we all belong to one body—the Body of Christ. That each of us is unique, special and necessary.

To have the privilege of celebrating the Eucharist whenever it is offered, is an opportunity for us to raise our voices in gratitude to God for the greatest gift that he has given.

To participate in the sacrament of the Holy Eucharist is to do so in response to the Gospel and out of freedom and not legislation. We are free to come and free to go. Free to be the person that God has created us to be.

Norval F. Pease once wrote a most challenging series of words which tie together the universal acceptance of all people by our Lord.

> *When God looks upon this world he sees in the foreground of the human picture not ideas, not things, but faces and to this all-seeing eye the billions of faces do not resolve themselves into a nebulous blur. They are not represented by statistics on a page but in each face a heavenly father sees mirrored life's dreams and disappointments—life's pain and pleasure—life's work and worship and the more we become like God the greater will be our concern for people.*

On this most festive and celebrative evening called Maundy Thursday, as we participate together universally with Christians in the Sacrament of the Holy Eucharist, might we recognize the power of freedom that is present. That through our meal together, God in Jesus Christ sets us free. It is this freedom which helps us to better understand what Luther meant when he said, "having been liberated by the Gospel, for me to return to the law, would be spiritual suicide."

Tonight, once again our Lord says:

This is my body; this is my blood

Given for you, for me, for each other! For which we say Thank you, Lord Jesus.

RONALD C. PETERSON
Minnesota Synod—LCA
Minneapolis, Minnesota

JESUS IS OUR GREAT HIGH PRIEST
Good Friday
Hebrews 4:14-5:10

"Priest," that is the key word that runs throughout the Epistle for Good Friday. I wonder what picture that word "priest" forms in your mind when you hear it? What do you think about when you hear the term "priest"? Do you think about a clergyman with a turn-around collar? That, after all, is the way that we use the word today. If that is the picture that is formed in your mind, then you will not be able to understand or comprehend what today's Epistle is talking about. You will miss the meaning. Jesus is called our priest. The meaning of that phrase is not to be found in the picture of the clergyman of the twentieth century, but of the Old Testament temple priest of the first century. To understand the priestly office of our Lord, we need to go back to the Old Testament and its categories. That is what the book of Hebrews is using as its basis for calling Jesus Christ our priest.

Old Testament Priests

The priesthood was an important order of society in Israel. Aaron had been appointed by God to serve as the first high priest of Israel. His descendants by hereditary right were to serve as priests. The job of the priest was to offer sacrifice for sins committed and to act as the intercessor between the sinner and God. The Old Testament is very specific on the rules governing the offering of the sacrifices, regulating the type of animal or grain sacrificed for each sin. And it was the duty of the priest, first in the tent tabernacle in the wilderness, and later in the temple in Jerusalem, to offer those sacrifices for the people. As intercessor he was also to pray for the people and to intercede in their behalf before the throne of grace. The priest was the only one permitted to enter the holy precincts of the temple to burn the incense as the symbol of the prayer of God's people. Israel saw the priesthood as its important link with God. Through the priesthood and the sacrifices that they offered in behalf of the people, Israel remained in touch with God.

It is that priesthood that is described in our text for today. The text reminds us that no one assumed the priesthood as a personal honor or distinction. Priesthood was by the appointment of God. For God had appointed the first high priest so that by extension all those who followed after the first high priest were likewise appointed by God. But while the priest was appointed by God and held a high position in the nation of Israel, he was not viewed as above the people. The priest was appointed and chosen from among men to act on behalf of men in relation to God. As a man the priest was just as subject to frailty and sin and temptation as any other man. As a man the Old Testament priest knew sin and weakness for he too had participated in sin and temptation. So the Old Testament priest could and did deal gently with the sinner because he too was a sinner. And as the book of Hebrew reminds us, the priest himself had to first offer sacrifice for his own sins, before he could offer sacrifices for the sins of the people. The priest was the important link between God and man, but still only a link, and a frail and human link at that. As important as that Old Testament priesthood had been, it was to be superseded by another priesthood, the priesthood of Jesus Christ.

The Priesthood of Jesus

The Old Testament priesthood becomes the point of both contrast and comparison with the priesthood of Jesus. As the Old Testament priest had been appointed by God, no one abrogated that status to himself, so Jesus was appointed to the role of priest. The appointment to priesthood was at his incarnation. God said to Jesus, "You are my Son, today I have begotten you." The song of the angels that announced the birth of our Lord to the shepherds became the great song of praise to the newly appointed priest of us all. When Jesus was born, it was more than the birth of another child in the nation of Israel. It was the appointment of a new priesthood.

Old Testament priests were human, and therefore susceptable to temptation and to sin. Jesus was human too, he was one of us. His birth assures us of the reality of the manhood of Jesus Christ. And as a man he knew temptation. He was tempted by Satan. He too had stood before the onslaughts of Satan who had wooed him with the seductive words, "just fall down and worship me, and I'll turn over the world to you. You won't have to undergo the suffering and death that you know stand before you." He had experienced the pangs of hunger and heard Satan say, "If you really are the son of God, then why don't you turn the stones into bread and eat. That's all you have to do. It would be so simple." Jesus had experienced the threat and temptation of the devil. But with one significant difference. He had not sinned.

So the new priesthood of Jesus was like the Old Testament in one way. It was a priesthood that was sympathetic to the sinner. It was a priesthood that had experienced temptation and the seductive invitation to sin. But the new priesthood of Jesus was also different in that the priest, Jesus, had never sinned.

Jesus the Priest Offers Himself

Priests functioned. They acted. They did. And Jesus as a priest also functioned, acted, and did. During the days of his flesh, his earthly ministry, Jesus as the priest interceded with prayers and supplications before the throne of his Father. He prayed for his disciples, for his people, and for the world. This function of Jesus the priest and mediator has not ceased. As our intercessor and our Advocate before the Father Jesus is still pleading for us. He is still offering in our behalf before the heavenly throne prayers and supplications.

But the real measure of priestly work was that of sacrifice. Goats, lambs, bulls had been offered in the Old Testament temple in behalf of the people. Now a new offering and sacrifice was to be laid upon the altar. But the place was not the temple. The place was a hill called Golgotha, the place of the Skull. The altar of the temple was covered with gold. The altar of the priest Jesus was the rough cross supplied as regular issue by the Roman army. The offering was not a goat or a lamb culled from the flocks of a Judean shepherd. The offering was the Lamb of God who takes away the sins of the world. The sacrifice was nothing less than Jesus, the priest, himself. There upon the cross-altar the priest of us all made the sacrifice for all people. He offered his life as the payment and ransom for us all. Jesus the priest learned obedience and became obedient to death on the cross. That death was in reality salvation. For that act of the priest, Jesus, was the payment that bought us back from sin and death and the power of Satan. God was acting in our behalf through his Son, and by that action was giving to us as a free gift, eternal salvation and life with him. Jesus through his priestly ministry became the source of our salvation.

Here is the significant difference between the offering of the Old Testament priest and the offering of the new priest, Jesus. The Old Testament sacrifice was killed and offered. That was the end of the sacrificial animal. It stayed dead. But the sacrifice offered in our behalf, the Lamb of God, did not stay dead. The third day that Lamb of God who had offered himself for us rose from the grave. The death of Good Friday gave way to the life of Easter Sunday morning. This is something that we can never forget. Even as we gather to celebrate and remember Christ's death for us today, we need always to project ourselves forward to the Easter resurrection. For it is the Easter resurrection that gives meaning to the death and the sacrifice of Jesus the priest.

Jesus the Priest Offers Us Grace and Mercy

What is the outcome of the priestly work of Jesus for us? The text says it clearly. Because of Christ's death as the Lamb of God, we have confidence to approach the throne of grace and receive there grace and mercy. Grace. Mercy. Those words are not abstractions but reality. Grace is the free and unmerited love of God for us. Grace is the means by which God has saved us and made us new creatures in Jesus Christ. Mercy is the forgiveness of our sins and the renewal of a relationship with God as his children and heirs. All of that happened because Jesus is our priest who offered his life as the sacrifice for our sins.

Priesthood is not just a category of the Old Testament. It is a category that summarizes what Jesus Christ did for us this day almost two thousand years ago. Jesus became our priest when he entered this world as a human being. As our priest throughout his earthly ministry, he prayed for his people. And finally, as the priest of us all, he offered his life for us, opening the way for us to come with boldness and confidence before God, knowing that we through him will receive grace and mercy.

Roger D. Pittelko
Lutheran Church of the Holy Spirit
Elk Grove Village, Illinois

BECAUSE OF THE RESURRECTION
The Resurrection of Our Lord—Easter Day
Colossians 3:1-4

Because of the resurrection, Christian churches around the world are filled with people, with the sight and smell of Easter lilies, with majestic hymns and stirring anthems.

Because of the resurrection, a unique feeling of joy and peace and love floods many lives.

Because our Lord Jesus burst the bonds of death and rose victorious from the tomb nearly two thousand years ago, the yearly celebration of Easter always seems to bring these feelings and sights to our lives.

Every year, from the Easters when we were young and gathered Easter eggs while still in our pajamas . . . to the Easters when we were a bit older and wore our first suit coat or special jewelry to the sunrise service, to the Easters when we sat in a pew together with our own children, every year these same feelings seem to be unleashed in our lives.

Yet I announce to you on the basis of Paul's words to the Colossians: the resurrection of Christ can have an effect on your lives not just once a year at Easter time, but each and every day of your life.

Usually at Easter we think of what the resurrection meant to Mary, to the disciples, and to the other followers of Christ. Today we're thinking about what the resurrection means to you and me. We're thinking what the resurrection means in your daily life and mine.

Life Is Transformed

The Apostle pens "you have been raised with Christ." That means you and I also participate in the resurrected life. Because of the resurrection, our life also is transformed.

In your baptism and mine we have participated in Christ's death and resurrection. In our baptism God has called us from death to life. No longer do we need fear that death will have the last word.

But more. Because of our participation in the resurrection, our daily life can be transformed. No longer do we need to be enslaved to those things which would drag us downward. No longer do we need to cling to old habits.

In a large city, a man caught another man in the act of picking his pocket. The would-be thief explained that he had been out of work and had gone hungry for days. What's more, he had once been in prison. When employers learned his name and thus discovered his prison record, they wouldn't give him a job. "Well," said the man to the pickpocket, "take my name, which has never appeared on a police record, and keep it clean." Fifteen years later this same man came into his office. A glance at this man's business card told him it was the very man to whom he had given his name. The man told how he had just become a partner in the firm which the other had recommended to him fifteen years earlier. "I owe it all to you, sir, and your generosity, and above all, I owe it to the gift of your name."

In the same way, you and I have had our lives transformed. In our baptism we have received a new name . . . "Christian" . . . a Christ-man . . . a Christ-woman. Paul put it this way: "Therefore, if anyone is in Christ, he is a new creation; the old has passed away, behold, the new has come" (2 Cor. 5:18). Think of it: because of the resurrection and our participation in it, you and I receive a new name . . . and a transformed life.

This is given to us, not because of what we are, but because of what he is . . . he who is called the Resurrection and the Life.

Life Is Renewed

But, someone may be saying to themselves right now, "My life may have been transformed once, but I've slipped into old ruts, old habits, old cynical ways whose grip I cannot seem to break."

Sure. It happens. Most of us know that experience. The Apostle Paul did too. Even he, who had met the Risen Christ on the Damascus road, and proclaimed his gospel all the way to Rome, even he confessed, "I do not do the good I want, but the evil I do not want is what I do" (Rom. 7:19).

That is why St. Paul urges us in our text to seek and set our minds "on things that are above," not things on earth. Paul knew the necessity of daily renewal, daily reminding ourselves who we are, and whose we are.

So did Martin Luther. The great reformer also knew the tempting power of evil. That's why he wrote in the Small Catechism: "our sinful self, with all its evil deeds and desires, should be drowned through daily repentance; and that day after day a new self should arise to live with God in righteousness and purity forever."

Who among us has not had blue Mondays, and irritable Tuesdays, and nervous Wednesdays and a whole pandora's box of bad days? All of us are in the battle of life and not above it. That's why it's so important to renew our faith daily in the Resurrected Christ. That's why it's so important to let this resurrection faith grip us, get under our skin, and work its way into every fiber of our being. That's why it's so important to do this each and every day of our lives and not just on Easter Sunday.

For years the famous preacher R. W. Dale of Birmingham, England, thought of the resurrection in terms of some intellectual doctrine. Then, through the influence of another preacher, the resurrection turned into a flame, and became a sun which brought life to Dale's entire being. From that time onward, Dale began the practice of including an Easter hymn in every Sunday morning service of worship.

Because of the resurrection, your life and mine can also focus on the resurrection and be renewed not just once a year on Easter, but weekly . . . yes, even daily.

Life Is Empowered

Yet someone still may be saying: "You speak of a transformed life, of a renewed life. That's all well and good. But I'm not the kind of person out of which Easter victories are made."

If you feel that way my friend, then listen. When Paul urges his readers to "seek the things that are above, where Christ is seated at the right hand of God," he is speaking of life empowered. With the demand to live the Christ-like life, Paul also speaks of the power to do precisely that! With the moral demand comes the moral dynamic. With the call to seek the things which are above comes the power from above.

Consider: all the forces of evil tried to win a victory on Golgotha with a hammer, some nails and a cruel tree. But the power of God was unleashed and Christ broke through with a victory over the grave in Joseph's garden. And *that same power* which took Christ out of the grave, is available to you and me today!

Because of the resurrection, the early disciples were driven tirelessly around the world of their day sharing the great good news. Because of the resurrection, countless persons since those first Christians have been empowered to live lives of faithfulness to the Risen Christ, even if it meant ridicule, hardship, and death itself.

Because of the resurrection, your life and mine can be empowered too. Because of the resurrection, the refrain of the Introit Psalm can ring in our ears and vibrate in our lives: "The Lord is my strength and my song, he has become my salvation."

Sure we slip back, mess up, miss the mark of what we were meant to be. That is why we are urged to look up and focus our eyes upon the cross of Christ "towering o'er the wrecks of time." We are to look to that empty cross and realize that forgiveness, the power to make a fresh start and a new beginning is available to us.

That's why our Lord and Savior said: "Greater works than these you shall do" (John 14:12). That's why Paul shouted: "We are more than conquerers through Him who loved us" (Rom.

8:37). Because of the resurrection, a transforming, renewing, recreating power has been unleashed and is available for daily living.

Life Is Enthroned

Now the good news of the resurrection does not end with transformation, renewal and power for this life. The Apostle Paul in our text would have us see beyond this life alone. He states: "When Christ who is our life appears, then you also will appear with him in glory." Because of Christ's resurrection, a hole has been punched in the darkness of death. Because of the resurrection, you and I are given a glimpse of light and life beyond the grave. The Easter Gospel and the good news of the Ascension shows us a Risen and Ruling Savior, enthroned as Lord of the universe, entrusted with all power in heaven and in earth.

Now that's not all. Paul emphatically declares that even though it does not yet appear that we too shall be seen with our glorified Christ, nevertheless, it shall be so. Listen to the First Letter of John: "We are God's children now, it does not yet appear what we shall be, but we know that when he appears, we shall be like him, for we shall see him as he is" (1 John 3:2).

The resurrected life does not end, but continues. Death is not a period, but a comma. Because of the resurrection, not even death shall separate us from the love of Christ, and from living some day in the presence of the glorified Christ.

Recall that at the Transfiguration, only Peter, James and John were present to see Christ arrayed in splendor. Now think of it! By the grace of God, you and I too shall some day see him in dazzling glory and join the throng around his throne.

Until then, you and I will still get up in the morning, eat breakfast, go about our work and have an evening meal. No one will notice a halo of radiant light around our heads. As Paul put it: "Our life is hidden with Christ in God."

But from the moment of our baptism, you and I have been joined to our heavenly Lord in an indissolvable communion. So when Christ Jesus shall return, the veil will be drawn back and we will be seen together with him. That's why we keep our eyes riveted on him and the things that are above.

Sure, some ridicule Christians at this point with the suggestion that the church is so heavenly-minded it is no earthly good. Yet, because of the resurrection and Paul's words in our text, you and I realize a greater danger is that we could become so earthly minded, we'd miss heaven altogether!

Besides, when you and I become grasped by the resurrection, by its power and glory for our lives, we realize that the trinkets for which we used to strive so desperately, "are not worth comparing with the glory that is to be revealed to us" (Rom. 8:18). Because of the resurrection, we know this is true.

RICHARD REHFELDT
Windsor Heights Lutheran Church
Des Moines, Iowa

CAUSE FOR JOY!
Second Sunday of Easter
1 Peter 1:3-9

Little Jack Horner is alive and well. And residing in any church you care to name. Sitting in his (or her) corner, he says, "What a good boy am I!" (That's an abridged version.) Of course, that nursery rhyme Jack Horner wasn't very subtle. He simply came right out and told any who would listen what a good boy he was.

Today's real live (but vaguely disguised) Jack Horners are much more sophisticated and subtle. But in one way or another they are proclaiming—to any who will listen—what good boys they are for having found Jesus! Or for having accepted him in their heart as Savior. Too often there is given off an attitude that makes me uneasy, an attitude which seems to give credit to the person who has accepted Jesus—as though that in itself is a good work. What a good boy am I. I accepted Jesus as my Lord and Savior.

Little Jack Horner is alive and well.

The Difficulty of Receiving Gifts

A real difficulty we have as human beings is to receive gifts. I have lost count of the number of people I know who are constantly doing good things for other people, but who find it hard to accept good things to be done for themselves. You know people of that sort—they're all around us. One typical example that comes to my mind is the lady who is constantly making cakes or bread or whatever to bring to someone in need. But when she herself is in need, she is very reluctant to accept help from someone else—because she doesn't want to put others to any bother!

I can't help wondering at such a time if all the cake-baking and bread-baking that she has done wasn't done with a conscious or subconscious motivation of establishing her worth. Or even so that people will say, "What a good person she is."

It is difficult for us to receive gifts. At first glance this appears to be a rather strange difficulty, but it is true. We feel a bit uncomfortable receiving something without keeping score so that we make certain of returning a similar amount. Or we would rather earn what is given to us—or in some fashion be able to say that we gave a respectable amount of service *in return* for the gift. We just can't stand still for being a gift-recipient.

There is no doubt that this trait has a wealth of positive value in it. It is desirable and necessary in our total human family for people to have the desire to earn their keep or to put in a day's work for a day's wages. No doubt about that.

But gifts are in a different category. If it is truly a gift, that means the recipient *has not* earned it because the earning aspect would take away the gift aspect.

And that's precisely the point where we inwardly resist a major theme of the Good News as given to us in Scripture: that salvation is given to us without any merit or worthiness on our part—and without our having to prove to anyone that we have earned it. Little Jack Horner is definitely out of place in the kingdom of God.

Important Words About Gifts

In his first letter Peter begins by speaking about the gift of salvation that God has made available for all of us. In the New English translation the words he speaks are stated, "This is cause for great joy" (1 Peter 1:6). The cause for joy that I feel compelled to speak about is stimulated by some very important words and phrases contained in those first few verses of that epistle. I refer specifically to "chosen," "gave us new birth," "inheritance," and "kept for you" (all from the New English Bible translation).

These words or expressions call our attention to a basic fact about this business of salvation: it is a gift. Those of us who are Lutheran Christians have had that fact drilled into us again and again—and intellectually we know it as well as we know our names. So that's nothing new.

Yet in the face of our knowledge of grace as a gift, we too often fail to defend that concept. Or worse yet, we allow it to be diluted within our own church by those who insist that their acceptance of God's grace is somehow to be conceived of as a good work!

In Defense of Grace

It is fashionable nowadays to take note of a sort of religious revival that supposedly is taking place in America. If it is happening, it isn't very Christian. It's religious all right. That's because those who are reviving manage to say the correct pious-sounding words—they've learned the word-formula—and they end up by rejoicing because they found Jesus! Yea team!

Sorry, but I am not buying it. Far too much emphasis is being placed on what *we* do as individuals in this home-grown religious revival. "*I* found it!" "*I* accepted Jesus in *my* heart." I, I, I. What a good boy am I.

I should hope that Lutherans will soon begin to object to the dilution and adulteration of our concept of Baptism. I didn't do *anything* to become saved or to "find Christ" or to be a recipient of grace. For one thing my parents brought me as an infant to the baptismal font of the church and there I was baptized into Christ. And in that act of God's (not my act) God made grace abundant for me. There is no way in which I can boast on what a good boy am I for being a Christian.

But I don't need to spell this out for Lutheran Christians or any others who accept the biblical concept of grace. What I do feel compelled to do is to point out how insidiously the religious revivalist cults always seem to turn the whole salvation thing around so that somehow *we* get a good measure of credit for it.

Oh, to be sure, never so clearly acclaimed. That's why I said "insidious." I won't rehearse all the routines—they are legion. I simply point out that Scripture denies much credit to us. We recall, for instance, at one point Paul says we can't even know what to pray for without the Spirit's guidance. And that we can't possibly call Jesus Lord unless the Spirit moves us to do so.

A Different Parade

Look for a moment at what the popularized kind of Christianity has resorted to today in an effort to impress the heathen. At least I suppose that's what it's for. There's this endless parade of the big wheels who suddenly "found" Jesus. It's the vice president of a steel company or the quarterback of a pro football team; or a movie star or a famous rock band leader or the latest

Miss America. Somehow they've learned to say the right words and so they're saved. Champions can do it, you can too! I'm totally unimpressed.

I'm much more impressed with the parade of people that Jesus presents to us. In his simple and quiet way Jesus tells us about the dregs of society that have been touched by God's love. His parade includes the town prostitute. And the crooked businessman. And some nondescript fishermen. There are many more in the gospels; look at who they are: the disinherited, the non-chosen, those without noble birth. And the beauty of the whole thing is that God gives them an inheritance, and chooses them, and gives them a new birth.

The great and mighty act of God, which can have its effect upon every human life, is that God looked upon us and gave us an inheritance. Gave us. And that's the constant nagging difficulty (the fact that it's a gift), and at the same time the unimaginable joy.

The Cause for Joy

Now let us return to a theme that I see coming through this opening chapter of Peter's first letter: a cause for joy. As I see it in Scripture, the cause for joy in our relationship with God is not that *we* have discovered him, but the simple realization that he claims us as his own. That is such an unthinkable mystery to me that I simply must stand in awe of the entire concept. The concept certainly leaves no room for me to boast, as though I had done something to make the concept valid.

To get the picture more clearly into focus, we need only glance at the significant words and phrases referred to earlier. One of those is the word "chosen." When I was in grade school and junior high, we often "chose up sides" for softball or football or whatever was in season at the time. The two best players were always selected as the persons to do the choosing. Inasmuch as I was never one of those two, I always stood expectantly, waiting to be chosen (hoping I wouldn't be the last chosen, because everyone knew the last guy chosen was the worst player). It never ceased to be a thrill for me to have this tough football player point his finger at me and say, "I want him." Chosen.

The reason God chooses me and you has nothing to do with our abilities or talents or goodness or badness. No credit line for us.

Or look at the word "inheritance." Whatever inheritance passes from a parent to a child certainly cannot be seen as something the child earned. It was the parent who built up the estate or invested the money wisely or whatever. And when that inheritance fell to the child, the only response making sense could be one of thanks.

The chief cause I find for joy is that God notices me, that he chooses me, that he bequeaths upon me an inheritance that I neither earned nor worked for.

Psalm 8 helps me to put into perspective what Peter is telling us. After the Psalmist reflects on all that God has made and how magnificent it all is, he asks, somewhat rhetorically, "What is man that you are mindful of him?" Then he answers, "You have made him just a bit lower than yourself." One of the most remarkable assertions in all of Scripture.

So Little Jack Horner is really quite out of place in the kingdom. We are there because God chose us to be there.

MERLE G. FRANKE
First English Lutheran Church
Austin, Texas

FIRST THE ENDING, THEN THE BEGINNING
Third Sunday of Easter
1 Peter 1:17-21

Have you ever walked into a theater during the last fifteen minutes of the movie? If, for example, you were to do that when the feature film was "The Robe," you'd find yourself in the middle of a tense trial scene before the emperor in Rome. You would watch two Christians standing up to a crazed monarch who can't absorb their irrational devotion to a resurrected Jewish carpenter. You would see them condemned to death, walking arm in arm to the execution yard. And you would watch the throne room and the raving dictator melt away, the entire background blending into a cloudy pathway as they step directly into eternity.

If you didn't know the story of "The Robe," you would probably say to yourself, "What an ending! What must the beginning have been like?" If then you stayed in your seat, you would soon see the beginning of the movie. And when the final scenes came by for the second time, you would be able to say, "I don't need to stay any longer. I know the ending!"

Most of us don't like to watch films that way. Sometimes it can't be helped. When it happens to us, though, we get a totally different perspective on the story. We find ourselves putting together pieces in a puzzle. We catch ourselves snatching clues we might not otherwise have seen. We anticipate things that ordinarily might have taken us by surprise.

Strange as it may seem, Christians live their lives like that! First comes the ending, and then the beginning.

God Has Already Finished the Story

The "end times" came with Jesus. His earth visit was light at the end of the tunnel. His ministry was the last chapter of the book. His death and resurrection were the kettle drum and cymbal crashes at the end of the symphony. When Jesus said, "It is finished," he wasn't just getting ready to die. He was saying: "This is the wrap-up; this is the end of the story."

In our town you can watch a television program called "The Last Word." It comes after the late show, just before sign-off. Jesus is the last word. His death and resurrection provide an exclamation point for emphasis.

Sometimes theaters or television stations re-run movies like "The Robe" around Easter time. Maybe you've seen it recently. You may recall in that story how the lines are drawn between two empires, God's and the devil's (in "The Robe," Satan's agent is Caesar). In the film both sides are in agreement about what happened out on Crucifixion Hill. Somebody's empire came to an end. Since that event *begins* the film story, the rest of the two hours has actors of both persuasions trying to prove that it is the *other* group that has lost and that *their* team is simply mopping up in pockets of enemy resistance.

Many contemporary theologians are taking pains to say that Good Friday and Easter Sunday are not opposite events (one for the devil, one for God) but, rather, both days are the same piece of cloth. On Friday God won and Satan lost. On Easter morning we have an instant replay of the same story: God won and Satan lost. On Friday the stage lights are down. On Sunday they are up.

Four Billion Hostages!

Medieval Christians often used the "ransom" picture to explain what was going on when Jesus died. Verse 18 of the text introduces this idea and, although it brings with it special problems as well, it has been one useful picture among several in getting at the meaning of the crucifixion (Martin Luther couldn't resist the ransom picture. He borrows directly from this text when explaining the Second Article of the Apostles' Creed).

The heart of the argument is that Satan has kidnaped the whole planet. God's commitment is to "bring 'em back alive." Satan agrees to a giant swap—the owner's son in exchange for the owner's servants. It would be like an extortionist surrendering twenty-five bank clerks and tellers in exchange for the owner's son, who controls a third interest in the bank and stands to inherit it all. But once the deal is arranged and the heir-apparent is bound and gagged, the kidnaper discovers, through carelessness and to his amazement, that his captive is an escape artist, a karate expert, and a weight lifter all rolled into one. The gangster simply cannot control his prize. Instead, he is crippled for life as the strong man makes his escape.

If you have a vivid imagination, you should, according to this picture, associate the thunder, lightning and earthquake at the crucifixion not with Satan slamming the jail door on Jesus, but rather with Jesus' smashing up the devil's living room furniture and breaking one of his legs.

That's the end of the story. That's the last word. The trick is, of course, to get the right reading on whose side was the winner. Jesus' life and death and resurrection really *were* at the "end of the times." What was ending was Satan's hopes for empire.

So Let's Begin!

Now that we know who the winner is (we've already seen the final reel) we can launch into living in the beginning. We know all about tomorrow. Now we can deal with today.

It should not be surprising that we structure our worship life and our community life by traveling backwards. It is the *end* of Jesus' life that gave Sunday to the church—his resurrection drove us to worship on that day. His death gave us the symbol that decorates our buildings and our church books, and gives meaning to our baptism. He died at 30 years. We die with him (in a water burial) at 30 days—or less! The end of his story is the beginning of ours.

Perhaps the most exciting aspect of starting with the ending, and moving backwards, is this: once we were bound (in bondage) to be winners. You only go around once, right?

Wrong!

The compulsion to slug your way through and end up "king of the mountain" is gone (have you ever noticed, incidentally, that nobody ever really wins that game?) We already know the ending. We know who the winners are. Now we're free to pitch our trophies in the trash and do some creative losing. Like losing our life for Jesus' sake.

In paraphrase, some first-century lookers-on observed Christianity and remarked, "Look at what great lovers they are!" Not much was said about their trophy cases. The text concludes with a formula for "creative losing." Behave, it urges, so that contemporary folks will have to say of you, "Look at what great believers and hopers they are!"

Is it not strange that faith and hope are key words for Jesus' followers? We already know the end of the story. Why should we sit in suspense *now* (suspense; questions not answered—these are the common denominators inherent in believing and hoping).

Dinner's Not Ready

Try this: at the end of the highway is a winner's circle. In its center is an enormous banquet table. There are name cards on that table for every one of us. But the meat is still in the oven and the candles are not yet lit. Have you ever tried to come to the table before dinner was served? I used to try that when I was young. My mother would tell me: "Dinner's not ready. Go outside until I call you." And she would banish me from the dining room. It was a kind of exile waiting for the meat to get done. But even the anticipation was delicious. My stomach was the loser for a while but I would find something useful to do. There was no doubt about having some of that dinner. There was a place set for me. It was only a matter of time.

The text says, "Conduct yourself with fear during the time of your exile." Another version (Good News) says, "spend the rest of your lives here on earth in reverence for (God)."

How shall we do that? The banquet is in our nostrils. The table is within sight. Our seat is reserved. We have time now to celebrate the future, stuffed full with promise for us. About that we already know. We have time to do so in a present that begs us to redeem what is lost;

to lift up what is fallen;
to put together what is broken;
to listen to the ignored;
to free the entrapped;
to forgive the guilt-driven;
to hurt with the hurting;
to celebrate with the happy.

We have seen tomorrow. We are richly burdened with today.

By our living and by our dying let us advertise the end of the story:
"The Lord is risen! He is risen indeed!"

MICHAEL L. SHERER
Redeemer Lutheran Church
Washburn, Iowa

I SIT AND LOOK OUT
Fourth Sunday of Easter
1 Peter 2:19-25

The Victory

He Is Risen!
He Is Risen Indeed!

So he is and so we shall proclaim. Certainly Peter has been proclaiming this for weeks in the epistle readings from his first letter. Let's remember a few of the words he shared two weeks ago.

> Praise be to the God and Father of our Lord Jesus Christ, who in his great mercy, gave us a new birth into a living hope by the resurrection of Jesus Christ from the dead! You . . . are under the protection of his power until salvation comes. This is cause for great joy, even though now you smart for a little while . . . under trials of many kinds (1 Peter 1:3-9, NEB).

And recall last week as well.

> It was no perishable stuff, like gold or silver, that bought your freedom from the empty folly of your traditional ways. The price was paid in precious blood—the blood of Christ. Through him you have come to trust in God who raised him from the dead and gave him glory, and so your faith and hope are fixed on him (1 Peter 2:17-21, NEB).

Suffering to Be Expected . . .

Having been reminded of the victory of God in Christ, we can move further into Peter's message to his friends about their life in an upset and darkened world.

We have clearly heard that this new life will call for "trials of many kinds" and that it did, in fact, call for the "precious blood of Christ." Suffering will be a part of the Christian's experience as sure as it was a part of Christ's. We should not be dismayed by this fact. Our lives should already be full of affirmations that living right-side-up in an up-side-down world is often a very painful experience. Yet, we always seem to be amazed when it happens. Our tendency is to look most often to the Scripture for comforts and guarantees—and they are there. But, with these promises, we often are amazed to find that we shall receive even more "pain and undeserved suffering" as we live them out. Suffering and bearing pain, because of our Christ-like behavior, is to be expected.

... and Celebrated

If we are looking only for jubilation, cheering, and comfort, then our text for today is not the place we should be seeking it. Peter bids us to hear the call, to see where Christ is going, and to follow. The comfort for today is to know that God rules everything in the universe for the sake of his people, the church; that we, by our faith in Christ, are part of his people; and, that suffering and pain which comes to us because of "having God in our thoughts" is known, honored, and celebrated by him. We are assured of God having both participated in our pain and loving us as we bear it. In the midst of suffering we dare to go on, trusting, to see where he calls. As Lilly Tomlin puts it, "It's easier to suffer in silence if you know that someone is watching."

He Calls Us Out

The first lesson for today from the Acts of the Apostles tells of Peter and the eleven standing up and addressing the Jews who had come from foreign lands to celebrate the festival of Pentecost. Empowered and emboldened by the Spirit, he said, "Repent and be baptized . . . save yourself from this crooked age." We have seen the crookedness of this age, have repented, and been baptized. Our life has been redeemed, bought back from futility, and given a purpose. The purpose, the same as Peter's and the eleven, is to proclaim the wonders of what it means to be made alive with Christ, and to show it forth in our lives. The goal is that brokenness might be healed and joy be restored to the whole of creation. For this we are all agents. We have been called to live our lives for others—for the world. That day, so many years ago, three thousand persons were cut to the heart and were baptized into the death and resurrection of Christ into a living hope. They saw in him a purpose for their lives.

Jesus, speaking through John's gospel, says of the Shepherd

and Guardian that "the sheep hear his voice; he calls them out. When he has brought them all out, he goes ahead and the sheep follow." Jesus will not be confined to the sheepfold, nor will he allow us, his people of promise, to remain self-indulgent and satisfied. He calls us out.

To See and Hear

Perhaps Walt Whitman, writing during the War Between the States over one hundred years ago, can help us to see and hear the meaning of God's call more clearly. The poem is from *The Leaves of Grass* and is entitled "I Sit and Look Out."

I sit and look out upon the sorrow of the world, and upon all oppression and shame,
I hear secret convulsive sobs from young men at anguish with themselves, remorseful after deeds done,
I see in low life the mother misused by her children, dying, neglected, gaunt, desperate,
I see the wife misused by her husband, I see the treacherous seducer of young women,
I mark the ranklings of jealousy and unrequited love attempted to be hid, I see these sights on the earth,
I see the workings of battle, pestilence, tyranny, I see martyrs and prisoners,
I observe a famine at sea, I observe the sailors casting lots who shall be kill'd to preserve the lives of the rest,
I observe the slights and degradations cast by arrogant persons upon laborers, the poor, and upon negroes, and the like;
All these—all the meanness and agony without end I sitting look out upon,
See, hear, and am silent.

And to Proclaim

Seeing and hearing all this, we must feel very inadequate and alone . . . silent. Dag Hammarskjold, in his book, *Markings,* said, "Pray that your loneliness may spur you on to finding something to live for, great enough to die for."

Obviously Christ could not afford the luxury of merely "sitting and looking out," let alone being silent. By words and deeds he proclaimed himself to be the Son of God with power. Nor can we, who have heard and seen the plight of the world around us, be silent. We have shouted, "He is risen indeed!" The proof of our words will be manifest in our actions.

We are called to follow Christ's example; to follow in his footsteps. Not in the steps of the lost, wandering, and misguided generation to which we belong, but in the steps of Christ who is the Way. We are called to be a part of the cure for the world and not mindlessly or selfishly a complication of the problem.

Having been redeemed and called, our lives are to be redemptive; that all the sheep may be turned toward the Shepherd and Guardian of their souls; that all the world, through us, may hear his voice, see his great love, and be found in him, always. Only then will the shattered world be healed and the angels sing again for joy.

Listen to Peter once more:

> It is for you to follow in his steps. He committed no sin, he was convicted of no falsehood; when he was abused he did not retort with abuse, when he suffered he uttered no threats, but committed his cause to the one who judges justly.

To Bless the World

Suffering? If you live his way it is sure to come; but then, so are the promises so to be fulfilled toward you, and through you, to the world. It was Nietzsche who said, "From a people who merely pray, we must become a people who bless."

So, let us all say Amen, and then, perform the same.

EDWARD M. RALPH
University of Georgia
Athens, Georgia

CALLED TO WITNESS
Fifth Sunday of Easter
1 Peter 2:4-10

Let's pretend! As we leave the sanctuary this morning, each one of us will be handed an envelope. It is not addressed to us personally. It is addressed to "a chosen race, a royal priesthood, a holy nation, God's own people," this congregation, this address, this zip code.

When we open the envelope, the message is short and simple: "As one of my royal, holy people chosen to declare the wonderful deeds of him who called you out of darkness into his marvelous light, would you, this week, select a person of your acquaintance least likely to know Jesus Christ, as Lord and Savior and go tell him/her, what it means to you to be chosen, royal, holy and to know the mercy of God. P.S. If this is inconvenient or you are too busy or you don't feel up to it, just throw this note away."

The pretending is over. We aren't going to burden ourselves with that decision today. But would it be an imposition? Is it right to expect this as a part of our ministry?

This text is freighted with thoughts of our being used by God in the ministry of witness and proclamation. And, of course, it begins with the greatest treasure we have received, our most precious possession—the Gospel of Jesus Christ. If we are to share that treasure as we ought, it will require of us our very best.

I begin with a word out of the last paragraph, "priesthood." The word layperson has never appealed to me since one of the saints in my life, a seminary professor and friend, refused to use the term. "Laos" refers to the whole people of God—"God's own people." We are ordained and unordained priests called to minister to one another and to "declare the wonderful deeds of him who called you out of darkness into his marvelous light."

Our Call

We must begin with our call. It is God who calls us through his Holy Spirit. Luther says it to and for us in the Small Catechism, "I believe that I cannot by my own reason or strength believe . . . but the Holy Ghost has called me . . . as he calls, enlightens and sanctifies the whole Christian Church." The sign of our call is our baptism. The daily renewal of those vows remind us of that call. It continually tells us to use Peter's metaphor that we are "living stones." That by the power of God, we have been "built into a holy priesthood." That the center and core of our priesthood is Jesus Christ, "a cornerstone chosen and precious." He is the foundation upon which we have been placed by the Holy Spirit. God is using us for his purposes, if we come to that living stone, the Christ. The call is valid, the cornerstone is here, the priesthood is ours.

Great scripture passage. Great metaphors. Great concept. Sounds good. What does it mean for us today?

We need to think and act in a ministry of proclamation and witness as a people of God. We need to see ourselves as not being alone. We need to understand our need for support. We need to understand the need to support others. We need to realize our unity. We need to continually nurture ourselves with the gospel in order that we can nurture others. It is a mutual aid package. Not to keep ourselves happy and content necessarily, but to strengthen us for our ministry.

How do we support, understand, nurture and strengthen ourselves? We *worship* together. We come together to celebrate the mighty acts of God in our lives. We *pray* together, here and at home and at work and wherever we are. We *pray* for each other all the time, not just when there is a tragedy or an apparent need. We *learn* together from each other. We *serve* together in the name of Christ without always naming him. We *witness* together. We give explicit witness to Jesus Christ as Lord and Savior.

This worshiping, praying, learning, serving and witnessing doesn't happen without effort and commitment. It happens when we want it to happen so much that we are willing to answer the call and be the chosen priesthood.

Called to Witness

When I was a boy, the last of the wide open spaces, a vacant end of a block, was about one half a block from the back door of my home. That undesignated playground was the scene of "life and death" games and activities. Many times at the crucial moment or when it was my turn to bat or my leaving would make the sides uneven, the call came from home. It was time to eat, chores to be done, time for bed, "where are you?" or just plain come home. Sometimes in the heat of the moment, I honestly didn't hear, sometimes I didn't want to hear and there were those times I heard and didn't respond. Strike a familiar memory?

The people of God are called on to declare his wondrous works —creation, salvation and direction. Do we not hear? Do we not want to hear? Do we hear and choose to ignore?

The call which brought us into our living relationship with Christ is the same call that calls us to witness together. However, this does not mean that it is always done in the company of another member of the chosen people. It does mean that when we witness, we know we are part of a great body of believers who are supporting us. We know this because we worship, pray, learn, serve and witness together. The strength of that being together in Christ is what makes us feel a part of the whole, even when we are alone in our ministry.

A Royal Priesthood

Let me share with you how I feel as an ordained priest. Whether in the courts, at the hospital, in the home or speaking to a civic organization, I am not alone. Christ is with me. You are with me. We are there together sharing the light and mercy that we understand because we came out of darkness and received mercy. Your strength is my strength. Our strength is Christ's strength. We minister together.

If as an individual priest you don't feel as I feel, we better do something about it. There has to be a way that we can support each other. If the things we are doing together make you feel like a "frozen" person of God rather than part of a chosen people of God, some self-examination of our congregation is in order.

Paul begins his first letter to the congregation at Corinth, it could be this congregation, by reminding them, "you are not lacking in any spiritual gift." Neither are we. We have the gifts but many times, because we feel inadequate or we are afraid of what might happen, we neglect. Some of us never take the gifts out of the box and use them. Others leave the gifts here or use them here but nowhere else. We don't transfer them to "the 12 o'clock noon today to the 11 o'clock A.M. next Sunday" world. Let us, as God's chosen priests, accept that we have the gifts Paul says we have.

What do we need as a congregation to use those gifts, to be chosen people of God rather than a collection of "frozen" persons of God? We need to use the gifts that are in us. We need to try. I'm sure you have heard "nothing ventured, nothing gained" many times. We need to try to talk about Jesus as our Lord and Savior over the coffee cups, around the water cooler, between classes, walking to the next hole, in the boat, at the bar, after dinner, riding the bus. Try it! Then if you feel uncomfortable or ill at ease, talk to another member about the witness you gave and share your feelings about it. That other member could be your spouse. If after that, the two of you feel inadequate, come to talk with your priest or evangelism committee. We won't ply you with all kinds of printed materials. We will talk with you. We will sympathize and empathize with you. We will be your support group. We will pray with and for you. We will give you all the help we can, personal, printed, or whatever you feel is necessary to enable you to try again.

One of the things that should result from this hour of worship is that we leave here feeling strengthened and supported. God has called on us to speak to others about him, because we ourselves have been called out of darkness into his marvelous light. Amen! Hallelujah!

DAVID R. GERBERDING
St. James Lutheran Church
Burnsville, Minnesota

THE PERFECT COMEBACK
Sixth Sunday of Easter
1 Peter 3:15-18

She came home in a rage. The casual encounter had involved a crisis of wills. The offhand comment now seemed enormously unkind. She had been put on the spot and her reply had been weak and witless. Hours later, she thought of the perfect comeback! In the privacy of her kitchen, she could imagine six good answers to that challenge that had shaken her confidence and upset her emotional balance.

We live in a world that expects the right answers to a host of pressing questions. Our involvement in the academic process teaches us the importance of right answers. Attending a college, getting a job, being socially accepted means giving right answers. "Do you take this woman?" is not one throwaway line in the familiar wedding ceremony, but a question that needs to be answered as long as the relationship exists. While every life situation seems to cross-examine us, it often takes a death in our midst to reveal the almighty size of the question mark of our existence.

The First Epistle of Peter is a vivid example of the New Testament consciousness that the Christian is always under interrogation. The author warns of testing in terms of persecution and suffering. In every relationship—slaves to masters, husbands to wives, citizens to the emperor—your conduct will be examined. So be ready to answer.

Rainer Maria Rilke is widely considered one of the greatest German writers since Goethe. His prose work *The Notes of Malte Laurids Brigge* contains a striking passage in which this gifted man ponders his call to say something meaningful to the world.

> One ought to wait
> and gather sense and sweetness
> a whole life long,

> and then,
> quite at the end,
> one might
> perhaps
> be able to write
> ten lines that were good.

The yearning of such an articulate man for ten good lines and his expectation that they will take a lifetime to produce, has a salutary effect on the Christian called to answer a questioning world. If only we had the quick mind and sharp tongue of an Abraham Lincoln. We would even settle for the latter-day cleverness of an Erma Bombeck or the marvelously-imagined comebacks of Snoopy. But we seem to lack both the talent and the time needed to properly prepare for the moment that demands an answer.

The Perfect Comeback: A Living Lord

Writing from "Babylon," a center of persecution and perversion, the author of First Peter advises: "reverence Christ as Lord." That simple phrase masks a cosmic revolution for the Christian. On the surface the monotony of seasons and times flows on with sad predictability. "All is vanity" sighs the preacher of Ecclesiastes. Nevertheless, the believer perceives

> Behind the scenes, a clandestine irruption;
> A fission in the world's grain,
> A benign conflagration...
> Convulsions at the earth's core
> The silent collapse of parapets.
> Moorings have parted
> And we are carried away into new latitudes.
>
> (Amos N. Wilder, Christianity and Crisis,
> Dec. 11, 1967)

"Reverence Christ as Lord." It is hard for us to measure the profound impact of that statement on the early believers. Those few words spell out the essence of their answer to life. After months of examination and "wilderness struggling," they had committed themselves to the cold waters of baptism and emerged proclaiming "Jesus is Lord." They dramatized that primitive creed by ritually dying to the old and rising with the Spirit's gift of new life. The elder from Rome invoked those sacred words of promise and proclamation to remind them of their precious share in the resurrection victory of the living Lord.

The church today is endeavoring to restore Baptism to its central position in Christian life and faith. Involving the total ministry of the church, we are attempting to recover the very cornerstone and lifelong dynamic of our existence. One wonders, however, if the average churchgoer is even minimally prepared for an "Affirmation of the Baptismal Covenant." We have grown so comfortable in the half-way house of our faith. Can we survive the flood that would sweep away the old ways, the safe assumptions and our lifestyle's status quo? Perhaps we need to hear again the Easter promise in this sacrament.

> We emerge from the baptismal grave with the sign of victory on our foreheads. That knowledge strengthens and cheers us in our life under the cross until in our own death/resurrection we share Christ's victory fully. That is what Luther meant by the singular statement "until fully baptized and strengthened" we pass out of this world and are born into the new eternal life. On the way we walk through life wet with the water of our Baptism. (Eugene L. Brand, *Baptism*, p. 122)

The Perfect Comeback: A Loving Life

"Wet with the water of our baptism," our lives speak eloquently of our living Lord. Spiritual graces such as the "gentleness" and "reverence" of our text are second nature to the redeemed. "Making a good defense" is not a matter of scoring debating points but the involuntary response of love.

"Lovers alone wear sunlight" wrote the inimitable E. E. Cummings. "Good behavior in Christ" is a vestment of beauty that clothes the Christian against the ill-treatment and malevolence of the world. As the word was enfleshed in Jesus, so he has called us to wear the servant's cloak and to "be his body in the world, living according to his example to bring peace and healing to all mankind.

The book of Acts deserves the place of honor as the First Lesson in our services during the Easter Season. It vividly documents the early church alive with the persuasive power of resurrection love. Philip preaching in Samaria, and, in the wake of the Good News—signs, wonders, "and many who were paralyzed or lame were healed. So there was much joy in that city" (Acts 8:17).

In the past few years religious conversation has become a socially-accepted phenomenon. To those who recall the many subtle prohibitions against our sacred words, it is surprising to find that "faith," and "Christ" are in fashion. Presidents and famous men openly witness to their conversions. Prime time is taken over by individuals and church sects to promote their causes on television specials. Bumper stickers and billboards shout "I've found it," and Jesus is openly discussed in air terminals and supermarkets. Perhaps we should be grateful *and* cautious!

Remember the mechanic who had a religious conversion. He talked about it continuously to friends and co-workers. His minister visited the plant one day and proudly said to the foreman, "I guess Bob is one of your best workers." "Sorry to disagree," replied the foreman, "but Bob stands around talking about his religion when he should be attending his machine. He is a fine fellow, and a good man when he works, but he still has to learn that when he is running that machine, his religion ought to come out of his fingers and not out of his mouth."

Talk about God's love is sometimes a way of escaping into generalities. Our Christianity ought to come out of our fingers, bodies, and total lives. In addition to "title and heading" we need to "subpoint and detail" our responsibility. One of the purposes of First Peter is to draw out the implications of the love of Christ in the lives of the baptized, and the unlimited nature of our call to obey his Holy Spirit. Even the extremes of suffering and death can be seen as part of God's will. Such catastrophies become positive opportunities for the Christian.

When we are bewildered by the critical attack of another person, sometimes we remember that beneath their antagonism lies a plea for help. Such insight inevitably draws the anger out of our response and gives us reason for patience and understanding. Perhaps, the Christian is being questioned because his world also wants to be brought to God—to know the Way, the Truth and the Life.

> You have tested us, O God,
>   tried us the way silver is refined.
> You have allowed men to ride over us prostrate;
>   we have gone through fire and water.
> Yet you brought us out into a place of liberty.

> Come and hear, all you who fear God;
>   I will tell you what he has done for me.
> Bless our God, you peoples,
>   Make the sound of his praise to be heard.

(Massey H. Shepherd Jr., *A Liturgical Psalter for the Christian Year*, pp. 46-47)

WALTER C. HUFFMAN
Lutheran Theological Seminary
Columbus, Ohio

MORE LIGHT FROM OUR ASCENDED LORD
The Ascension of Our Lord
Ephesians 1:16-23

The ascended Christ is here, present among us through his Word, to give himself to us. We do not observe the Ascension by paying our respects to a departed Lord, but by listening to the Word of our very present Lord.

The English writer, J. B. Phillips, once wrote a fantasy in which a senior angel described to a junior angel the visit of Jesus, the Prince of Heaven, to our world. After Jesus, the Prince of Heaven, returned to heaven, the whole earth turned dark, and the junior angel became quite distressed. However, the senior angel told him to be patient, and while he waited, little pinpoints of light began to appear all over the world until the whole world glowed with a soft light. In other words, when Jesus the Light of the World, left this world physically, he did not leave his followers in the dark, but now enlightens them, individually, so that each of us becomes a little Christ, a little light, in our dark world.

In Luther's explanation of the Third Article of the Apostles' Creed, he says, "I believe that I cannot by my own reason or strength believe in Jesus Christ, my Lord, or come to him; but the Holy Spirit has called me by the Gospel, and *enlightened* me with his gifts . . . " In that one word, "enlightened," Luther compresses together the tremendous experience of the new birth which the Holy Spirit imparts to those who come to faith in Jesus Christ and receive baptism in his name.

Becoming a Christian, and receiving the Holy Spirit, is a most *enlightening* experience. It's like awaking from a dream in which you dreamed that you had died, only to awake and find yourself fully alive. It's like living for years in darkness without the gift of eyesight, and then suddenly having your eyes start working, and you see for the first time a blaze of light, color and beauty surrounding you on all sides. How eternally thankful each of us ought to be whom the Holy Spirit has called by the Gospel and *enlightened* with his gifts!

St. Paul's prayer in the Epistle for today suggests that there is *more light to be had!* Let us join St. Paul in praying to our ascended Lord that he would further enlighten us through his Word and Spirit.

Enlightened in the Knowledge of God

St. Paul was never one to settle for "dimly lit" Christians. In the verses preceding, he gives thanks because he has heard concerning the Ephesian Christians, "of their faith in the Lord Jesus" and of their "love toward all the saints." That was a great beginning, but then he goes on to pray that, "the Father of glory," would give them, "a spirit of wisdom and revelation in the knowledge of him." Apparently, not all Christians have that "spirit of wisdom and revelation" or it would not be necessary to pray for it. And probably the word "spirit" should be capitalized, since it is the Holy Spirit who imparts wisdom and revelation—especially when that wisdom entails insight in the nature and ways of God.

And how desperately mankind needs this enlightenment—this Spirit of wisdom and revelation in the knowledge of God. Our world—yes, some church members, I fear, don't even know yet that God wills to deal with us on the basis of grace and mercy, not on the basis of merit and reward.

Recently, columnist Ann Landers told a correspondent, "A place in heaven is not for sale. And neither is peace of mind. There are no shortcuts or free passes to the pearly gates." In reply, a college student wrote, "Ann, you gave a Jewish answer to a Christian lady. Small wonder you goofed. According to Jesus, a seat in heaven can be bought." Then he quoted Matt. 25:31-36 and 40. Ann Landers, in turn, consulted Father Theodore Hesburgh of Notre Dame University, and he wrote in reply that Ann Landers was perfectly correct. He said that the reader merely put a different interpretation on the word, "buy," and then went on to say that heaven can be *earned* by helping others, but not *bought* by helping people. Yet, according to the teachings of both Christ and his Apostles, *heaven can neither be bought nor earned,* so Father Hesburgh was just as wrong as the correspondent.

Do you see why we need to be enlightened as to the knowledge of the true God? The reason so many think heaven is on a pay-as-you-go basis is because they are not enlightened—they have no idea how *generous* and *loving* the true God is. The whole New Testament fairly shouts at us that heaven can neither be bought nor earned, but that heaven and eternal life is the *free gift* of God, won for us by the sacrificial death of Jesus when he died for us on the cross; and that the *gift* of heaven and eternal life is ours when we repent and accept God's gift in faith. And until we know that our God is the kind of God who wills to deal with us on the basis of his grace, rather than our performance, we simply don't know the true God.

The kind of thinking that supposes it can earn, merit, or buy eternal life, is in the dark; it is *unenlightened* by the Spirit of God. It is oblivious to the perfect righteousness which God's Law requires; and that God cannot countenance in the least, wrongdoing on our part. The unenlightened mind hasn't the slightest idea of how deeply sinful and unworthy we really are in the sight of God, and that never in a million years of intense striving, could we earn even a smidgen of heaven's real estate. For, as the prophet says, "all our righteous deeds are like a polluted garment" (Isa. 64:6). Therefore, we need to be enlightened as to the righteousness, truth, and goodness of God, as well as to the depths of our own sinfulness.

And when the Holy Spirit comes, he does that for us. He shows us our sin in all its crushing and damning weight. He breaks our pride and batters down our self-confidence, and makes us face up to our failure. Then, when we know ourselves to be guilty and justly under God's judgment, he shows us Jesus, "who loved us and gave himself for us"; who stepped into our place and took God's judgment upon our sins in his own person. He shows us a Father's forgiveness and an amazing grace offered to every broken spirit and contrite heart. And that's quite a *revelation* of God's way of dealing with us.

St. Paul says that Satan, the god of this world, "has blinded the minds of the unbelievers, to keep them from seeing the light of the gospel" (2 Cor. 4:4). In other words, to picture God as a heavenly employer who only awards eternal life and heaven to the superior performers—this is satanic blindness. It is the devil who would like us to picture God in those terms. But the Holy Spirit enlightens us. He teaches us that God is our Creator and Father, and that he doesn't despise any of the works of his hand; that he wills to deal with us as his children whom he loves and not as his employees or slaves.

What earthly father or mother would keep their children at home only on the condition that they made themselves valuable enough and worked hard enough to deserve their food, clothing and rent? What five, or ten-year-old child today could possibly work enough to pay for their room, board, clothing, education, medicine and so on? And if human parents, sinful as they are, don't accept only those of their children who can pay their own way, how much less is this true of our gracious Father in heaven? Thus, Jesus told his disciples, "Fear not, little flock, for it is your Father's *good pleasure* to *give* you the kingdom" (Lk. 12:32). "You don't have to worry, there's nothing that pleases your Father more than to be able to prepare a kingdom for you and then to *give* it to you, for no other reason than that he loves you." Therefore, this is *the basic enlightenment,* to know that the true God is a God who wills to act toward us in grace and generosity in the person of his Son, Jesus Christ.

Enlightened to Our Hope of a Glorious Inheritance

St. Paul also prays that the Holy Spirit would "enlighten" the "eyes of our hearts" so that we would know the hope of the glorious inheritance God has promised us.

How many of you gave any thought this past week to the fact that someday, through Christ, we who believe, are going to be in heaven, and there will enjoy a joyous and glorious inheritance with the saints of God? My point in asking this is, that too often we have only the vaguest, weakest hope of heaven and eternal life. And because our hope is vague, weak, minimal, so also the *affect* that this promised inheritance has upon us is also weak and minimal.

But if you and I could only spend five minutes in heaven and experience the joy and happiness, the strength and perfection of body, mind, and soul that will be ours, we'd be so impressed, so overwhelmed by it all, that for the rest of our lives we could scarcely think or talk of anything else.

Oh, that the Spirit would open our eyes to this! Oh, that he would pull back the veil from the eyes of our hearts and give us some appreciation, some insight, into the glorious inheritance God has prepared for those who love him! How our hearts would sing for joy! How we would pour disdain and scorn upon the ridiculous and petty trifles that get us so upset and cause us constant anxiety and discouragement!

But, we're not that way are we? Either we've never really gotten hold of the vision of our inheritance, or we let it fade swiftly from our eyes, and pretty soon we are fretting over trifles, majoring in minors, piddling with the picayune, upset with the insignificant and unimportant. And so, we ought to pray daily with St. Paul that the Spirit would enlighten the eyes of our hearts so that we *know the hope* to which we are called, and the riches of his glorious inheritance in the saints.

Enlightened to the Greatness of His Power in Us

St. Paul would also have Christians to be enlightened about "the immeasurable greatness of his power which is at work, in us who believe."

Most of us, I guess, are at least dimly aware that God is at work in our lives. But if you're like me, his power seems terribly weak at times, primarily because I can't *feel* it. "If only God's power would come upon me like waves of the ocean and make me feel as strong as Samson, so that I could go out and wrestle lions!"—then, I suppose, I'd be more aware of the "immeasurable greatness of God's power" which is at work in us who believe.

Yet, the Holy Spirit must enlighten our hearts so that we begin at least, by faith, to perceive just how great that power is, which is at work in our lives, in spite of the fact that we don't always feel it.

You see, God's power which is at work in us, is so quiet that we might foolishly suppose it is really quite weak. But, in fact, it is God's power, a power that is invincible, infinite, and indestructible. In 1 Corinthians, Paul says that, "the foolishness of God is wiser than men, and the weakness of God is stronger than men" (1 Cor. 1:25). When God decides to do something, he has a way of clothing himself in utter weakness, and then he does what he has in mind. And so it is with God's power *in us*—since it operates so silently, so quietly, we mistake it for weakness, when in reality, it is far more powerful than any other force at work in the entire universe.

In fact, St. Paul says the power at work in us is the very same power that was at work in the life, death and resurrection of our Lord—the *unfailing* power that sustained him in all his trials; the *courageous* power that enabled him to resist the devil and to stand confidently before Pilate, Caiaphas and Herod; the *hidden* power that enabled him to accept the cross even though his human body sank beneath its weight; the *quiet* power that enabled him to hang on the cross without complaint, recrimination or bitterness; the *compassionate* power that enabled him to pray for his tormentors even while he was being tormented; the *awesome* power that quickened his lifeless, cold body in the tomb and raised it to new life; the same *tender, devoted* power of the Father that restored Jesus to his heavenly home, and there exalted him as King of kings, and Lord of lords—this same gentle, yet invincible power of God, is at work, Paul says, "in us who believe."

My friends, we need to be *enlightened* about that. We need to be aware that when we feel so weak; when we are down on ourselves and feel hopeless and worthless—that God's power is there to uphold, strengthen and sustain us. We need to have our eyes opened so that we realize that—though God is a God who hides himself, and that our real life as Christians is, "hid with Christ in God," nonetheless, when we are seemingly at our weakest, then God is at his strongest in us; that through trials and sorrows, through labors and defeats; through opposition and failure—in all these things we are more than conquerors through him who loves us.

Our ascended Lord, who now dwells in the light and glory of eternity, has by no means deserted us or left us in the dark. Through his Word and Spirit, he stands ready to enlighten and strengthen all who believe in him. May we all join St. Paul in earnestly praying that the Spirit would open the eyes of our hearts—to *know the true God* in all his grace and love; enable us by faith to *grasp the greatness* of our heavenly hope and inheritance; and *perceive and believe,* the immeasurable greatness of his power which is at work in us who believe.

HENRY F. FINGERLIN
Shepherd of the Hills Lutheran Church
Littleton, Colorado

THE PASSION OF THE CHURCH
Seventh Sunday of Easter
1 Peter 4:13-19

In the last full week of the month of January in the year 1977, a cultural event of enormous significance occurred in our land. Millions of Americans tuned in to TV, night after night, for eight consecutive evenings, to watch a dramatization of Alex Haley's novel *Roots*. This was the story of his own family, from the days of his great-great-great-great grandfather in Africa, through his capture and deportation as a slave to the American colonies before the Revolutionary War, through their trials in the early years of the 19th century, up to the Civil War, and freedom and independence in the years of Reconstruction.

It was a stirring story, and we Americans came to share the lives of the principle characters: their sorrows and sufferings; their shame; their pain; their tragedies; their recurring triumphs and victories; most of all perhaps, their essential nobility as human beings. It was an incredible experience for most of us —to live through those terrible days with these people, as if we belonged to them and they to us. That had not happened to us, as Americans, before; it is not likely to happen again, in just the same way. I mark it as a cultural milestone of enormous significance.

What affected me, at least, so movingly throughout the whole experience was the realization that, through most of their lives, these people were suffering, bearing a terrible burden of oppression and shame and pain, and without any reason or cause. The young African abducted to the slave ship was a symbol of that for me: he could not comprehend what was happening to him, or why. The question recurred night after night in the series: Is this really happening to me? And why? What have I done, what has my family done, to deserve this?

The Question of Suffering

That is the issue the author of the First Letter to Peter is addressing to his friends. He's trying to give them some answers to their questions about suffering. The first three chapters of his letter have put the question of suffering in the context of a kind of sermon on themes from Christian baptism it may even represent a selection of quotations or allusions from a primitive baptismal liturgy. Now in Chapter 4 the focus narrows from suffering in general to the specific trials of this specific group of believers. And they're suffering, apparently, for no other reason except that they are believers.

It's pretty much of a certainty, then, that this letter is addressed to Christians who are being actively persecuted because of their faith. Perhaps Nero is the Roman emperor at the time this letter is received; perhaps Domitian or Trajan. In any event, under all three of them, the infant community of Christian believers began to assume a kind of Passion in imitation of Christ's own suffering: believers were burned at the stake, fed to the lions, hounded out of their homes and cities. It cost something, in those days, to believe.

And there is a sense in which it will always cost something. One of my teachers says, "It is the church's destiny always to be under accusation by the world." Perhaps we're not fed to the lions in the arena, these days. But perhaps that other accusation is equally difficult to bear: the unspoken indifference to your faith by friends and neighbors, or even by members of your own family; the mindless inattention by the rest of the world, to those "things of the Spirit" which you take to be passionately important. There is suffering there, and accusation, and trial. And to those of you who feel that pain, for the sake of your faith, the author of our text says "Rejoice!"

The Economy of God

He cites five reasons why suffering for faith might be a part of God's wider economy, God's plan for his world. I'll list them off just briefly.

First, in verse twelve, the author suggests that suffering for faith may be a kind of test: "Do not be surprised, beloved, that a trial by fire is occurring in your midst. It is a test for you, but it should not catch you off guard." In much the same way that manufacturers in Detroit take pains to test each new model of automobile, perhaps the trials of the Christian represent a kind of test for God's new model for humankind. We are a new humanity; perhaps we might expect to have that newness tested; that fresh and unimagined dignity that goes along with being sons and daughters of the King, reborn in his Spirit, equipped with his lavish gifts, not lacking any good thing. If that's who we are—as our Baptism assures us—we might even welcome the tests, the trials, and rejoice in them! We are God's new model for humankind! What a privilege! Put us to work!

Second, and more mysteriously, the author suggests that our suffering for the faith is a part of Christ's own passion: we "share Christ's sufferings" (v. 13). That is a notion the Apostle Paul considers elsewhere in Scripture: the presumption that in our own pain, we "fill up" or "complete" the sufferings begun by Christ himself. The mystery of Christ's own passion and death is deepened and widened, awesomely if that is true. Because you see, it suggests a congruence between the Lord's gift of himself, in his death, and the gift of our own pain, the sinews of our own lives stretched out like this. In Baptism we are "sealed by the Holy Spirit and marked with the cross of Christ forever . . ." Our own sorrow—could it be part of the meaning of that mystery that we are to serve as Christ to each other, even in this?

Third, we're assured that our sufferings can be a sign of the presence of God's Spirit, and his comfort, in our midst. "You are blessed, because the spirit of glory and of God rests upon you" (v. 14). That's the assurance that even in the face of suffering, we know that we will not succumb; God has sealed us as his own, and his Comforter is with us. "I know that he who vindicates me is near," my defense attorney, so to speak, who will not allow the verdict to go against me.

Fourth, our suffering for faith can be a witness to non-Christians. "If one suffers as a Christian, under that name let him glorify God." Can adversity convert the hearts of those who see it in action? We've wanted to believe that ever since poets and playwrights began to tell our human story. I'm thinking of the death of Romeo and Juliet, in Shakespeare's classic: a death which finally brings reconciliation to their feuding families. I'm thinking of the courageous death of the Puerto Rican boy in *The Pawnbroker*, which serves to offer the old man his own first stirrings of compassion. Suffering can often make a stunning witness to the love of God. And those who see are changed.

Fifth, adversity is a sign of the coming kingdom of God: "You may rejoice and be glad when his glory is revealed." When his glory is revealed! What a hint of goodness, freshness, completeness, yet to be: every wrong made right, every wound and infirmity made whole, every tear wiped away! That is the promise of the coming of the kingdom of God. And our own sorrows, our own shame, may be a preview of that day. "Dear friends," the author of John's First letter tells us, "What we shall be has not yet been revealed, but when it is revealed we know that we shall be like him" (1 John 3:2).

There is a final injunction in our text: "Therefore let those who suffer according to God's will do right and entrust their souls to a faithful Creator." Our response to adversity is suggested there in two words, *faith* and *obedience*. In whatever pain you bear, this is God's wish for you: that you may trust in God's unfailing love, in spite of everything. And that you may commit yourself to do his loving will.

PAUL F. BOSCH
Lutheran Campus Ministry
Syracuse University
Syracuse, New York

THE MIRACLE OF PENTECOST—THEN AND NOW
The Day of Pentecost
Acts 2:1-21

The three great Festivals of the Christian church are Christmas, Easter and Pentecost. At Christmas and Easter, services are filled, these are very special days. But Pentecost is just another Sunday. Even the business world which is quick to take advantage of a good thing, has not been able to make much of Pentecost. But maybe there is no need. With Mother's Day coming before and Graduation Day coming after, Pentecost is not needed for its commercial value.

Whatever the reason, Pentecost—The Day of the Spirit—and our celebration of the beginning of the church, has not inspired the imagination of Christians as it should.

However, this seems to be changing. One of the fastest growing denominations in the world today is the Pentecostal church. It may not be the biggest, but it is the fastest growing. What do they do in the Pentecostal church? They speak in tongues, they are very enthusiastic. They are not satisfied with one Baptism, they believe in a second Baptism, Baptism by the Holy Spirit, that fills them with ecstatic power.

And what lies behind this experience, which has made inroads into all denominations, seems to be a hunger for direct experience of God. Not knowledge about God, but knowledge *of* him, which becomes apparent through the ability to speak in tongues. For such a movement, Pentecost—the Day of the Spirit—is a very important event.

The Story of Pentecost

What did happen on that first Day of Pentecost when the Holy Spirit came to the church in a very special way? In the tradition of that day, Pentecost was a kind of memorial day. Everybody got the day off from work. They gathered to celebrate the spring harvest and to remember the time in history when Moses received the Ten Commandments on Mt. Sinai. Pentecost was a day to celebrate God's direction and the purpose given to his people in his law and sustained in the fruitful harvest. This was the Jewish Festival of Pentecost. Literally, Pentecost means fifty days after the Passover feast.

But what happened to the disciples on that first Pentecost? They were gathered together in one place. As yet they were unsure of themselves, of their power to proclaim the gospel, and the exact nature of their mission. Mostly they sit around and wait. Suddenly, their presence was shattered by the noise of a strong driving wind. They saw what appeared to them tongues like flames of fire spreading over and resting on each person there. Everyone touched became filled with the Holy Spirit. The disciples began to speak in different tongues. Moving out into the street they encountered the devout people who were in Jerusalem for the Pentecost festival. When the disciples began to speak in the various languages of the people, they were met with bewilderment. Amazed and perplexed that Galileans were speaking, they asked, "What does this mean?" Some went so far as to answer, "They have been drinking."

What Does It Mean?

It is a good question to ask, "What does it mean?" There is no doubt that the events of the first Pentecost were very important for the life of the church. William Barclay writes that "we may never know precisely what happened on the Day of Pentecost, but we do know that it was one of the supremely great days of the Christian Church . . . from that moment the Holy Spirit became the dominant reality in the life of the early Church."

Søren Kierkegaard told this parable about a king who had some horses. He had a coachman to train the horses and drive them regularly, but in an economy move the king decided to dismiss the coachman and drive the horses himself. However, because the king had used his coach only rarely, the horses, which the coachman had kept in top-notch shape, soon became sadly out of condition. They could not make even the shortest trip without becoming winded.

And so the king decided to give the horses back to the coachman that he might drive them regularly. Kierkegaard observed that this is what God does with his saints. His apostles and saints were just ordinary men and women, but they were driven. Oh, how they were driven! They were driven by the Spirit of God.

In the Old Testament Lesson for today we heard again the prophecy of Joel that someday God would pour out his spirit upon all flesh. In his sermon to the crowd, Peter identifies that prophecy with the events of that Pentecost day. Indeed, the gift of the Spirit was a turning point for the disciples. It was a fulfillment of the promise that God would come to them and enable them to remember, to teach, and to act out all that their master Jesus had said and done. They were driven by the Spirit of God.

When we read the entire Book of Acts, it becomes apparent that the author, Luke, does not intend to give a complete report of the activity of the disciples as they begin their missionary work. Rather we are given a sweeping view of how the message of the risen Christ led from the city of God (Jerusalem) to the city of the Emperor (Rome). We can see how the evangelical message penetrated to the "ends of the earth, and how Caesar is conquered by the Lord Jesus Christ. This is the main theme and passion of Luke. And the events of Pentecost set the stage for the "beginnings" of this movement.

The Pentecost Miracle—Then

On the basis of Peter's sermon to the crowd, it becomes clear that it is not because of the noise or the speaking in languages that startled the listeners. But it was through the content of Peter's message that the listeners became conscious of something happening. It is not because of some unusual or ecstatic behavior of the disciples, but on account of the foolishness of the message of the cross that some believe the speakers to be full of sweet wine. Here as elsewhere in Scripture, the uniqueness of the report is not to be found in the details of the miracle, but in the central scandal of the Gospel. And it is this combination of Spirit and Word which brings the church into being and gives it power. As Dale Bruner has observed, "To be filled with the Holy Spirit is to want others to know God's deeds in Christ. The Holy Spirit moves men to praise the 'mighty works of God.'"

It is this combination of the Spirit and the Word that is essential for us if our Christian community is to go forward. The power of the self-giving love of God allows a new beginning.

The Pentecost Miracle—Now

The Pentecost miracle is precisely that joyful-fearful event when the word suddenly reaches me, when it jolts me and sweeps me off my feet, when it "clicks." Then this word quickly shows that it is a dynamic thing, and that the symbols of movement and elemental force, suggested so naturally by the images of fire and storm, simply point up its power as it bursts into my life.

Thus when we speak of the miracle of the Holy Spirit we are confessing that something has come to us which we didn't comprehend before. Suddenly something that had previously left us cold and had meant no involvement at all gets through to us.

I hope this decisive point becomes clear to you—that is, God gives us his spirit so that we may fellowship with him and be led to do his will. In that way we are not left alone to our own ways or our wishful thinking about life.

We mean things when we speak of the Holy Spirit. We mean him who enlightens us, so that what was dark is now radiant. We mean him who calls us inside the sanctuary, where the windows begin to brighten, recounting to us the mighty acts of God. We mean him who, speaking out of flames of fire, makes dead Christian teachings burn again.

We don't come to any of these discoveries if they are not given to us. Such grace does not allow itself to overpower us. But whoever has empty hands and a great longing that they be filled, whoever says to his Lord, "Nothing in my hands I bring; Thou, O Lord, art everything," falls heir to the promise that he will not fail, but that he will be accepted.

And the promise is sure. God's Spirit has been poured out upon us. The prophecy uttered by Joel a long time ago has taken place. The early disciples did not remain a group of morose, defeated, shrinking men and women, but they went out as conquerors. The change was real and lasting. They went out boldly to win the world for Christ. They launched out unafraid and kept the channels open for that power of the Spirit.

Pentecost comes again to remind us that a handful of people once utterly transformed a sick society and gave it new life. What they did then, is equally possible today.

We are the church, individually and corporately. And God lets himself be known to us and through us. Knowing God and doing his will, we become part of the leavening influence commissioned by Christ himself. To pray earnestly, to serve despite the cost, to worship as an act of faith, to give as an expression of sacrificial love, to serve through involvement, to study the Word as discipline for your life, to let the mystery of the sacraments speak, to know the genuine fellowship of honest relationships—this is what it means to let the Spirit work in your life.

Waiting, wanting, hoping, and working to let God's Spirit come alive in your life is to realize that there is more to life than merely man's will and way and wisdom. The Holy Spirit is God in action—challenging us to action! He is the breath of God shaking the foundations of the world, your world and my world.

CHARLES H. MAAHS
Atonement Lutheran Church
Overland Park, Kansas

CHILDREN OF THE TRIUNE GOD
The Holy Trinity—First Sunday after Pentecost
Romans 8:14-17

It isn't hard to understand why this particular text was chosen as one of the Epistles for Trinity Sunday, for in this text the redemptive activity of the three Persons of the Holy Trinity is portrayed in a truly marvelous manner. Our text speaks of a God who calls us into his family and who allows us to address him as Father. It speaks to us of God's Son, Jesus Christ, who shares his life with us, and makes us fellow heirs with him of all the grace and glory our heavenly Father has to offer. It tells us of the Holy Spirit who enables us to believe that we really are the children of God, no longer slaves but free, free to live gladly and joyfully without fear, with all of the security and glory that comes to those who are heirs of God the Father and fellow heirs with his Son Jesus Christ.

Sons and daughters of the Triune God, we are; loved of the Father, redeemed by the Son, called to new life by the power of the Spirit. "Children of God," says St. Paul, "and if children then heirs, heirs of God and fellow heirs with Christ." And in our text this morning St. Paul talks to us about what that means, how it is that we became children of God, and the privileges and characteristics of that life which is ours as true children of our heavenly Father.

Led by the Spirit

Children of God are, first of all, those who are led by the Spirit of God, and when St. Paul uses language like this he really has two very particular things in mind. First, he is talking about the folly of trying to save oneself, and how it is only by the Spirit of God that we can be called the children of God. Throughout the seventh chapter of Romans—the chapter just immediately preceding our text—St. Paul has been talking about how impossible it is for us to be saved by our own virtue or power or goodness. Even those who try with all their being to live virtuous lives and to fulfill the demands and purposes of God's law must admit their failure. It's all very frustrating! Paul says, as he confesses in the closing verses of this chapter, "I do not understand my own actions . . . for I do not do the good I want, but the evil I do not want is what I do. . . . Wretched man that I am! Who will deliver me from this body of death?" (Romans 7:15, 19, 24). But then in the very first verse of chapter eight he has his answer: Christ will! "There is therefore now no condemnation for those who are in Christ Jesus." If we are to be the children of God, it will not be *our* doing but *God's*. Only by the leading of his Spirit can we become the children of God and fellow heirs with our Lord Jesus Christ.

But St. Paul has yet another thought in mind. When he speaks of being led by the Spirit of God he is thinking not only of the *source* of our new life but of its *end and purpose*. Throughout this eighth chapter of Romans, in the verses immediately preceding our text, Paul has been saying again and again that our new sonship in the Spirit must show itself in our life and actions. "Walk not according to the flesh but according to the Spirit" he says. It's simply no good *claiming* to be the children of God, and then not *living* as the children of God. If we are truly led by the Spirit it will show—in the kind of lives we lead—in the compassion we have—in the love we share—in the forgiveness and reconciliation we offer—in the joyful service we render. To be the children of God means that something very special has happened *within* us by the grace and power of the Spirit. It also means that by the grace and power of that same Spirit something very special is happening *through* us—and it is only by such spirit-filled and spirit-motivated lives that we can truly be called the sons and daughters of God.

Members of God's Family

But having said all this Paul now goes on to his next great point. The sonship we have in Christ is real. It is no pretending. God does not say "I will think of you as though you were my sons and daughters," but he says, "you *are* my sons and daughters in the fullest sense of the word." To underscore this truth St. Paul uses several Greek words that are very significant. The first of these is the word adoption. We have been adopted into the family of God, Paul is saying.

Now in the Roman world, adoption was something which was taken as seriously as it is in ours. When you were adopted into a family you truly became a part of that family. How true this is can be seen from the practice of the Roman emperors who frequently chose their successors not from the sons born to them but from sons whom they had adopted—a general, perhaps, or some leading government official—whom they had selected as best qualified to rule the empire after them. You see, to their way of thinking, adoption was so real that an emperor could even pass the inheritance of an empire on to somebody who was an adopted son, and could give that person privilege even over the son of his own issue. That's the sort of thing St. Paul is talking about when he uses this particular word. He is writing to citizens of Rome where the Emperor Claudius had just adopted Nero to be his son and heir to the empire. So St. Paul knew they would understand the full weight of his meaning. When God adopts us we become truly his own, with all the grace and privilege which that entails.

There's another significant thought involved in this concept of adoption. In the Roman world and culture there was a concept known as *patria potestas*, which meant that the father was the absolute lord of the manor and of the family. What the father said went! And that was true not only when a person was under age, but was true his whole lifetime long. Now when an adoption took place in the Roman courts there was a very elaborate ceremony in which the person being adopted was transferred from the patria potestas of one to the patria potestas of another. A great deal was made of the fact that a person now no longer had any allegiance to the old father but had allegiance to the new father to whom he was henceforth to give his loyalty, obedience and support.

Sometimes it happened that a man would adopt the slave of another man and make him his son and heir, and when that happened the concept of the patria protestas had special meaning, for it meant that the slave was now free. He was no longer under the bondage of his former master but a free man able to serve his father not in fear but in love, living no longer in servitude but in sonship. That's what St. Paul is thinking about when he says in our text that we have not received the spirit of slavery leading back to a life of fear, but the spirit of adoption to live freely for our Lord. We no longer have anything to do with that old father, Satan. We are no longer in his power, he no longer has any claim upon us, and there is no need to be filled with fear. For now we are under the protection, the patria potestas, of a new father, our heavenly Father. Now we are free as his sons and daughters to serve him without fear in righteousness and holiness all the days of our lives and forever.

To reinforce this, Paul uses the word *tekna*. That's the word that our text translates as "children." Now *tekna* is a word that was ordinarily used only of children born into a family, and in introducing this word Paul leaves us with a very beautiful thought. Because God has adopted us, we are his children in every sense of the word. Fully and completely he has made us his own. We are now even his *tekna,* his natural children reborn by the power and grace of the Spirit.

Sharing His Glory and Suffering

One more thought the Apostle has for us. To be sons and daughters of God means to share fully and completely in the life of Christ, and that means sharing both his glory and his suffering. Both the glory *and* the suffering! That's something we often forget. Glory we anticipate, and grace we come to take for granted, but suffering is something else again. It is something we do not expect, and we often fail to remember that to follow the way of Christ means to follow him also to the cross.

That's something St. Paul couldn't forget, nor could any of the other disciples. For them, opposition to the Gospel and life they proclaimed way a day-to-day experience, and they came to realize only too well the full implication of the Savior's warning, "If they persecute me they will also persecute you." But this has not been a part of *our* regular experience. Rarely does it come to us that we are called upon to suffer for his name and for his truth's sake. And when it does happen it shocks us. We feel that something is terribly wrong, that we have been done a gross injustice. How is it possible for us to suffer when we have done something that is right and good?

Yet that's precisely what we do need to expect. The sons and daughters of God in every age, including our own, have discovered that when you truly stand for something it is almost certain that there will be someone to stand against you, and sometimes that opposition has taken some very violent and painful forms. But rather than being outraged by that, we need to take heart and see it as a sign that we really are the sons and daughters of God—and fellow heirs with our Lord Jesus Christ.

When the Apostles in Jerusalem were put in prison for preaching the good news of Christ's resurrection, they rejoiced that they had been counted worthy to suffer for his name's sake. More recently, when a modern-day apostle found himself condemned by his church for insisting on preaching the Gospel, he confessed that there was some pain in that, but then went on to say that there was joy and glory in it too, for the Lord had always said that we were going to have to suffer for his sake and it was good to know that he hadn't been forgotten. That's the way Christ's people have always felt in the face of suffering for Christ's sake. They have seen it as a sign that his favor rests upon them—that their service to his name was of enough consequence to warrant opposition.

This is not to suggest that Christians ought to seek martyrdom, or deliberately make themselves obnoxious in order to be able to prove by their rejection that they are on the Lord's side. But it is to say most emphatically that living by the Spirit and facing opposition just naturally go together. Jesus once said, "Beware if all men speak well of you." If we have never faced any opposition it may only mean that we have never stood for anything. In any event, one thing is certain, if we wish to share in the glory of Christ, we need to be ready to share in his suffering too.

And the glory will come. St. Paul says, "I consider that the sufferings of this present time are not worth comparing with the glory that shall be revealed to us." And that's true, for "eye has not seen, nor ear heard, nor has it even entered into the heart of man what God has prepared for those who love him." But there is glory right here and now too—the glory of knowing that we are his, that his life is within us, that he has called us to be his own, to live under him in his kingdom, to serve him. Rejoice, therefore, sons and daughters of the Triune God!

HAROLD F. DICKE
Grace Lutheran Church
Cleveland Heights, Ohio

GETTING RIGHT WITH GOD
Second Sunday after Pentecost
Romans 3:21-25a, 27-28

Some moments in life shatter us. An engineer with nineteen years of faithful service for an aircraft corporation finds himself out of a job. After months of unsuccessful job hunting, he says in lament, "What am I going to do?" A woman sits stunned as her fourteen years of marriage comes to an end. She hears those unbelievable words from her husband, "I don't love you anymore. I want a divorce!" Sobbing her heart out, she says, "What am I going to do?" A person visits the doctor. He gives him a battery of tests and then calls him in for consultation. "I don't like what I see in these tests," he says. Even before he can finish the diagnosis, the person asks, "Doc, what can I do?"

If these shattering moments come in our work, in our marriages, and in our health, they also come in our spiritual lives.

There are those moments when a person wakes up to find that he has drifted away from God. His life is spiritually empty. This awakening may come in any number of ways. It may come through listening to a religious radio or television program. It may come as one sits down in conversation with a Christian friend, or it may come in one of those shattering moments of having lost a loved one who is very young. These moments do come. A person then says, "I need to get right with God."

Struggles with Sin

In the 16th century an Augustinian monk by the name of Martin Luther had a similar struggle. He had a problem of trying to find peace with God. His discovery of peace with God became one of the sparks of the Reformation. Something as basic as one's relationship with God was at the very heart of the movement for reform in the church over 450 years ago.

In a day of moral laxity some may wonder whether people are concerned about a subject such as sin. Carl Menninger has written a book entitled *Whatever Became of Sin?* In it he questions whether we have lost our sensitivity to sin. However, there are people today who have become very sensitive to the sin in their lives. Their consciences begin to throb and ache. They feel there is something lacking. They want to know that their lives are right with God. "What must I do?", they ask.

Some people who have this struggle and search for a sense of peace with God often plunge into church work. With a frenzy they volunteer for this and that. They feel that if they just work hard enough, they can win God's favor. God will then overlook all the things they have done or failed to do. Like a mountain climber, that person tries to scale the spiritual heights, struggling laboriously up and up. Such a plan of trying to take heaven by storm may not bring the peace for which we long. It may be like trying to walk up an escalator that is traveling down. For all their efforts, they are fighting a losing battle.

The more a person looks into God's word, the more one becomes aware of God's demands. Take the Ten Commandments. The first one is, "I am the Lord your God. You shall have no other gods." The harder we try to live up to that commandment, the more we become aware of the concerns that crowd God out of the number one place in our lives. The difficulty of our situation is pointed out by Jesus when he said, "I say to you, everyone who commits sin is a slave to sin." Our situation is like being in quicksand. The harder we struggle the deeper we sink.

God's Better Idea

The Living Bible states our situation clearly. "No one can ever be made right in God's sight by doing what the law demands. For the more we know of God's laws, the clearer it becomes that we aren't obeying them. His laws serve only to make us see that we are sinners" (Romans 3:20). We try and try to be what God wants us to be, but we sink more and more into feelings of failure. We become aware of the extent of our sinfulness. How, then, can we get right with God?

In his book *Touch of the Master's Hand,* Charles L. Allen tells a legend about a man caught in quicksand. Various religious leaders come by. Confucius sees him and remarks, "There is evidence that men should stay out of such places." Buddha comes by and says, "Let that life be a lesson to the rest of the world" Mohammed, on seeing him, says, "Alas, it is the will of Allah." In an effort to cheer the man, the Hindu says, "Cheer up, friend, you will return to earth in another form." However, when Jesus sees him, he says, "Give me your hand, brother, and I will pull you out." Our Lord doesn't stand and cheer us on with remarks similar to the popular commercial, "We try harder." Rather, he reaches down to give us his hand and lift us up.

God has shown us a different way. Not by our trying harder ... not by our striving to keep his laws. God says, I will accept you and declare you "not guilty" for the sake of Christ who takes away your sins. When we hear about God's way of getting right with him, there is something within each of us that says, "But that's too easy. There must be more to it than that . . . just accepting and trusting Jesus Christ. There's got to be more than that!"

No Coupons to Clip

We live in a time of bargains and free offers. Most of us clip the coupons out of the papers and magazines so that we can take advantage of the special bargains. There are no coupons in any newspaper or magazine to compare with this. God's fabulous offer is this. If we trust in Jesus Christ, God will declare us "not guilty." Our sins will be forgiven. We will be made right with God. Now our acquittal is not based on our good deeds—on the things we have done and avoided doing. It is based on what God has done for us already in Christ. It is based on our faith in him. St. Paul's letter to the Ephesians states it clearly, "For by grace you have been saved through faith" (Eph. 2:8).

The gospel is so simple and so beautiful. Yet we insist on complicating it. We want to make it something we must achieve, something we ourselves must do. When we try to complicate it, we destroy the salvation it offers and the peace it brings. The glorious gospel is this: God has shown us a different way to get right with him. The gospel way is not by being good enough. God's way is putting our hand in the hand of Christ. "We trust in Jesus who, in his kindness, freely takes away our sins" (Romans 3:24, LB). It's so simple. Why do we insist on making it complicated.

A Freeing Faith

What is the result of trusting Jesus Christ to take away our sins. The result is peace and freedom. We are at peace, because we are not struggling to live up to the law, to win God's favor. We relax in the knowledge that Christ did it all at Calvary. That victory can be ours by our faith in Christ. Faith like that is a "freeing" faith. John says in his gospel, "If the Son makes you free, you will be free indeed" (John 8:36).

What does this freedom mean? One thing it means is that God releases us from working and striving for our salvation. He frees us to work for others in Christ's name as evangelists, as people who care about others, as "little Christs." Think of it in this way. A woman is preparing to have her baby. She has arranged with her mother that when the baby arrives, her mother will come and help for two or three weeks. The mother comes when the baby is born and handles the housework. She does the cooking, she takes care of the needs of the other children. In doing that, she frees her daughter to give her full time to the most important thing, that of taking care of the new baby. The mother is released from one responsibility and freed to work at another responsibility, the loving care of her infant child.

Scripture tells us that God has shown us a different way of "getting right with him." He uses Christ's blood and our faith as the means of saving us. Through Christ's sacrifice, God frees us from the futility of trying to work for our salvation by a hundred percent compliance to his commandments and laws. He frees us to be what St. Paul says we are in 2 Corinthians 5:20, "... ambassadors for Christ, God making his appeal through us." God frees us from trying to work out our own salvation. Instead he lays upon us the challenge of bringing others to a faith in Christ Jesus and to the joy of having a right relationship with God.

God's Greatest Gift

Let me illustrate what this passage in Romans is saying by this story. Several months ago I became aware that there was something I really needed for our home. I decided I would look around. When I finally found one in a retail store, the price was extremely high. It was beyond my budget. So I found that the trading stamp redemption center had the item in their catalog for one hundred and seventy-five books. I decided I would work for it, so I began saving stamps. I went to all the places that gave stamps. Those places are becoming fewer and fewer, you know. I saved stamps, carefully pasting them in the books, anticipating the day when I would be able to buy what I really wanted. Members of the family would borrow a book now and then for something they wanted. It soon appeared that I was fighting a losing battle. I didn't know if I would ever have enough books. One day a dear friend came over to visit, unexpectedly. He said, "Here, I brought you something."

"For me?", I said, and began to unwrap it. To my absolute amazement and utter delight it was the very thing I had been saving to get. "What do I owe you?", I said.

"Nothing. It's a gift."

"But these are very expensive," I argued. "Let me pay you something."

"No, no! It's a gift. I love you and I want you to have it," the friend said.

I accepted the gift and said thanks. I could hardly believe it was true. A gift! What did I do to deserve it? Nothing!

He merely said, "I love you. I want you to have it."

So it is with God. God comes to us, busy as we are, pasting our stamps of good deeds done in our little books. And God says, "Trying to be good enough? Trying to keep the law? You will never make it. Here, let me give you a hand. My Son Jesus Christ has already paid with his life so that I might give you the gift of a new relationship between us. Here, just take it."

With amazement I raise my hands and take it. It is mine—a gift! All I did was receive it. So it is that we are saved by faith in Christ and not by the good things we do.

CHARLES A. ENDTER
Our Redeemer Lutheran Church
Garden Grove, California

HOW YOU CAN HAVE A STRONGER FAITH
Third Sunday after Pentecost
Romans 4:18-25

Abraham did not weaken in faith. I wonder why? So often my faith does weaken...

Abraham grew strong in faith. I wonder how? I'd like to have stronger faith...

Abraham grew strong in faith as he faced up to two fundamental tests: The test of the *unknown* and the test of *discouragement*. Faith grows strong as it comes to understand, accept, and enter into these two tests.

The Test of the Unknown

"By faith Abraham obeyed when he was called to go out to a place which he was to receive as an inheritance; and he went out, not knowing where he was to go" (Heb. 11:8). God tests our faith with the unknown in order that we may learn to obey his word.

Weak faith wants all kinds of supporting evidence that what I am about to do will turn out all right. Maybe I know that God wants me to do something. But then I look around to see if—well, if it's likely to work out. What will other people think? Are the circumstances right? What if such-and-such happens?

When faith obeys God's word in the face of the unknown, we are delivered from our dependency upon the support systems of this world.

*The Call Into the Unknown Forces Us
to Face Up to God's Plan for Our Life*

God had a plan that he wanted to work out through Abraham. With Abraham God wanted to make a new start in raising up a people who would believe and obey him. So he called him away from the idolatries of the Chaldeans which would continually tempt him away from God. He called him away from family and friends whose way of life would undermine God's purpose with the family that would be born to Abraham. He called him to go to the land where God, in his sovereign will, had determined to work out his plan with his chosen people.

The call of God need not be dramatic. It may simply be related to one's station in life. Every married person is called to be a husband or a wife. School-age children are called to be students. The owner of a business is called to be an employer.

In any of these ordinary situations of life God can call us into the unknown. It does not mean that you will necessarily pick up and move. On the contrary, the call may be to stay right where you are and enter into the uncertainties of the situation that faces you.

A woman had been going to a marriage counselor. After three months he told her to get a divorce. "Your husband is impossible. You'd better begin thinking about building a life for yourself and your two daughters." Some of her friends gave her the same counsel. But then her own mother came to see her. "You have a vow," she said with unaccustomed sternness. "And don't think you can blame all this on your husband. There are some things in you that need to change too."

That was a call into the unknown that was as real and challenging as a call to pick up and move to another country. In the face of that call she had to ask herself, "Is this word of my mother really God's word to me? (God often speaks to us through the counsel of others.) Am I ready to abandon the idea of divorce when our marriage is so shaky?"

For a while she toyed with the idea that perhaps the counselor was right, and her mother wrong. After all, he was professionally trained. But something in her knew that that would not stand up under scrutiny. What the counselor said was comforting, but what her mother said was true. She decided to do what her her mother was telling her to do. She closed the back door of divorce and went on in her marriage. In the face of the unknown she obeyed God's word. And faith won a battle.

Several years later—and many battles-of-faith later—she said, "When I gave up the idea of divorce I knew I would need God like I had never needed him before, because humanly speaking it was impossible. I think it was the first time in my life that fatih in God became a practical necessity for my everyday life."

The Call Into the Unknown Forces Us to Live with Uncertainty

When God calls us into the unknown it is no mock exercise. It means living with a real measure of uncertainty. It may involve basic changes in our way of life.

A businessman confided to a friend, "If I report my income and my inventory exactly the way it is, I may have to go out of business. It's crazy. Between the competition and the government you're virtually forced to doctor the figures if you want to stay in business." This man took seriously God's claim upon his life. He was finding it increasingly difficult to live in the shadowland of moral hypocrisy. But shaking free of it was not easy either. It meant facing the very real possibility of losing his business.

The element of uncertainty is what forces faith to grow. When we leave behind a support system in obedience to a word of God, then we become dependent on God. And that is what faith is, depending on God.

The Call Into the Unknown Forces Us to Depend on God Alone

A call into the unknown sets before us this challenge: "Are you willing to break free from whatever kind of support system you may be depending on, and to depend on God alone?"

High school and college age young people—are you willing to leave the country of conformity? Are you willing to give up your dependency on the approval of your peers? If God calls you to a different code of morals, a different modesty in your dress and speech and behavior, a different standard of honesty in your school work, a different integrity in your personal relationships, are you willing to be . . *different*? Is it enough for you to know that you have God's approval?

Members of a congregation of Christian people—can you break free from the bondage of super-private individualism? Are your ears open to a call from God that would bring you to a place of greater interdependence within the fellowship of believers? You came together on Sunday morning, and maybe an evening or two during the week. But after that you retreat to your own four walls and live out your thoroughly private lives. The Body of Christ cannot be built with such loose joints. If God calls you to commit yourselves to one another in further ways, to take responsibility for one another, to encourage and exhort and correct one another, to give up those things that hinder the fellowship, and to be available to one another not according to your convenience but according to the needs of the body, are you willing to lay down your personal life-style?

We may say that we love God, but God tests that at the level of our love for one another. "He who does not love his brother whom he has seen, cannot love God whom he has not seen" (1 John 4:20). We may think that we trust God, but God tests that at the level of our attitude toward those who come to us in his name. "He wo receives you receives me" (Matt. 10:40).

What "unknown" has God raised up to challenge your faith? What support system are you being asked to leave behind?

God calls us as he called Abraham—into the unknown. There

faith is tested. There faith takes leave of the comfortable country. There faith steps out in naked obedience to God's word. There faith grows strong.

The Test of Discouragement

"He did not weaken in faith when he considered his own body, which was as good as dead because he was about a hundred years old, or when he considered the barrenness of Sarah's womb. No distrust made him waver concerning the promise of God." God tests our faith with discouragement in order that we may learn to *trust his promise.*

Weak faith has little appetite for endurance. It rejoices easily in a promise, but loses heart when the fulfillment is delayed. Common sense takes over. Maybe we misunderstood. Or maybe it was meant only in a spiritual sense. The gap between our experience and our faith-expectation is too painful to endure, so we lower our expectations.

When faith trusts God's promise in the face of discouragement, we are driven to reach more deeply into the strength and grace of God.

Discouragement Forces Us Back to the Promise

Several times when discouragement weighed heavily on Abraham, God called him back to the original promise and re-established his covenant with him (See Gen. 15:1-6, 17:1-19, 22:15-18.). Times of discouragement are occasions for bold remembering!

When Martin Luther was afflicted with doubt and discouragement, when God seemed to have allowed every vestige of faith to be stripped away, he would return to God's foundational promise, and affirm, "But I am baptized!" This was not a foolish hoping in a magical rite. It was a dogged return to the promise of baptism, that he had been grafted into Christ. It was a trusting in God's promise when all evidence and all experience seemed to argue to the contrary.

God speaks promises over our lives at many points. Inevitably these promises must face the test of discouragement. They will never come to full flower unless they are so tested.

How seriously do we take the promises that God speaks over our lives? How many husbands and wives, in a time when their life together is mired down in discouragement, return to the promise that God spoke over their marriage, "The two shall become one?" How many Christians enter into a work of service in the community trusting in the guidance and blessing of God, then succumb to discouragement when their service encounters opposition, or continues to go unnoticed?

God's work in our lives can only be built on the strong rock of his promises.

Discouragement Forces Us to Recognize Our Own Weakness

Abraham coolly considered the situation: He was almost a hundred years old, his wife Sarah was past ninety. God had promised them a child, but to have a child at their age would be contrary to all human experience. Nothing but the intervention of God could bring the promise to fulfillment.

Discouragement brings us to just this place—the place of helplessness, where we recognize that God alone is our hope.

Many a parent has been brought to that point in the business of raising children. "When they are little," a friend once told me, "you can direct their activities. But when they grow older you can only bear them up on the weary arms of prayer."

God speaks powerful promises over parents and children. "Train up a child in the way he should go and when he is old, he will not depart from it" (Prov. 22:6). But that promise is never fulfilled unless we pass the test of discouragement.

Discouragement brings us to the end of our human possibilities, where we see our helplessness, and our need of God. There we learn that God's commands and God's promises (they are two sides of the same coin) are not something we accomplish, but something God accomplishes with us and through us.

Discouragement Drives Us Into Closer Union with Christ

"In the days of his flesh Jesus offered up prayers and supplications with loud cries and tears" (Heb. 5:7). In Gethsemane he poured out his soul to the Father in an agony of blood and sweat. Yet even in his suffering the one thing he clung to above all else was the Father's will. When all human comfort failed, when discouragement pushed him to the point of anguish, he knew that the one thing he could finally depend upon was his relationship with the Father.

God allows discouragement to teach us the true nature of faith, and that we may see faith grow. Faith is not a mere agreement of the mind to certain truths. Martin Luther grasped the true nature of faith when he wrote, "Faith is a sure trust and confidence of the heart, and a firm consent whereby Christ is apprehended; so that Christ is the object of faith, yea rather he is not the object, but, as it were, *in the faith itself Christ is present!"*

In a time of discouragement my wife found all her praying reduced to a single supplication, "Take my hand, dear Father, and lead Thou me." Discouragement strips faith of all its accessories. One is left clinging to the reality of God alone. It is like a pruning. Everything is stripped down to the central trunk in which the life is housed, and then stronger, more beautiful life comes forth.

You may have wondered why you have had to face so much uncertainty; why God seemed to be calling you into the unknown. Now you know that he has a divine purpose. He is teaching you to obey his word. And that word leads always to Christ.

You have looked discouragement in the face; like Jesus himself, you may have cried out to God. Now you see that through the discouragement God has been teaching you to trust his promise. And the heart of his promise is Christ.

Faith is a personal union between the believer and the risen Christ, which is brought into our hearts by the Holy Spirit. To grow strong in faith means to grow strong in my relationship with Christ. To grow strong in faith means to have his lordship gain strength in my life. To grow strong in faith does not mean that some part of me called "faith" gets stronger, but rather that Christ in me gets stronger. For faith is nothing other than that, *Christ in me.*

Strong faith is not something reserved for a handful of supersaints. *You* can have strong faith. Because you have a strong Christ.

LARRY CHRISTENSON
Trinity Lutheran Church
San Pedro, California

SAVED FOR LIVING
Fourth Sunday after Pentecost
Romans 5:6-11

Those who never really get around to living often have the most difficulty dying. Dying, unfortunately, is something we are all going to have to do. Those who work with the terminally ill tell us that people who do not believe they have lived a full life often feel most cheated as they die. They sense that there is still so much to do and now so little time to do it.

Death is always a companion on life's journey. Its positive function is to gently remind us that tomorrow's life is never as sure as today's. Often we try to avoid any thought of death. We attempt to escape its reality. Death is something that happens to the other fellow. Like the husband who says to his wife, "Honey, if one of us dies, I'll go to Paris." Yet a consciousness of death encourages us to live our life rather than simply pass through it. Death puts life into a context—it encourages growth and positive living—with each day seen as possibly the last. It encourages us to seek meaning for our lives—especially ultimate meaning.

God Is for Life

God has always been on the side of life. From the moment he breathed on some dust, and it became a man, he has affirmed life. Although we were made in the image of God and called to walking the high road together with our Maker, we chose rather the low road of disobedience and sin. In the process we became enemies of God. Not satisfied with our own magnificence as God's most wonderful creation, we were conned into thinking we could be something we could never be—God himself. We fell for the devil's ploy and thereby fell from God's favor. Like God, yes! But never his equal. Never God.

Now at the point of our disobedience God shows his unreasonableness. Our text says, "While we were yet sinners Christ died for us." Not when we deserved his love but rather when we needed it. In our weakness he gave us the strength of his forgiveness.

Who Is Worth Your Life?

Who is important enough to die for? Think a moment before you answer. Give up your life for someone else, and in the process never see a beautiful sunset again, never smell the fragrance of another rose, never enjoy another kiss, never be with another person you love, never complete another goal, or fulfill another dream. Who is worth your life? Who is that important to you? Other than a member of your immediate family, I doubt if anyone is. Well, Jesus died not only for members of his immediate family but also for weak people and unrighteous people and unworthy people and sinful people—people like those who live all around us and like the person who lives within us. Yes, Jesus thought we were worth dying for. In Jesus, God shouts from earth that his love is greater than our rebellion.

Recently I read of a pastor who received a letter from a son of his parish who was in the Air Force. The young man was also active in the community. The letter read, "I work for a rescue squad. . . . Well, last Thursday about 7:00 a.m. we got a call on a stroke victim . . . we responded . . . when we got there we found a 62-year-old woman—unconscious but still alive. I monitored her vitals while my partner called for an ambulance . . . while he was doing that, she stopped breathing and her heart stopped! I started ECPR and mouth-to-mouth. We continued this for ten to fifteen minutes. We put her in the ambulance and she opened her eyes! People talk about how they'd get high . . . but that is the ultimate high . . . saving someone's life with your own breath and hands!"

With hands and breath Jesus saved our lives as we were dead to sin. Hands stretched out upon a cross. And as his last breath made its way from his lungs up and through his lips, the gap between God and man was closed. Now it becomes possible for us to make an appointment with eternity—to live as that woman lived. He gave his breath for us, but unlike the woman, we will live forever.

Moping Not Necessary!

Belief in Jesus puts us in the company of the saved. The saved no longer exist on this earth—they live! A Christian doesn't have to be a mope. But we see Christian mopes all around. It is not necessary—even more, it's uncalled for. Sure Christians have problems. No one escapes problems. But when they enter our lives they either become a permanent house guest, or their visit can be short. We can solve our problems as we remember God's promises of deliverance and then beckon an indwelling Christ to help us do battle. For, you see, Jesus saves us for living. Beauty need not be blurred, purpose need not be lost, joy need not be occasional, humdrum need never describe our lives.

Outside and Inside the Christian Life

Those outside of life in Christ have little more than death to look forward to. Although they are physically alive, their life is only a mockery of what God wants it to be. Outside of Christ their visions seldom reach higher than the curbs lining the street. They are the walking dead, and when they finally lie down to die, they have only the wrath of God and separation from the Father awaiting them.

The good news for us today and for our limited tomorrows is

that the death bell never tolls its final ring for those who love the Lord. For when we believe and then fall asleep in Christ, we are justified by his blood and thereby declared righteous. When God looks at us he does not see what we are, but what we have. When he sees Christ in our hearts, then he declares us, "Not guilty." Jesus makes us right again with the Father and makes heaven a certainty. We are also reconciled with God and thereby delivered from his wrath. Jesus not only saves us from the tragedy of a life which merely exists but also saves us for a wonderful eternity with him.

Help Also in Dying

And when we believe in Christ he even helps us in dying. I'm not saying that dying is easy for the believer, but I do know it is easier. For the believer lives life until the last breath. He also knows that the time span between death and heaven is merely the blink of an eye.

Martin Luther was a man who knew how to live and how to die. At two o'clock on the morning of February 18, 1546, he suffered a series of attacks around the regions of the heart. Doctors were quickly summoned. It became clear he was dying. In spite of his weakness, he recited several passages of Scripture and repeatedly commended his soul to God. Finally, Jonas, one of his fellow reformers, asked in a penetrating voice, "Reverend Father, are you willing to die in the name of the Christ and the doctrine you have preached?" Luther, rallying his last bit of strength, replies, "Yes" so distinctly that the fourteen people standing around his bed all heard him. He then died and joined the community of saints.

In his later years no longer did Luther tremble at the rustling of a wind-blown leaf. Instead of calling upon St. Anne, he was able to laugh at thunder and jagged bolts of lightning. He was able to live and to die with the assurance of God's love and forgiveness. "He who through faith is righteous shall live." He believed those words of Paul both in life and in death. Life in Christ provides us with much reason for rejoicing—even while we are dying.

In Christ Yields Great Benefits

There are great benefits for us who are more alive than dead. In Christ, no longer need the feeling of guilt breathe its stagnant breath upon us. In Christ, no longer need our failures parade their ugly faces before our eyes. In Christ, no longer need we keep coping with shame, uneasiness, and lack of confidence. In Christ, no longer needs grief's tentacles suck energy from our veins. We can rejoice in God because Jesus has made life possible and much more than that—livable.

The day we were born into this world was not the greatest day in our lives but rather the day we were adopted by God through Baptism and then later came to know his Son as our Lord and Savior.

In the Old Testament a great man of God, named Moses, one day spoke to the children of Israel. He said, "I call heaven and earth to witness against you this day, that I have set before you life and death, blessing and curse, therefore choose life, that you and your descendants may live, loving the Lord your God, obeying his voice and cleaving to him."

God says to us again today, "Choose life," another way of saying, "choose Christ—have a close walk with him." For in Christ we are saved for living—both now and later.

JOHN H. KRAHN
Trinity Lutheran Church
Hicksville, New York

WITHOUT PARALLEL
Fifth Sunday after Pentecost
Romans 5:12-15

A most popular phrase generated recently is, "tell it like it is." Many times, doing just that creates hurt, upset, anger, frustration, and discomfort. However, Paul states very concisely just how it is in his letter to the people at Rome.

This changed new man starts with very real facts in a very real world and relates how his experience brings meaning to him. The experience Paul had is itself the result of the impact of the real acts upon him. . . . "Therefore as sin came into the world through one man and death as the result of sin, so death spread to all men, because all men sinned." No one could stop, avoid, or escape its power.

The Reality of Sin

Speaking boldly, Paul says the reality of sin brings about the present state of affairs. We have an inward disposition of rebellion against God, stemming from self-exultation. It has always been that, and is closely bound up with our inward desire to have the best of everything for ourselves, regardless of the consequences. We look after number one, self. We want to be in control and we express this in actions that are real and assessable. We become conscious of this desire many times every day as we read our newspapers, listen to our radio broadcasts, and watch the TV. We hear and see confirmed the fact that sin is very visible and real. The result of all this is death, death as a power that denies human worth, dignity, and potential.

In preparing this sermon I went back to review in my mind what I have seen, heard, and just read within the last week. It's all there—robbery, death of a victim, war and famine, violence, hurt, and death. A recent novel which relates in vivid pictures how inhuman people can be is *Roots*. That novel was turned into a giant TV production and portrayed how those feeling good about themselves, desiring to have the best, made other persons serve them, captured, enslaved, inflicted inhuman treatment and degradation on them. This novel gives us only a short period of time when we compare it to the whole of human history. It further reveals only one of the examples of our inhumanity to others and our attitude of superiority over others.

God then judges us, and that judgment results in condemnation through the laws given at Sinai. This law judges us guilty; it reveals our willful actions and disobedience against the will of God quite visibly. For who among us can say that we are good when contrasted with the law? The law of God opens the door for us to see what we are, what we do, and ends up condemning the disobedience.

Judgment and Mercy

There is no parallel to man's disobedience to God, his living under the reign of sin and death as these very real things control our lives; but Paul tries to make a parallel and in so doing shows us that there is something much greater. Picture yourself along with all the rest of humanity in one boxed canyon. There is only one way out and this is blocked by a massive gate locked and bolted. In this canyon are many open graves just waiting to swallow up this humanity. Everyone in there is subject to digestion by the earth.

Mercy comes and stands before this gate and is crying over what is seen and wishing to enter, to heal, to relieve the pain and the sorrow, to save this humanity. Mercy realizes that she can pity, but not relieve; she can see, but do nothing about it.

"Why?" Mercy cries out. Answering her own question, "Because Justice has barred the gate and I cannot move the bolt." Justice comes to the gate and says, "You cannot enter—you are right; a law has been broken and it must be honored; therefore all must die!"

It is at this point, while her tears stream down her cheeks, she is joined by the Son of God. Turning to him, Justice says, "My demands are very strict—without the shedding of blood, there will be no setting right." And so the Son says, "OK, I hear and understand your terms, but let all the wrong be upon me and let Mercy enter and hold off this comedy of death." Justice says, "Fine, that is easy for you to say. How do I know that you will fulfill my demand?" "The time will come and I will follow through; take my word for it," says the Son of God.

Justice and Grace

The time did come. The covenant made with justice was to be fulfilled. In his humanity, this Son of God took to himself all the sin of mankind. He took it to a hill called the Calvary, carrying his own cross, followed by his crying disciples and jeering humanity, he climbed the hill just like a lamb being prepared for sacrifice. This is the day on which the covenant is cancelled. The covenant is nailed to a cross and the cry echoes over the whole of the world, "It is finished." In his humanity, the Son of God took all our sins to the cross and death died his own way when touched by his godliness. Death died in the struggle of darkness, and in the tremor earthquake; and it was then above all this noise that the echo of the angels was heard again, "Glory to God, on earth peace and good will to all people."

"God's free gift is not at all to be compared to the trespass." His grace is out of all proportion to the fall of man. The effect of the trespass is "vastly exceeded by the grace of God, and the gift that came to so many by the grace of the one man, Jesus Christ."

So it is that the free gift of God stands without parallel. There is no balance between the fall of man and the reign of death, compared to the grace and love of God. God makes righteous the whole of his beloved humanity. It is his act of righteousness that is his ongoing activity, a divine activity taking place visibly and knowingly within the field of human experience. And this righteousness is revealed to us. It is God's saving power. Paul knew it was accomplished for him; we must realize it is accomplished for us and, like St. Paul, pray for the zeal to spread this good news to the rest of the world.

You and I as the church of Jesus Christ are now called to respond to this free gift and act of God by sharing, showing our righteousness as it has been revealed to us by reaching out to those who still remain victims of people and death. We are called to live out our baptism as we minister in our mission to the whole of the world. It is in this mission of the Word, in worship, witness, learning, sharing that we reflect the love shown to us in Jesus Christ. This love is all and total self-giving. We live out this love in our acts of doing and giving; through feeding and being advocates of justice to those who know not the just; to love and to heal through missionary and medical personnel; to send others where we cannot go. Multiply this by the list of many ministers throughout the United States and Canada, on six continents, in town and city.

"Lift up your heads O gates lift up ye everlasting doors that the King of Glory may come in. Who is this King of Glory"—the psalmist knew and cried out, "It is the Lord, the Lord of Hosts." The enemy of God received his mortal wound in Jesus Christ, and so our thanks to God who has given totally and completely his gift through his Son Jesus Christ, our Lord. Go you now to all the world proclaiming this good news of God's grace and love.

JAMES E. BENNETT
Berkeley Hills Lutheran Church
Pittsburgh, Pennsylvania

WHAT'S IT LIKE?
Sixth Sunday after Pentecost
Romans 6:2b-11

What's It Like?

"Hi, Mike. I haven't seen you since the wedding. How's it going? What's it like being married to Kathy?"

"Oh, marriage is fine. But you have to keep a close eye on the budget to keep it all together. But it's better than being single."

Did Mike answer the question? Did he even hear the question? Or possibly he heard only a part of the question. He was asked—"What's it like being married *to Kathy?*" The question he answered was—"What's it like being married . . . ?" He spoke about marriage rather than Kathy.

Many times we speak about the state of our existence (our activities) rather than (the state of) our relationships. Often we find ourselves more comfortable with the impersonal than with the personal. For some it may be easier to speak in general about marriage, rather than to speak about their specific experience—relationship. Although it is for sure that anything a person would mention about marriage in general would be colored by their specific relationship, it is much more difficult to speak in terms of persons than it is to speak in terms of activities, circumstances, or situations.

What's It Like Being a Christian?

For example, how would we reply if asked what it was like being a Christian? "Well, we have services every week at 10:30 a.m.; and, of course, there is Sunday school for the kids at 9:30 a.m. The council meets on the third Thursday of the month. The ladies get together to study the Bible each month. We had a mission dinner last year in May. The kids go on trips now and then—retreats, conventions—you know that kind of stuff. We'll have an ice cream social this summer. We collect money for the hunger drive. The men take their turn ushering."

Is that what it means to be a Christian? I suppose for some people, yes. How boring! The answer was about things, activities. But it was not an answer to the question—"What's it like being a Christian?" How can anyone ever speak of marriage and never mention the name of the person they are married to? How can anyone speak about being a Christian and never mention the name of Christ? And yet it is done all the time—probably more times than not. We speak of impersonal things rather than our personal God—the relationship we have with him.

Learning, But Not Living

I know a young woman who is single and is very eager to find someone she considers suitable to marry. You can see in her anxiety that she is willing to be satisfied with less in order simply to have something—someone. I'm concerned about her a great deal. I've often thought if I had the world to give, if it were in my power to hand out "suitable mates," I would give her one. In my concern for her (and since I don't have any spare young men around) I suggested that she might share with God her feelings of anxiety, of loneliness, or indecision in her relationships. I asked her if she had ever told him how she felt. No.

Along in the conversation she said, "Maybe I should go back to church." Here was a young woman living alone, carrying many unnecessary burdens, very much alone, not recognizing the power, the strength available to help her—not necessarily to find a husband—but to help her see, to understand, to live . . . in whatever circumstance. With the eyes she had, she could only see one kind of person of a certain status. With new eyes, her whole view would open up and would include many more possibilities, hopes, dreams.

She said she had attended a parochial grade school, gone to a Lutheran college and had learned about God and Jesus. But no one had ever *personalized* him for her before. She thought God wouldn't care about her search for a husband—and besides what could he do about it? What good would it do to tell him? She didn't know that the answer to prayer is not always that God changes the world or delivers us our request postage paid—but rather that if we make ourselves available to him, the answer might be that we are changed. She had learned—but was not living. Maybe she was not ready. Maybe she forgot she was baptized. Or maybe she met too many people who talked about the church, the mission dinner and forgot to share Christ with her; and so what she had been given was put in storage. It's easy to speak about marriage and not Kathy. It's easy to fall into the rut of talking about the church rather than about Christ. It's easy to talk about a thing, an event, and forget the person.

The McDonald's-Kresge Syndrome

It's so easy for learned words to come out of our mouths and not be connected to any feeling or reality inside us. I occasionally stop at McDonald's for lunch. When I have received my order and paid, I hear the same thing every time—"Thank you. Have a nice day. Come again." "Thank you. Have a nice day. Come again." I could go on typing the same words as if they were a continual flowing from a computer. They are the same. It's as if the employees are programmed (which they probably are) to treat the customer in a certain polite way with certain polite words. When shopping in Kresge's, I will hear these words at the checkout counter, "Thank you for shopping at Kresge's. Thank you very much. Come Again." With this one clerk—the words never vary. The tone never varies. And her facial expression never varies. What is the result? I no longer hear them. And if I do for a moment, what they are saying means nothing to me. They are just words run over and over on a tape. It isn't anything special for me. They are the words for a "customer" but not for me as a person.

How well are we programmed in the church? We know the words, the phrases, the expressions, the answers to this or that question. Maybe we are programmed too well? Maybe the right words come out and are no longer connected to a reality inside us. Maybe we can even get to the point and speak of relationship after it has long been dead. Maybe that is why some people don't want to listen. We have nothing to say. The message we have—if programmed through a computer—comes out like a tape with no variation in tone, expression, or facial muscles. Maybe we give no indication that we are speaking about a life and death matter for us and for them. That is easily tuned out—just like the same smooth tones of commercials. Where is the message about a person for another person spoken by a person?

The Message

What do we *have* to tell someone? Or do we just have neutral facts that really don't influence us at all or don't need to be mentioned. When we do mention them as we have learned them, do they bore us as well as others? We might ask what is the message? What do we have to tell? But the answer that would come back would be on a tape reeling around and around saying the same words, facts over and over. Rather we need to ask first what is the relationship. For it is this answer that will tell us what the message is. Without relationship we have no message to tell. Without relationship we fall into the McDonald's-Kresge syndrome—splashing the same non-message on everyone. The words may be right—but they have no meaning because the person who speaks them no longer finds meaning in them. They say them because when you work at McDonald's that's what you say at that point. When we're a member of the church, there are certain things we say at certain times because *we belong to a church*. Would the words we say—the feelings we express be different if we remembered that we don't belong to a church as much as *we belong to Christ?*

The Relationship

The message throughout the Bible is that God loves us—God loves you. God loves me. It sounds nice. But maybe it's just a tape. What does it mean? What action has he taken so that we might know that? What is the relationship? What has Christ done for you? What do we have to say? What do we have to tell other people? How can we direct another to Christ through prayer if we have never found value in it ourselves? How can we speak of someone if we have never met him—if we have no relationship with him—or if we have a relationship on his initiation but left it behind? We can only tell what we know. If we try to tell what someone else knows—we are a tape with no expression—no message at all.

Paul speaks of the relationship in the dramatic terms of life and death. He was answering the people who thought that because of Christ, because of grace, that they could sin all the more to receive all the more grace. He told them they were far off base. Didn't they know that in Christ their life was different having passed through death itself to a whole new life?

More Than Words

As a Christian, what does that mean? How do we know that to be true for us? Is it so because someone told us? Is there any evidence of its truth in our lives? Have we ever died and risen again? In Baptism by the water and the Word, our sinful self has been drowned and a new life is growing. Words on a tape? A programmed response? No, we can see it happening day by day. (1) "You know that old witch Beatrice? I wouldn't be caught within 10 miles of her." (2) "I feel sorry for Beatrice. She's had many difficulties and sometimes just isn't in the best of spirits." (1) "That old Joe Smelts is a lazy, no good bum." (2) "Yeah, I saw Joe yesterday. He's a very friendly man." When we go from No. 1 in each case to being able to speak No. 2 honestly, we have died and rose. In union with Christ there's the opportunity for changes every day. There is the hope of becoming (like him). There is the hope of seeing. There is the hope of hearing for the first time.

Yes, we have been baptized. So? Can we see the death—the drowning that takes place each day? Can we see the new life—the new attitudes, the new values, the new understanding, the new insight that coms to us? We can. In union with Christ we are continually dying and rising again—giving up judgments for understanding. Paul's words are not pat answers—we can see and hear the evidence of them today.

Other Voices

Matthew speaks in the Gospel for this day of the losing and the finding of life. Losing life is letting go of all that which is of no value to us; and finding life is listening to Christ—living in intimate relationship with him through prayer, worship, study —acknowledging by action our rebirth in Christ. The person who holds on to life retains what he was born with—a life under dominion of sin. The person who lets go indeed loses that life of sin and is given a new one in Christ.

The lesson from Jeremiah speaks of a yoke that must be carried—either a light one or a heavy one if the first is rejected. Hananiah spoke of release and freedom. Jeremiah spoke of servitude for a purpose. If we remove the one, another heavier, unbearable yoke will be ours. For example, the young woman I mentioned earlier. She had forgotten the new birth, the yoke of Christ, and on her own was burdened with even . . . .

The next time you have the chance to tell someone *what it's like* to be a Christian—skip the mission dinner and get to the point. Tell them who you are related to, what he taught you today, and what he did for you today.

DAWN M. PROUX
Glen Flora Lutheran Church
Glen Flora, Wisconsin

SAINT AND SINNER

Seventh Sunday after Pentecost
Romans 7:15-25a

Our text this morning talks about an experience that most of us have faced. How often have you felt just like St. Paul? How many times in your life have you experienced that what you really want to do you don't do, and that the things you most despise you find yourself doing? What you know you want and ought to do sometimes you find yourself incapable of doing. What you detest most in others and yourself, you find yourself doing. We've all had that kind of experience. We know it well. Christians throughout the centuries have had that experience.

Luther was fond of talking about himself as saint and sinner at the same time. He knew in a most personal way the struggle of St. Paul. He, more than most, desperately struggled to control his every thought and action, but to no avail. It was only after he found the secret of God's forgiveness through faith in Jesus Christ that he could boldly confess he was saint and sinner, but living moment by moment in God's forgiveness. Paul's passionate struggle and search for an answer helped Luther and other heroes of the faith and is capable of helping us experience God's good news for us today. Let's meditate on this text—focusing on the topic, "Saint and Sinner" . . . living freely in God's forgiveness."

Who's Talking?

Some Christians miss the point of this text. They suggest that in Romans 7 Paul is talking about his life before he was converted. Some Christians even make the assumption that after conversion, it's possible to live without this tension. A careful study of the text and other parts of Paul's writings reveals just the opposite. Paul is talking about his personal struggle after his conversion experience. He's talking about the Paul who Jesus confronted on that road to Damascus. He's talking about a Paul who at times experienced being caught up into the seventh heaven. He's talking about a Paul who had the courage to face councils and governors. He's talking about a Paul who could rejoice in all things. He's talking about a Paul who could give thanks and sing for joy even in a prison cell. Paul, who was a hero of the faith, cried out: "I do not do the good I want, but the evil I do not want is what I do . . . who will deliver me from this body of death?" As we identify with the text, it's the real me, it's the real you, that experiences this tension. We're not talking about a time when we did not belong to Christ. We're talking about ourselves, baptized into Christ's body, called by God's Holy Spirit through the Gospel, loved of God, but still in tension. It's a real tension and it makes us cry out with Paul: "Who will deliver me?"

Understanding the Tension

Another problem people sometimes have with this text is a misunderstanding of what is meant by the struggle between *flesh* and *spirit* in New Testament literature. Many people correctly criticize the Christian church and accuse it of separating flesh from spirit, or mind from body. Sometimes Christians have talked about human personhood in a way that denies the unity of the person. Again, a careful study of biblical material reveals an emphasis on the wholeness of the human person. The Greek philosophers are the ones responsible for separating flesh and spirit, mind and body. Unfortunately, many Christians have given the same impression. Our Judeo-Christian heritage, however, sees a unity of the human person. People can't be divided into mind, body, soul, spirit. God interrelates with total persons, not just some spiritual part of us.

When Paul talks about the struggle of the flesh against the spirit, he's not talking about the body in conflict with mind. Flesh must never be equated with body. When Paul talks about flesh warring with spirit, he's talking about a force that permeates every part of us, our mind, spirit, soul, body. Flesh is a very technical word which means that there is a driving force within each of us that would center life on ourselves. We become the center of the universe. Our self acts as if we were God. People, circumstances, experiences are used by us for our selfish purposes. That's the source of greed, lust, anger, hatred, murder. It's a driving force within us. Paul calls it the power of sin at work within us.

When Paul talks about spirit of the law of God at work in our mind, he's talking about another force which permeates every part of us. It's an energy, a desire, which empowers us to love, to serve, to give, to affirm, to care, to risk our self, to share, or in other words, to be motivated by God's Spirit for life and peace.

In some sense, Sigmund Freud talks about these forces to which Paul refers when he talks about life and death forces in the human person. Of course, he didn't talk in Christian categories, but his descriptions are very much related to the realities Paul describes. It's the struggle between two different kinds of energy that Paul and we experience. It's a struggle of sin and the law at work within us and the force of God's Holy Spirit. That's why, many times, what we want to do, we don't do, and what we don't want to do, we do.

Searching for Resolution

What's the solution? Can the tension ever be resolved? What's the answer? Is there a solution? Is there an answer? What have you found in your own life? How have you experienced the struggle? Where did Paul find hope?

It would be easy to reply with a quick theological quip. Of course, Jesus Christ! But what does that mean? Paul seems to be saying, that the recognition of this struggle is the first step in dealing with it. You can't possibly find any kind of resolution without facing the problem. Too often we Christians act as if the conflict does not exist. I believe that's why Luther once told Melanchthon to sin boldly! Too often, like Melanchthon, we live with a veneer of piety and outward goodness that makes it impossible for us to face the depth and the force of the conflict which wars within us.

Luther also once said that the "World at its best, is the world at its worst." In the best of human action, there is often the assumption, that the struggle no longer exists. It assumes a goodness in human kind which is not there. In recent history, the beauty and naivete of the young people of the sixties—putting flowers into gun barrels gives eloquent testimony to that heresy. Young students, on one Maundy Thursday during the sixties, on our campus, put flowers over the door posts instead of blood to symbolize that a liberation, a new exodus, could occur in a different way. The shedding of blood was no longer necessary. Results in our own country, in South America, in Africa, and in the Middle East, show how far removed from reality that assumption was.

One of the revolutionary leaders of the sixties, Stokley Carmichael, speaking on University of California campuses, proclaimed tht capitalism was doomed because it assumed a sinful nature of human persons and that only a system that accepted the goodness of persons could survive. Capitalism may indeed be dead, but not for that reason. No system which does not adequately consider the radical alienation of human persons will ever be able to work for peace and justice among people. The resolution of this problem will never be accomplished by denying its existence. It's only when we face in the depth of our being the extent of the struggle is there a way to find hope.

Some Clues

The Old Testament lesson for today gives us a clue. The word from Zachariah is a joyous one: Rejoice greatly, O daughter of Zion! Shout aloud, O daughter of Jerusalem! Lo, your king comes to you, humble and riding on an ass, on a colt, the foal of an ass." The children of Israel were able to receive the message. Their liberation was coming not from their own political manipulations, not their own military might, not their own clever schemes. Those had all failed. They were in exile and they knew it. The God of Abraham, Isaac, and Jacob was delivering them, and it was a different kind of king who was to do the job. They had given up trust in themselves. They had recognized their plight, and at that juncture, they were capable of receiving deliverance, not from themselves, but from God.

It's like that in our own lives. Some of you have perhaps read the book by Charles Colson, one of the Watergate crew who became a Christian. At one point, he says that only when he found himself in prison did he become really free. Only when he recognized the evil he was involved in and turned to the grace and mercy of Jesus Christ, did he really find freedom. Sometimes, it's difficult to accept such testimony, because it comes from a "battlefield conversion" context. When someone like Colson proclaims such deliverance; or when Eldridge Cleaver faced with possible conviction has such a conversion, we sometimes become skeptical, but we shouldn't. God can also use those situations and similar experiences though less traumatic, in our own lives to bring about change. Solzhenitsyn, the Russian author, talks about the people that are truly free in Russia, are those in prison. People who truly recognize their condition, or who have and then know there is no one to fear, are the people truly free.

The Yoke of Jesus

The Gospel for today gives us the answer. The fear we experience, the struggle we experience between flesh and spirit, all comes because there is something in life which makes us think we can solve our own problems, justify our own actions, become our own righteousness. Paul talks about this as law. There is something in our own makeup that tries to find security in ourselves. The message of Jesus is just the opposite. Listen to the Gospel for today: "Come to me all who labor and are heavy laden, and I will give you rest. Take my yoke upon you. The yoke of Jesus is acceptance. We can depend on someone other than ourselves. There is forgiveness. Paul concludes this discussion about the struggle of flesh and spirit in Romans 8 with these words: "If God is for us, who is against us? He who did not spare his own Son but gave him up for us all, will he not also give us all things with him?" That's the yoke of Jesus. That's the message we need to live in the tension of flesh and spirit.

Implications

Are we ever free of the struggle? What would you say? How can we live with these warring factions? Recently a psychiatric staff working with counselors in our local juvenile treatment center helped them understand one perspective for living with the different forces within us. It came very close to the message of Jesus. There are many facets of our personhood. Sometimes the shadow side of ourselves feels it is about to be kicked out. We don't really take seriously our shadow side or fleshly side, and so it raises its ugly head to take control. It wants recognition, so we fight it. It fears it will be destroyed. That's why, many times, we can't do what we want. The solution is not to fight that side of ourselves, but see it as accepted, forgiven, part of ourselves. Given such treatment, the flesh can't take over.

The power of the Spirit gives wholeness and we become an integrated person. That's what Luther is talking about when he calls himself saint and sinner at the same time, living moment by moment in God's forgiveness. That's a different life style, and it's why Paul could say: "Thank God for our Lord Jesus Christ." You and I, too, can live in Christ's forgiveness as saint and sinner at the same time. The yoke of Christ is easy. His burden is light. The law can't condemn. Flesh and Spirit both are accepted and loved. We're free. At last made whole.

HERB SCHMIDT
University Religious Council
Santa Cruz, California

LIVING THE DOUBLE LIFE
Eighth Sunday after Pentecost
Romans 8:18-23

Life is very complicated and we are called to live in painful tension between love and hate, joy and sorrow, justice and injustice, good and evil, hope and meaninglessness, reconciliation and estrangement, life and death, the present and the future. Amid all of this, the believer in Christ is meant to live a double life. Our text today from the resplendent eighth chapter of Romans speaks to this.

When the Lutheran Church in America met in convention at Kansas City in 1966, it adopted a manifesto entitled "God's Call to the Church in Each Place." This double life was indicated in its opening statements—"This is God's world: the object of God's love, the arena of man's achievements, and the scene of man's struggles. This is God's time: exciting and full of hope, confusing and plagued with anxiety. The Church is

God's people: the new humanity in Christ, called into being, sustained and empowered by the Holy Spirit."

The Believer's Temporary Distress

As St. Paul writes to the Christians at Rome, he is painfully aware of the troubled state of the present world. He looks about him and sees the decay, the violence, the broken relationships of life. For a moment he sounds very pessimistic about a dying world. But then he remembers who he is and who God is. He looks down the road of life and writes, "I consider that the sufferings of this present time are not worth comparing with the glory that is to be revealed to us." Here Paul addresses himself to hope. He sees his struggles as being very temporary.

In Southern Germany, a short train ride from Munich, is a beautiful little city of Dachau with a population around 25,000. It is famous in World War II history because on the edge of the town was the huge Nazi concentration camp which housed some 206,000 political prisoners during the period of 1933-1945 in critically over-crowded conditions. A couple of years ago my wife and I took the train out of Munich and then a little bus out to this camp. The Americans insisted that this remain an infamous memorial of those dark days. Some of the barracks are still standing, the ovens are still there and now a large museum is there which shows horrible evidences of man's inhumanity to man. Barrack number 26 was for the clergy. It was a cold, windy, bitter day when we were there. We thought of the thousands who had suffered and died there and of believers who comforted each other with these words of our text: "I consider that the sufferings of this present time are not worth comparing with the glory that is to be revealed to us." Paul had something similar in mind when he wrote to the Corinthian believers: "We are afflicted in every way, but not crushed; perplexed, but not driven to despair; persecuted, but not forsaken; struck down, but not destroyed; always carrying in the body the death of Jesus, so that the life of Jesus may also be manifested in our bodies."

Paul paints a graphic picture here of the longing for a different new day—a being "set free from the bondage of decay." When the Hebrew people were enslaved and oppressed, they too dreamed their dreams of the new earth and that reconstructed world with their worship centered in Zion. Suffering comes to everyone. It often seems like it is so unevenly and unfairly distributed. It falls on the good and the bad—upon innocent children as well as upon guilty parents. The magnitude of human suffering which sits on the doorstep of the world community is impossible to imagine. The hungry people of Asia and Africa, the exploited and often voiceless farm worker in California, the thousands of refugees in camps throughout the world—all long to be set free. To live is to have a share in suffering. The Christian has a God who knows all about suffering. He suffered the suffering of rejection, the suffering of loneliness, the suffering that always accompanies evil, the suffering of goodness being trampled into the dust. He knows all about it. That is why he can so eagerly identify with our suffering. Here in our text we are reminded that the believers' suffering and distress in life is only temporary.

The Believer's Magnificent Future

Paul believes in the transitory nature of human suffering because he has an overview of life. There is more to our existence than the here and the now. God has a glorious plan for the future of all believers. God had the plan before the creation of the world. It was a difficult plan because it involved God's full identification with evil. A Holy God embraced evil so man could be set free. Paul had that overview of life when he wrote, "What no eye has seen, nor ear heard, nor the heart of man conceived, what God has prepared for those who love him."

Francis Bacon had on his bookplate an engraved picture. It was the picture of a small ship sailing out between the great Pillars of Hercules into an uncharted, unknown sea. Inscribed on the bow of the ship was its proud and defiant name: "More Beyond." That has always been the exhilarating truth of our Christian faith. We are creatures of time and eternity. This little world of time and space is a small fragment of something much larger than itself. There is more beyond. No wonder Jesus said, "Let not your hearts be troubled; believe in God, believe also in me. In my Father's house are many rooms; if it were not so, would I have told you that I go to prepare a place for you? And when I go and prepare a place for you, I will come again and will take you to myself, that where I am you may be also." What a fantastic promise! How wonderful to know that heaven is a vast empire where suffering and death cannot reach. We can leave behind our failures, our tears, our regrets.

Our text speaks of the Christian hope. This hope is a gift of God. It is a hope which reminds us that our suffering is temporary—that our destiny is a serial story. The real glory of it lies in the words "To Be Continued." Over and over again the New

Testament makes this crystal clear. Remember how our Lord said to Martha: "I am the resurrection and the life; he who believes in me, though he die, yet shall he live, and whoever lives and believes in me shall never die." The resurrection of Christ spells out hope for all believers. It says that nothing can finally stop God—not even crucifixion and death, for God is God. Because Christ arose from the tomb, we have a final and adequate answer. The tomb which could not hold the Lord of life cannot hold those who share in his eternal life. "May the God of hope fill you with all joy and peace in believing, so that by the power of the Holy Spirit you may abound in hope." Believers who have accepted God's acceptance have a magnificent future.

The Believer's Power in the Present

We live for the future but at the same time we are challenged to live in the present and to live meaningful and productive lives. We can't do this in our strength and intellect. There is power available to become what God would have us be. He wants to reveal himself to us in all of his fullness so we can respond to him with abundant living. This revelation comes in a very special way through the Scriptures.

A very popular writer today is Dr. Francis Schaeffer, who is the founder and director of L'Abri Christian Retreat Center in the Swiss Alps. Here countless students, professors, doctors, writers, pastors, scientists, musicians, and others came in search of the meaning of life. One book, among many which he has authored, is entitled "He Is There and He Is Not Silent." Isn't that a tremendous and beautiful title? Here he writes about the dilemma of man in trying to explain his existence. With evangelical confidence he points to the biblical revelation that God is there and he may be known and experienced by man. He is there and he is not silent. He desperately wants to communicate with us and tell us who he is and who we are and what he has done and will do for us. The crisis of our time is that so many are not aware that he is there and that he is not silent.

The first lesson today is from Isaiah 55. Beautifully it sets forth that he is there and he is not silent. Listen to it again. "For as the rain and the snow come down from heaven, and return not thither but water the earth, making it bring forth and sprout, giving seed to the sower and bread to the eater, so shall my word be that goes forth from my mouth; it shall not return to me empty, but it shall accomplish that which I purpose, and prosper in the thing for which I sent it." This is how God operates. His key desire is to accomplish his mission in our hearts. The Gospel for this day deals with the parable of the sower. Here, too, is pointed up God's key desire to have the seed fall on good soil so people will hear the word, understand the word and bear fruit in Christian living. As St. Paul writes to young Timothy, he emphasizes how the believer can receive power to live in the present—"All Scripture is inspired by God and is useful for teaching the faith and correcting error, for re-setting the direction of a man's life and training him in good living. The Scriptures are the comprehensive equipment of the man of God, and fit him fully for all branches of his work" (Phillips Translation).

The Order for Confirmation in the Lutheran Church is an impressive and usually a very emotional experience for the pastor as he lays hands on the head of the kneeling youth and says the following Prayer of Blessing: "The Father in Heaven, for Jesus' sake, renew and increase in thee the gift of the Holy Spirit, to thy strengthening in faith, to thy growth in grace, to thy patience in suffering, and to the blessed hope of everlasting life." Those few, tremendous words sum up the truth that there is power available for the believer as he makes his journey through life. The blessing is for the present and for the future—our double life.

It is not easy to be a human being because life gets very complicated and difficult at times. It is not easy to be a follower of Christ but over and over again in Scripture we are promised that there will be one alongside of us to empower us. This One is the gracious Holy Spirit, the Counselor. Romans 8 closes with this incredible promise: "In all these things we are more than conquerors through him who loved us. For I am sure that neither death, nor life, nor angels, nor principalities, nor things present, nor things to come, nor powers, nor height, nor depth, nor anything else in all creation, will be able to separate us from the love of God in Christ Jesus our Lord." St. Paul is very eloquent here and it almost seems like he can't find enough words to share his enthusiasm about God's great, loving concern for his people.

Paul was very much aware that he was a fellow struggler, a saved sinner, a sinner and a saint at the same time. But he was also aware that in Christ life was a throbbing expectation. Beyond the horizon of this life there would be a full realization of what adoption into the family of God really means. You and I are challenged to live this double life of the believer. Do we avail ourselves through Word and Sacrament of the power to face up to the situations encountered in life? Do we keep ourselves aware that there is a power of love and truth and right alive in the world and it works when we allow the Living Christ to dwell in our hearts and control our decisions? Do we claim that eternal hope anew each day—that hope which is totally dependent on what God is and does? Someday may we all step out into eternity with our hand in his.

PHILIP A. JORDAN
Trinity Lutheran Church
Fresno, California

GOD KNOWS YOU!
Ninth Sunday after Pentecost
Romans 8:26-27

St. Paul, in today's Epistle, has little comfort for the great majority of Christians, for most of the time Christians are not in need of special comfort. We go from day to day borne along by a gracious and providential God, with only minor ripples crossing our path of life. That's cause for thanksgiving to a heavenly Father who satisfies our daily needs "even without our prayer" as the Catechism puts it.

It's when the turbulence hits that questions arise as to the providence which seems suddenly to be lacking. Then the doubts assail us. Then all of that glib talk about a caring Father in heaven seems like just so many pious words and phrases concocted by unthinking people who have never been trapped in the vortex that draws them into the abyss.

What do you do when in the abyss? What strained words can be used to restore faith and hope? Where is the gracious God in those moments of despair? Why does he withdraw his face in just such a time as this when he ought to be nearest? Why is he at times so very distant, so deaf, so callous to our need?

Sighs Too Deep for Words

Today's word from St. Paul is for those who lament. In fact, as you may remember from last Sunday's Epistle, there was a lot of talk about "groaning":

"We know that the whole creation has been groaning in travail together until now; and not only in creation, but we ourselves, who have the first fruits of the Spirit, groan inwardly as we wait for adoption as sons, the redemption of our bodies."

A fallen world and a fallen race experience together that "bondage to decay" which is the awful consequence of man's rebellion against his maker. It is as though there is a great St. Andreas fault cutting through not only California, but around the girth of the whole globe—creaking, sighing, groaning in agony with the pain akin to childbirth.

And even we, who have the first fruits of the Spirit of God—who have already been assured that we are his children—we sometimes groan inwardly until what we hope for becomes real.

So where is God in all of this? Why must a sense of abandonment be added to our pain? Why in our greatest weakness and helplessness is the source of strength beyond our reach? Is God so weary of human woe that he hides his eyes from our plight?

It is for those who sigh inwardly that St. Paul has written these words, full of comfort and assurance. He wants us to know that even our groans are heard, for "the Spirit helps us in our weakness; for we do not know how to pray as we ought, but the Spirit himself intercedes for us with sighs too deep for words."

Three times in this context, St. Paul uses that word for groaning: the creation groans; we ourselves groan . . . and now, the Spirit of God himself intercedes for us with unutterable groanings. "And he who searches the hearts of men knows what is the mind of the Spirit, because the Spirit intercedes for the saints according to the will of God."

This is marvellous beyond our expectations. When the pressure is on, when our understanding becomes dulled through pain, when we wrestle with conflicting thoughts and do not know how to pray as we ought—then the Spirit himself intercedes for us. He fuses, as it were, our anxious sighs with his own and brings them before the Father for interpretation. "He who searches the hearts of men knows what is the mind of the Spirit."

God Knows You

So don't lose heart; *God does know you!* He has not forsaken you, or closed his eyes and ears to you. He is not unaware of your times of bodily and spiritual weakness. Only Christ experienced the ultimate agony of God-forsakenness; now those who live in him need never fear abandonment. Though crucified in weakness, he "lives by the power of God" (2 Cor. 13:4). And it is precisely at the moments of our greatest helplessness that we can discern the undergirding power of God. His fatherly care continues though we are unaware of his presence. Always in the midst of the storm he brings us this assurance: "My grace is sufficient for you, for my power is made perfect in weakness" (2 Cor. 12:9).

This brief passage in Paul, so rich in its assurance for the distressed, is akin to one in the Old Testament. In Psalm 139, the writer contemplates his relationship to God—or rather, God's knowledge of him:

"O Lord, thou hast searched me and known me! Thou knowest when I sit down and when I rise up; thou discernest my thoughts from afar. Thou searchest out my path and my lying down, and art acquainted with all my ways. Even before a word is on my tongue, lo, O Lord, thou knowest it altogether. Thou dost beset me behind and before, and layest thy hand upon me." Such knowledge is too wonderful for me; it is high, I cannot attain it."

Indeed it is! Here is the highest knowledge—something after which our soul yearns, and in which it finds rest even though it is incomprehensible. For to know—even in part—that God's concern is inextricably interwoven with our daily life—is to have knowledge that cannot be surpassed. To have all knowledge, but to be ignorant of that, is to grope in the darkness.

God Is Near

God is not a God afar off, but a God who is near. The Psalmist asks: "Whither shall I go from thy Spirit? Or whither shall I flee from they presence? If I ascend to heaven, thou art there! If I make my bed in Sheol, thou art there. If I take the wings of the morning and dwell in the uttermost parts of the sea, even there thy hand shall lead me, and thy right hand shall hold me." Just as little as we can escape from his presence, so little is God's presence removed from us. Did not Jesus assure us that "even the hairs of our head are all numbered"?

Yes! God does know you! He knows you in your greatest weakness—when you are at your wit's end, he does not forget you. He who has given you his Spirit sees and hears and searches your heart's groanings and shares your agonies.

Why should we think that anything can escape God's notice? Should not we live in the same awareness of God's nearness as the Psalmist did? For he affirms that God's knowledge of us encompasses the whole of our life from the moment of our origin, from the time when we began to be:

"For thou didst form my inward parts, thou didst knit me together in my mother's womb. I praise thee, for thou art fearful and wonderful. Wonderful are thy works! Thou knowest me right well; my frame was not hidden from thee, when I was being made in secret, intricately wrought in the depths of the earth. Thy eyes beheld my unformed substance; in thy book were written, every one of them, the days that were formed for me, when as yet there was none of them."

From embryo to clod of earth—through the whole span of life from beginning to end and into eternity—"thou knowest me right well."

Therefore, "how precious to me are thy thoughts, O God! How vast is the sum of them! If I could count them, they are more than sand. When I awake, I am still with thee" (Psa. 139:17-18).

There is no fleeing from the Spirit, nor any flight of the Spirit from us. For he himself intercedes for us with sighs too deep for words.

Do not ask how this is possible. Do not inquire into the processes and the means whereby God's knowledge of us is so complete and perfect. Think only of the truth that he who has guarded and kept you since your secret beginnings, guards and keeps you even now. Be mindful only that even as your words make their way from your mind to your tongue, your thoughts are already known to him. And that even when words fail—when there has been enough of talking, and time only for groaning and sighing—even then, God's Spirit, in touch always with your spirit, interprets to the gracious One the desires and needs of your heart.

Is it presumption to say that? Is it saying too much about God whose concerns for an entire universe would seem to exclude such personal concern? Sure, he moves the countless swirling galaxies; he guides a million Milky Ways; he knows the location and purpose of every mysterious "black hole" in space.

But he demonstrates his concern for us by sending us his own Son, that we might know he is a God for us and not against us, nor indifferent to our needs.

He does know you as fully as he knows me. Together we can pray:

>Lord, as a pilgrim on earth I roam,
>By foes surrounded, far from my home;
>Whate'er betide me,
>Walk thou beside me,
>Shepherd divine!
>
>Thou art my refuge; grant me, I pray,
>Strength for each burden, light on my way,

Balm in my sorrow,
Grace for tomorrow,
Saviour divine!
Wilhelmi Malmivaara

OSCAR SOMMERFELD
Director of Communication—ELCC
Saskatoon, Saskatchewan

IN SPITE OF EVERYTHING
Tenth Sunday after Pentecost
Romans 8:28-30

Not Everything Works for Good

Everything works for good? Everything? That's hard to believe. Everything includes earthquakes, heart attacks, human failure, ruined lives, and death. Those things work for good? That sounds like there is in every cloud a silver lining. That reminds us of the pious statement that suffering builds character. I do not accept that as axiomatic, because clouds sometimes rain down nothing but destruction, and suffering has broken as many people as it has built up (if suffering itself is able to do anything one way or another). The premise that some good must come out of every evil, it seems to me, is untenable.

It has long been considered a Christian principle or philosophy that there is a beautiful, beneficial side to everything, including the most heinous crime or the most devastating disaster. And so, we have been imprinted with messages about an ideal world that transcends the one we know and see and feel everyday. I perceive that as a way of affirming good in the face of evil. It really seems more like a way of denying evil, and it also raises questions about the reality of what we might call the good. Are we not dealing with illusions rather than truth?

Each of us choose what is good for himself or herself, knowing that there is suffering and sorrow all around. The values to which we are exposed every day, especially through the media, suggest that avoiding pain and having pleasure is the greatest good in life. The message is "live it up," as though there were no evil, no suffering, no ugliness. I wonder how we can come to any positive affirmation of life, if we cannot take evil seriously. If avoiding and denying becomes a way of life, how can we live at all? If we are not with everything, with the whole of it, we are not with any of it in any real sense. If the good we embrace only gets us around the evil rather than through it, we are not where Christ took on everything, who found good not in some place above suffering but in God whose love was present in the midst of pain. He knew the purpose of God, because he lived in the real world and knew that the Father loved it. Jesus did not show us a better world; rather he revealed the goodness of God which is enough for living in this world in spite of everything.

That is disturbing to us, not only because of the secular values that infiltrate, but also because some forms of Christian piety—all of it suggesting that good comes if we look on the brighter side of things. All my life I have heard Christians stating that God has some blessing in store for us, even though we may not see it, whenever some evil befalls us. I have known many people who inhibit grieving, repressing guilt, and deny reality, because they believed that Christians should not cry, lament evil, or, even get angry when tragedy occurs. How often I have heard well-meaning Christians attempting to comfort a troubled soul by asserting that some good will come from all that is now being suffered. Cheer up! It can't be all bad! Really?

There Is Evil That Kills

The context of Paul's words says otherwise. The law of sin and death which dogs us all is not a good. Accusation and oppression are evils. Setting the mind on the flesh is not a good. Worship of self and of things—of anyone and anything above God—is an evil that destroys the spirit. Because of it we kill and are killed. A creation subjected to futility, subject to bondage and decay, is not a picture of something good. It means that the old order—this world, this life which we know and sometimes consider the greatest good of all—indeed it might be the only "good" some people know—is doomed. And I don't read Paul affirming any intrinsic good in tribulation, distress, persecution, famine, nakedness, peril, sword, or death. In fact, what we call good, like life, angels powers, height or depth, can be a potential threat to the Christian. By them some people have separated themselves from the love of God. No good will come from that. Not even God is glorified in that. That is the ultimate evil.

Finding some good in evil is difficult enough. To affirm that it comes to those who love God is almost too much to believe. That's like saying that those who really love God will find the good in no matter what happens. I don't know how it is in your life, but I don't confess week after week that I can't find the good in all the things that happen around me or to me. I confess that I don't love God as I ought. Maybe that's why I don't find the beautiful life in my everyday life of struggle, conflict, and pain—I don't love God. Maybe if I loved God more, I would see good everywhere. Is that what's wrong with me? If that is so, then I work the good, because I love God. And that is an even greater illusion, not just that I imagine I can find the good in everything, but also that I can make it—if only I can love God enough. That, too, is not good. It remains an illusion of the evil one.

God Is Able to Work Good Nevertheless

Paul's reference to "those who love God" is probably another way of referring to those who are Christians, those who believe in God's love. What could be more difficult than that, than to believe in God's love in spite of everything? What greater good could there be than that there is no evil—nothing at all anywhere, anytime, any place—that can cancel out the love that God has for us. No matter what happens to any of us, whether we call it good or bad, God is working his good purposes nevertheless.

That's what Paul is affirming in this chapter, that God's love stands in spite of everything, that he has taken the initiative to choose us and call us to himself, as he did with Abraham and Amos and Jeremiah, and Paul himself. Even though evil has invaded God's good creation, even though we pass our days under the law of sin and death, even though evil surrounds us, the grace of God is not nullified. The image of his Son prevails, the one Paul calls "the first-born among many brethren." The power of sin and evil, writes the apostle, was condemned to death and died in the humanity of Jesus Christ, who was made in the likeness of sinful flesh. That is where and how God met the evil that threatens our existence everyday. And precisely when it appeared that evil had won the day, that the death of Jesus marked the triumph of the evil one, God raised his Son to life, to be the first specimen of his new creation, to show that he is God, good and gracious, whose loving purposes for his people cannot be wiped out. In spite of everything his good lives, his will is done. Because of Jesus Christ we are forgiven, we are destined to share in the resurrection. All things, even all evil, are subject to that good.

There is a persistence in God to bestow on us the good that has been in his heart from eternity. Paul nails that down with the words "foreknew," "predestined," "conformed," "called," "justified," and "glorified." Nothing could stop God from loving and saving us. For that reason he gave his Son as the sign and seal of what he wills for us in spite of everything. In Ephesians 1:3-10 Paul cites the same premise and promise. We hear the same good news in today's gospel lesson, where our Lord himself describes the relentless love of God, a searching grace, like a merchant selling everything to obtain a pearl of great value, like a fisherman gathering in a great catch. There is no doubt that God will have his way for us in spite of everything.

He Loves Us in Spite of Everything

There is not good in everything that happens. There is much evil that we touch, that we do, that must die if we are to live. The good that we believe in is not an illusion about something good that survives when the evil has passed. The good we share is not some pious maneuver, to find a world that doesn't exist at the expense of denying a reality that needs to be faced. We believe the good news that God loves us in spite of everything. And anyone who believes in that love believes in God because of his love that cannot be killed—and therefore we believe in him, if we know him at all—in spite of everything.

"In everything God works for good." That means we can really live, that we can embrace the whole of life, enduring even the pain of accusation, loss, and judgment, since God's love stands and the work of Christ avails. We can dare to hope, to love, to do good, because nothing can defeat God or us. We have the courage to accept birth, to be vulnerable, and to die, because we are already being conformed to the image of Jesus Christ. Since there is no doubt about God's will being good and gracious for us, we have the knowledge and certainty that in and through all of the twisted, tangled skein of life God is bringing us along to enjoy with him forever what he has always planned—his love —in spite of everything!

RONALD C. STARENKO
Church of the Savior
Paramus, New Jersey

GOD IS FOR US

Eleventh Sunday after Pentecost
Romans 8:35-39

Some of Paul's most solid Christian writing is packed into the first twelve chapters of his letter to the church at Rome. For some, his eighth chapter is the high-water mark in his ministry of Christian writing. The whole of that chapter is a joyous celebration. It is a hymn of praise composed by a man who, imprisoned by his human nature and beaten to his knees by an improper use of the law, had been liberated by Jesus Christ. We, too, understand his experience: certainly not with his intellectual and emotional intensity, but we do understand it substantively. Like Paul, we too have agonized over the good that we wanted to do but left undone, and the evil that we pledged ourselves we would not do yet somehow did, and looking desperately for a way out, were set free by Jesus Christ.

Some Contemporary Responses to Paul's Victory Song

One does not treat massive personal liberation lightly. Paul goes all out in testifying to, marvelling at, being grateful for the love of Christ that did for him what neither he nor others could do. Surprised by joy, he is ecstatic about God's love, yet rational, too. Nonetheless, his superlative adjectives may turn some of us off. In this age of empty rhetoric when a heavyweight boxer is "the greatest," a breakfast cereal, "dynamic," and the King Kong movie, "fabulous," Paul's rhetoric is suspect to some.

Listen again to parts of Paul's eighth chapter. "The sufferings of this present time are not worth comparing with the glory that is to be revealed to us." He could not prove that sweeping claim. It is a declaration of faith and an expression of hope. In our own day, many people who suffer from cancer know days on endless days when they feel that the sufferings of this present time are larger than any "weight" of glory that awaits them beyond the grave. Again, Paul keeps insisting that God is at work in all things with those who love him. Gerdler the Jew, Von Stauffenberg the Catholic, and Bonhoeffer the Lutheran clergyman—key figures in the plot to assassinate Adolf Hitler in July, 1944—must have thought, however briefly, after that abortive attempt, that not only was God not at work but that God had turned his back on decency in Germany. Candidly, I had days like that in the spring and summer of 1968 after the assassinations of Martin Luther King and Robert Kennedy. Having had my share of hardship in the civil rights movement since 1961, and from protesting the war in Vietnam since late 1964, an awful lot of meaninglessness would engulf me on occasion.

But here in today's Epistle, the closing verses in Romans 8, Paul is still at it, piling those superlatives one on the other. "What," he asks in his own new hour of continuing hardship (arrested and headed for Rome), "can separate us from the love of Christ?" Then he answers with one claim after another, each of which seems too sweeping to hard-pressed Christians in our era. Nonetheless, Paul insists forcefully—giving no quarter, allowing no room for debate—that nothing can separate us from the love of Christ: not affliction nor hardship nor persecution nor hunger nor nakedness nor threat of violent death.

That simply does not square with reality is our complaint in this age of deep alienation from God, and from one another. Affliction and hardship stripped away the faith of many people as they died week after week in Nazi concentration camps in the late thirties and early forties. And today in the ghettos of America — and in other nations — affliction and hardship strip away the last smidgin of faith of millions of hard-pressed people. And persecution? Certainly the majority of preachers and lay leaders in our Protestant churches go all out for cheap grace, cut "the whole counsel of God" in half by avoiding God's demands. They accommodate the Word of God to contemporary culture, trimming it to fit institutional and professional survival. One small threat from well-heeled church members to cut their giving unless the pulpit steered clear of civil rights and the War in Vietnam in the sixties was enough to send most modern "prophets" back to Tekoa. And the people I know intimately—hundreds of clergy among them—give in before persecution begins, turn their backs on God's demands at the first intimation of personal criticism. Permissive with themselves, avoiding self-discipline, they are permissive with others, careless with God's truth and man's truth as well. In this era most church people turn tail and run at the first threat to their security and to the institutional well-being of their churches. The first wave of criticism does most of us in. Few get in deep enough to be persecuted.

What about hunger and nakedness and peril? In our overpopulated, under-fed, world—a world divided socially an economically into what we call "four worlds"—the people of the third and fourth worlds, literally starving and naked and in peril, are so frustrated and angry and weak and disheartened they scarcely think of God at all. And God's people scarcely think of them either, which is part of their plight—and ours.

And when it comes to threat by sword, it is difficult to find Christians who stand firm. For every Bonhoeffer who risked his life in Nazi Germany, a half million Germans went along with Hitler to get along. For every Berrigan speaking for truth in America in the 1960s, two million Americans swallowed their moral indignation and made no protest against the war in Vietnam, and for every Martin Luther King millions swallowed anger and humiliation to stifle protests against the emotional genocide committed against Blacks in our society. The church in America has millions of card-carrying members; it has precious few cross-bearing Christians.

So here in this text from Romans—at least at a hurried first reading—it appears that Paul overstated the claims of the Christian life. At a deeper level, that is how one might feel—and on occasion does indeed feel—when he himself is in the valley of the shadow or overwhelmed by the evils of our depersonalized society.

The Reason for Paul's Victory Song

But to read the passage in a casual way is to miss altogether what Paul was getting at. He is not suggesting that affliction and hardship and hunger and nakedness and peril and the threat of death cannot cause a Judas to betray, prod a Peter to defect, or lead him, Paul, for that matter, into sessions of deep depression. His eye is not on *our* faith or on *our* hope. Not one whit. His eye is fixed unswervingly on Jesus Christ. He is urging us to look objectively at reality. He is testifying to what God has done for you and me and all people. Paul is not saying that *we* are able to love him with a love that will not let him go. He is declaring that God in Christ loves *us* with a love that will not let *us* go. So, we sing: "There's a wideness in God's mercy like the wideness of the sea," and we must come back to this again and again.

Paul is saying essentially in the first twelve chapters of Romans—and especially in the eighth chapter—that the only reason we can have faith and entertain hope as Christians and the only reason that we can love God is because he first loved us, and because his love never runs out, is never selective, never petulant, never arbitrary, never powerless. Here is a clean statement of Paul's Christology; and the heart of it is that the Father of Jesus Christ *is God for us,* and that when God is for us, nothing —including our own flawed selves—can finally put us down. In Christ, we can claim his victory over sin, death, and the demons.

C. K. Barrett goes to the heart of God's self-revelation in Jesus Christ: "Love is . . . the essential activity of God himself, and when men love their fellowmen they are doing (however imperfectly) what God does." That is the Bible's central message: God is love. One of the winsome traditions from the first century Christian community attaches itself to the aged Apostle John who, feeble, unable any longer to fashion a structured discourse, kept saying over and over to his congregation, "Love one another." A rock tune in the sixties was titled, "Love Is a Verb." God's love, cognitive as well as emotional, is indeed his activity. He is seeker, finder, savior because he is always the indefatigable Lover. W. E. Woodyard nails it down: "Love is an event God initiates and in which man participates." Precisely! We are forever getting the cart before the horse, trying to love on our own. We fail at it as long as we are too proud to acknowledge that we are first loved by Another, the holy God, and accept his authority in our life and over all life. It is because God loves us that we can, with critical judgment, put our faith in him. It is because God loves us that we can have confidence in ourselves and in other selves to build the good society for the sake of the kingdom of God. God's active love is the ground of our faith, the sure reason for our hope.

Listen again to Paul on God's central activity: "I am certain that nothing can separate us from his love: neither death nor life, neither angels nor other heavenly rulers or powers, neither the present nor the future, neither the world above nor the world below." Nothing, literally nothing, in all creation can keep God from loving us. That's the heart of Paul's Christology. And he's exuberant about what that love can do: liberate mortals in bondage to their perverted nature, fashion a new community of the committed, turn the world right-side-up. So, for our day, Paul claims that even though we travel to the planets in outer space we cannot outrun the reach of God's love, and that the demonic forces in our institutionalized lives cannot overwhelm the power of God's love. He is saying that no matter how many things we achieve or earn or receive in this life, no matter how affluent we become or how hard our dying may be, God does not give up on us.

God's Love—The Greatest Power in the World

When Paul writes (1 Cor. 13) that love is the greatest thing in the world he is not going sentimental on us. He is remembering the central activity of God in Jesus Christ: his love that accepts us as we are, his blood that cleanses us, his power that enables us to rise and start again, his determination to finish on the other side of heaven's line all that he began in us here and now. Paul is also remembering from experience that love works in and through us; that it is, like truth, a constructive, recreative force. We also know from experience that when all else fails—persuasion, manipulation, threats, fears, coercion, force—love alone succeeds. It is the greatest constructive power in history and human experience. When the prodigal son came to his senses

—that is, when he remembered that his father still loved him in spite of, indeed because of his degradation—he saw clearly that he did not have to live with the pigs, that he could go home —and he did! So with you and me. We are not destined to be degraded by self and society; we can go home to the Father any moment we choose. We can love God because he first loved us. We can serve God because he first served us. We can live in his presence because he is always with us in the world.

If only talented Freddie Prinze had known, remembered, and claimed God's love, his troubles would not have overwhelmed him. If only Hitler had known, remembered, and claimed God's love in the early 1920s, his frustration, bitterness, and racial prejudice would not have compelled him to mislead a nation. If only Johnson and Nixon had known, remembered, and claimed God's love, their ego-driven needs for power would not have compelled them to lie to, manipulate, and mislead the American people.

So, Christians—whether fulfilled or frustrated, following or faltering, and in spite of all the ambiguities of life and history—make claims for Christ as sweeping as Paul's! Because God was in Christ reconciling the world to himself, we, like Paul, dare, delight, and are constrained to declare to the world that it can be reconciled to God. And those who choose in their freedom to be reconciled—to love him who first loved them, to do his commandments, to take up their cross daily and follow him—experience new life as persons and take their places in the new community of persons serving him who first served them. It is the only way to *live*.

WALLACE E. FISHER
Trinity Lutheran Church
Lancaster, Pennsylvania

THE STRUGGLES IN CHRISTIAN WITNESSING
Twelfth Sunday after Pentecost
Romans 9:1-5

Prayer: Lord, we thank you for the wonderful Grace you have given to us. It fills us with pain to know there are others who appear not to have come to full realization of the Gospel and all the joy and peace you want to give. Help us each in our witnessing that it may be the best witness of you possible. In Jesus' Name. Amen.

There was a man, very well to do, born to an influential family, educated in Jerusalem. He had wealth, prestige and power. One of his teachers was the famous Gamaliel. He was filled with zeal for his tradition. If he had lived in America we could have called him an "All American Boy, patriotic to the enth degree." With his education, family background and experience he was possibly in line to take a high position among his countrymen. As a young man he was an active participant in the persecution of Christians. He was a man of strong feelings and strong actions! He had so successfully completed one mission in Jerusalem that he was given permission to go to Damascus, to continue that mission. His devotion was so intense to his religion and to the religious authorities that he felt he was rendering the highest service to God.

This same man, after his conversion experience on the road to Damascus became one of the greatest of the Christian missionaries. I don't believe his character, personality, or whatever you want to call it, had changed that much. But the direction of his devotion to witnessing and sharing, preaching and teaching the Gospel of Jesus Christ did change. The dedication and devotion which had been part of his personality were still part of that same personality, but now from a Christian perspective. He had strong feelings of concern for those with whom he had first been a part. That man is the man Paul, who in our text speaks about the intensity of his feelings for his former colleagues, friends, countrymen; the same men with whom he had studied, worked, been involved in carrying out what he felt was the Lord's will. They are God's Chosen People, former friends, who were now his enemies.

Some of us have probably felt this same kind of love, concern, even pain over some member or members of our family, maybe not specifically over a "religious problem" but over a person and his problems, his relationship with himself, with someone else, or with God. And how we have wished in some way that we could get through to them. That in some way they could come to realize the truth, Christian truths of the Gospel, the Christian life style and wishing that there were something that we could do to help them realize the ultimate truth, even to the point of suffering in their place. I know as a pastoral counselor I have felt that way and really wished I could trade places with some of them out of deep sincere love and concern. That is how strongly Paul appears to be feeling, the depth, the intensity. He expressed how strong his love was for the Jews that he would have been willing to be eternally damned in their place! Not often, but maybe once or twice this kind of depth of feeling has been present in me, but Paul wrote it down—how strongly he felt.

So here, right after this strong victorious Chapter 8 in Romans, I hear Paul struggling with his love and concern for Israel, his people both by nationality and heritage, and how painful he feels for them. J. T. Forestell in *Proclamation* is correct when he writes that "Paul is not dealing with the eternal destiny of individuals, Jews, or Gentiles, but with the role of individuals and collectivities in history in God's plan of universal salvation." To me he's talking about the witnessing and the struggle going on in Paul.

God's word in the Old Testament speaks about Elijah's struggle too in witnessing. The struggle of the disciples with their fear in the Gospel account may also reflect a similar struggle, their lack of faith and courage. We may identify with the concern, fear, struggle, lack of faith and trust in the power of God which we individually may have in our love and witness as Christians. Paul deals with the struggle which he had; in witnessing to his own people. Let us look at Paul's struggle and at our struggle and learn from God's Word how to take courage with faith, to love and struggle and witness in sharing God's love.

The Depth of the Struggle

Paul appears to have been an emotional man. He had strong feelings and he was willing to express the depth of those feelings which he had for his own people, the Jews, who refused to accept Jesus Christ as the Messiah. He felt this way, I believe, because he recognized the freedom of saying "No" which every individual or group has. He had said "No" and he had witnessed the stoning of Stephen. He had heard the prayer, "Lord! Do not remember this sin against them." I believe he had heard Gamaliel saying in the Council, "Leave them alone, for if this plan of theirs is a man-made thing, it will disappear; but if it comes from God you cannot possibly defeat them." He knew the struggle that he had gone through . . . the Damascus road experience. . . . He knew how hard it might be for them, but his love was so great.

It is like Jesus, who wept over Jerusalem during that final week, whose tears were not the product of the moment but of a constant grief. Paul is conveying how strongly he felt. It is good to express our own feelings. I don't know whether there was anger on the part of Paul to the Jews or not, but there was pain and sorrow over them. This was the depth of his struggle, his pain, his love for them.

How strong have your feelings been to a person or group? Are you first willing to recognize how much you do care for them, how important they are to you? Are you willing to take the risk, as was Paul, to share those feelings? He was willing to take the risk! Are we? Are we willing even to make ourselves vulnerable? Moishe Rosen, Director for Jews for Jesus, in his booklet, *"How to Witness Simply and Effectively to the Jews"* writes, "Make a policy that limits your witness to only those Jewish people with whom you have a friendship." This truth of sharing applies generally in most of our witnessing. In the Word of God Community in Ann Arbor, the emphasis in witness is especially on loving, and how carefully it should be done. So in witnessing, we need to recognize in ourselves just how strongly we feel about the person, or the group and express it as did Paul—but it is not easy, it's a real struggle.

The hymn of the day is "Fight the Good Fight"; I used to see the struggle as being on the outside with the enemy there. But a new kind of significance comes when I realize, more and more, that the fight, the struggle is within me. Here, is where I can and must first deal with it. That fight, that struggle is very great. It was great for Elijah, for Paul, for the disciples in the boat, and Peter in the water as he was sinking.

Understand the Person

If the focus in Christian witnessing is on the person and on the Gospel, then we won't need to be so worried about ourselves and what we are doing or not doing, because the priority and sensitivity would be on the other person.

To me, listening is one of the first, and most important aspects of witnessing. To hear, to learn, to determine where the person is with his problems and concerns is an important beginning. Look at Jesus' ministry and witness to the Samaritan woman at the well, or to people that he healed. He asked questions. He was sensitive to the people, not just because of his divinity, but his humanity and the importance and value of that person. So we must listen.

As Rosen indicates "Probably the best way to engage a person's mind with yours is to ask a sympathetic question and to be genuinely interested in their answer." Focus on the person. Try to understand the person or the group.

There was a man in the first parish which I served that, in my own mind, I put on a 10 year plan. I thought it would take 10 years for him to become a church member. I couldn't understand why he had such a strong resistance to Holy Communion. Then I learned from his childhood and his religious impressions how kneeling had to do with the old sawdust trail revival meetings. He didn't want anything to do with what he remembered. I had to understand that background and feeling before any real sharing could be accomplished. Truly we must know and understand the person both good and bad, successes and failures, hurts and concerns. The Old Testament phrase of "a word fitly spoken" to me refers to "knowing and understanding" where the person is. Then we can see and recognize that which is so meaningful to the person and how God's Good News can speak to that need.

Share Your Faith

Paul wrote it down in his witness. Jesus spoke it according to the need of the people. Not all, but some heard and understood. Paul himself, though he'd been saying "no" over and over again, was open at the time to the conversion experience. He could have said "no," but he did not. That, I believe, was all part of what the Holy Spirit had been working. Different people who have experienced a rebirth have told me that it had started long before the specific experience. Our personal witness, which we share, may not immediately precede the full awareness. It may be much later. But the Word must be spoken in love. And if we are sensitive and share with that person then this is all that God asks, and we need to trust his power to work through his Holy Spirit, through his Word. I need to be ready to give account of what it means to me, not to all, but to me! The Scriptures and the encouragement to the Scriptures is one of many steps. We are not called to convert, only to witness, hard as it may be. The Spirit will lead us if we are open.

And then we, like Elijah, like Peter sinking in the sea, like Paul, can continue to trust in him. And his answer—"My grace is sufficient," "My power is made strong in weakness"—will give us the strength we need. Witness and trust in God's great power and might to work! Pray for the willingness of many to hear and respond.

PAUL F. REYELTS
St. Peter's Lutheran Church
St. Clair, Michigan

MISERERE
Thirteenth Sunday after Pentecost
Romans 11:13-15, 29-32

Mercy is a rarely heard cry these days. More often we hear cries for justice, demands for equality, or calls for vindication. Even Gary Mark Gilmore, awaiting his execution for murder in Utah, isn't pleading for mercy in an attempt to escape the firing squad; and the opponents of capital punishment argue simply that death is not the answer to curing crime, even for a convicted killer.

But mercy was a well-known cry in antiquity. Much of the world of that day hung on the sleeves of mercy. The masses of the people were desperately dependent on the mercy of the few. That was a harsh, cruel world—the world of the prophets and patriarchs and apostles—and human lives were often worth far less than the whims and whimsies of the ruling class. Slaves and captives, those trophies of military conquests; the crippled and handicapped, whose hopes for cure or assistance were usually shattered; or those few pathetic elderly who survived the typical early-death of those days . . . All of them knew the tender thread by which they existed from day to day, and much of that was at the mercy of those on top.

So, when the Scriptures use the concept mercy to describe God —our merciful Father in heaven, and to describe the plight and plea of humanity—"Lord, have mercy upon us," they do so in a world which understood much better than we what mercy was all about.

Yet while mercy was well known among the ancients, it was nevertheless a rare treat. The sheer dimensions of need, the masses crying for mercy, tended to whittle down concerns and callous the ears of the privileged. It was, I suspect, as frustrating then as now to determine how to alleviate the tremendous amount of suffering and human need. Today we who care are often also overwhelmed by the needs of others around the world, so much so that we tend not to act at all.

This morning we want to listen to Paul's lesson regarding mercy, to appreciate again God's mercy toward us and his mercy in a merciless society and world. We want to understand it in terms of our *plight,* our *pleas,* and God's *promises* of mercy.

Our Plight

God's mercy toward us is necessary because of the plight of us all. That is, whether we want to acknowledge it or not, we are in difficulty when it comes to our spiritual health as well as our need for daily bread. We may have adequate resources to live on and enjoy even some of the luxuries of life, but not only are we dependent upon God for daily bread, we are absolutely dependent on help from outside when it comes to our relationship with him.

The natural human tendency is to pride ourselves in being better than others; less in need of God's help and deliverance and mercy because we are more conscientious, more moral, more generous, more thankful than others. We don't have to look very far to find satisfaction in being a cut above a lot of other people! That spells p-r-i-d-e, that basic sin which severs human relationships and gets between God and us.

That was one of Israel's basic problems. The people of God began to think that they had such an inside track with him that they, the creatures, could dominate the Creator. Carefully crafted religious routines began to displace simple faith and loving service. Even in the church of that day a caste system developed and the ordinary people were at the mercy of the system.

Sadly, that describes much of the history of the Christian church as well. God's people have continually had to wrestle with attempts, individual and corporate, to take center-stage away from God. Paul, with a sweeping stroke of his pen, puts to route such religious pride when he writes in this same letter to the Romans, "For all have sinned and come short of the glory of God." The *plight* is common to everybody, no matter how saintly or prestigious a person is or thinks he is: "*all* have sinned and come short ..."

Only when that condition of need is grasped and understood is a person in a position to appreciate and, by faith, to appropriate mercy. Mercy is useless if it is unneeded; it lies dormant and ineffective where it is neither wanted nor treasured. Paul points out that Jewish pride and Gentile pride are really no different, both suffer the same consequences! Isaiah, centuries earlier, had written of those who prided themselves in their religious performances, "We have all become like one who is unclean, and all our righteous deeds are like a polluted garment" (Isa. 64:6).

Our Pleas

While the common plight of all is affirmed by Paul, and the judgment—"The wages of sin is death"—leveled, the need for mercy must be satisfied. It is one thing to know that you have a disease, it is another thing to seek help and to accept the cure when it is offered.

God's people, sensing their need, have echoed throughout history the Psalmist's plea, "Lord, have mercy upon me, according to thy loving kindness" (Psa. 51:1). Mercy, not justice, is the answer to our plight. Too many of us are like the lady who, when she got the proofs back from the portrait photographer, marched to his studio and stormed, "Mister, these pictures don't do me justice." To which the photographer quietly replied, "Lady, you don't need justice, what you need is mercy!"

We can be grateful that God did not deal with us directly in justice. His love intervened and Jesus Christ became the object of the Father's justice. The absolutely fair and impartial judgment of God upon our sin would be more than we could possibly bear. Sin's wages would consign us to everlasting death. But Jesus Christ, the sinless Son of God, willingly became the target of divine judgment. He took upon himself the searing wrath of God against sin and evil, and he himself bore our sins in his body on the tree, that we might die to sin and live to righteousness" (1 Peter 2:24).

Our plight generates our pleas for mercy. In the liturgy this morning we sang, "Lord, have mercy upon us. Christ, have mercy upon us. Lord, have mercy upon us." That ancient hymn, the *Kyrie Eleison,* erupted from people in need as a king or patron passed by. It was both a plaintive cry for mercy as well as a strong affirmation that, if anyone would dispense mercy, it was the individual to whom they directed their pleas. It was also a plea raised by ten lepers "who stood at a distance and lifted up their voices and said, 'Jesus, master, have mercy on us.'" (Luke 17:13). And in today's Gospel, the Canaanite woman, reduced to despair over her daughter's illness, cried, "Have mercy on me, O Lord, Son of David . . ." *Miserere mihi,* in one form or another, has been chanted and cried by the people of God throughout history.

God's Promises

The common plight and pleas of God's people are met with promises of never-failing mercy. The "God who consigned all men to disobedience" is the God who has done so "that he may have mercy upon all." Recognizing the inability of people to meet the standards of divine law, God in love and mercy provided a way for their salvation.

Old Zechariah, father of John the Baptist, saw and sang of God's promises coming to fruition, "Blessed by the Lord God of Israel, for he has visited and redeemed his people . . . to perform the *mercy* promised to our fathers . . ." (Luke 1:72). Mary, the girl of tender youth who was informed by the angel that she would be the mother of the Christ, replied, "And his mercy is on those who fear him, from generation to generation" (Luke 1:50). Paul, who had come out of a system of legalism as a Pharisee, appreciated what mercy meant and wrote to the Ephesians, "But God, who is rich in *mercy,* out of the great love with which he loved us, even when we were dead through our trespasses, made us alive together with Christ (by grace you have been saved)" (Eph. 2:4). And Peter, the shamed denier who knew the need for mercy, wrote "Blessed be the God and Father of our Lord Jesus Christ! By his great *mercy* we have been born anew to a living hope through the resurrection of Jesus Christ from the dead" (1 Peter 1:3).

The promises of God are that his gifts and his call are irrevocable. We can depend on his mercy to undergird us in our need, to strengthen us in our calling and commitment. Centuries ago the Psalmist knew the comfort and assurance of God's never-failing mercy, when he sang, "Surely goodness and mercy shall follow me all the days of my life, and I will dwell in the house of the Lord forever." So we raise our voices in supplication and in confidence that mercy is ours, through Christ our Lord. *Miserere mihi;* Lord, have mercy!

DALE D. HANSEN
St. Luke's Lutheran Church
New York, New York

HE PUTS US IN OUR PLACE

Fourteenth Sunday after Pentecost

Romans 11:33-36

This sermon is the result of a dialog process between the pastor and six members of the congregation. During the Epiphany season of 1976 the pastor invited the following people to join in a weekly discussion group: a freshman coed, a mother of three elementary school children, a middle-aged widow, a young male engineer, an architect who is the father of four college-age young people, and a professor of public health who is the father of four college-age young people, and a professor of public health who is the father of two elementary school children. Each week they discussed together the lessons for the following Sunday. During the discussion the pastor took notes. From the discussion he prepared the sermon. The committee members attended the worship service and received a copy of the manuscript. The following Monday they met again and gave their reactions to the sermon before they began their discussion of the lessons for the next Sunday.

This group of lay people was gathered together again to repeat the process for this sermon on the Epistle for the Fourteenth Sunday after Pentecost. This sermon is the result of their dialog, discussion and reaction to the preached sermon. The sermon was revised following the discussion of their reactions.

"O the depths of the riches and wisdom and knowledge of God! Who can explain his decisions? Who can understand his ways? Yet all things were created by him, and all things exist through him and for him. To God be the glory forever! Amen" (TEV).

The face of the young father radiated with joy as he talked of the fantastic event he had experienced. "Pastor, I have believed in God. I knew he existed. I knew he had created this world. Yet in many ways he was so abstract for me. Now he is so real, so personal. Being there in the delivery room, seeing what was happening, being a part of what was happening helps me know, even forces me to know, that there is a God. When my daughter was born, I was there. They gave her to me to hold right away. As I looked down and saw that squealing, wiggling little girl, I was overcome with the magnificence of the creative power of God. It was like the first day of creation all over again. I guess in a way for her it was the first day of creation. Really, only God could do something like this. During the first weeks of my wife's pregnancy, she was so sick. I thought, 'God, how could you do this to her?' Then in the labor room, I saw how much she was suffering. Yet as the Bible says, when the baby was born, all the pain was pushed out of our minds as we looked at our daughter. I had a part in that. God let my wife and me be partners with him in creation. I don't really know why he has done this. I don't understand why he devised this intricate process of creation of new life or why there is pain and then joy. But he does it. I know he does it. I believe in him. I thank him and I praise him."

A mother described how she had felt while watching her first child leave for kindergarten all by himself. The first few days of school, she had walked with him. She was worried about the two busy streets he had to cross. Yet she knew that soon he would have to go by himself. That day as she looked out the window, she thought, "God, why can't he stay a little boy? Why can't I keep him home with me and protect him from the danger that is outside: not just the speeding cars, but the unkind people too? Why does he have to grow up and face the problems which exist in this difficult sin-filled world?" The woman related that her feelings changed, though. She said, "Pastor, I remembered something you said once about God's letting us be free people. You said that God in his love lets us make mistakes and get into trouble. He lets us go against him and sin. If God didn't, then we would not be free. We would be like puppets. God would not be loving us if he did not let us make our own choices, even whether or not we want to love him. I had never understood that concept. However, that day as I sat and watched my first child walk alone down that sidewalk and turn and wave to me, it became a little clearer. I wish God had made life easier for us. Yet maybe his wisdom is beyond ours, at least beyond mine. I know I have to let my son grow up and be free. I guess God has to let us be free. I see a little more now that he really knows what he is doing with us."

The face of the man was worn and downcast. You could see the load was so heavy for him. His wife would never walk on her own again. The stroke had paralyzed her. She could talk a little, yet her speech was slurred. She would never be able to do anything for herself again. Anxiously he said, "She has been such a healthy woman, a good woman. Why did this come to her? Why didn't she just die rather than face the prospect of years living like this? What good can come from this? Why would a loving God let something like this happen? What am I going to do? You know I am not a patient man. I guess I am going to have to learn to be patient. But what a way to learn. Yet I guess all I can do is hope and trust in the Lord. I have nothing else."

"O the depths of the riches and wisdom and knowledge of God! Who can explain his decisions? Who can understand his ways? Yet all things were created by him, and all things exist through him and for him. To God be the glory forever! Amen."

These words of St. Paul to the Christians in Rome can be repeated over and over again in the life experience of every Christian, for all of us face situations and experiences of life which are beyond our comprehension. The wisdom and actions and decisions of God can never be understood by finite persons. St. Paul was aware of this. In his letter he had been talking about what seemed to be inconsistencies in God's actions and attitudes. Immediately preceding this beautiful hymn of praise and thanksgiving to the wisdom of God who orders everything for the salvation and good will of people, St. Paul had written, "For God has made all people prisoners to disobedience, in order that he might show them his mercy." That does not make sense to the human mind. That is not the way humans treat one another. St. Paul says we can thank God for not treating us as we treat one another. In his wisdom, he gives us his love in a way that is almost incomprehensible to us.

A son once said to his mother, "I knew you loved me. I always knew it. I never really knew it, though, until I had disobeyed you, and you still forgave me. I guess that is when I knew you really loved me." That must have also been the feeling of the Prodigal Son when his father hugged him. All his words of what he would do to make up for his mistakes were silenced when his father held him and called for the clean coat and the ring of sonship.

God, our Father, in his wisdom knew he had to let his children be free people. He took the risk because he wanted us to know how great and deep his love really is. Maybe disobedience to him is the only way that we will be able truly to understand what his love is all about. God permits us to be disobedient. He lets us be free to make our own choices. Many times we make the wrong choices and do great harm to ourselves as well as to the people around us and the world God has created. God even permits us to turn against him. Yet he is always there ready to forgive, to take us back, to turn us around and shower us with his love and mercy. That love cannot be accepted unless the ones who are to receive it have a free choice in the matter. True love lets us be free to be who we are. As the mother said, she had to let the child grow up. She had to let him be who he is to be. It still hurts. Yet if she did not do this, she would not really be loving the child.

There are pains and aches inside the heart of a parent when a child leaves home. How the hearts of the parents of our forebears must have ached as they watched their sons and daughters get aboard rickety little ships to sail across the fierce, stormy Atlantic to a new land. They realized they would probably never see them again. Yet they had to let them go for their own good. These aches and pains are also experienced by God as he sees us make our mistakes, create our own miseries, face the consequences of errors in judgment, face the devastating results of the accidents and the calamities of our physical world. What a horrible way to let us live! Yet what a beautiful self-sacrificing way for God our Father to let us live!

The Lord our God is the Divine Creator. The psalmist reminds us, "It is he who has created us and not we ourselves." That is a fact we should recognize and not forget. He is in charge. Still the Lord our God is also the Divine Lover. His love is expressed to us most completely in the cross of Jesus Christ. In Jesus God came into the world to show us how deep and all-encompassing his love is. He came to show us that he understands what our life is like. He was willing to endure death itself to show us the magnitude of his love. For God so loved the world that he came in Jesus to put us in our place.

During my student days, I received a grade on my first paper which I thought was lower than I deserved. I went to the prof, who also was my advisor. I explained my position to him. Then he explained my position to me. He let me know I might have been a star at my small school, but this was the larger world of the university and I was not the creme de la creme of the student body. I had better recognize it now if I wanted to get anything out of my years there. I had better understand just who I really was. As I came out of his office, I met a friend and I commented, "Boy, did he put me in my place!"

To this day I am grateful to that professor for being concerned enough to put that brash new student in his place so that it would be possible for him to see himself as he really was, and then do something about improving. That professor cared. He told me so in a rather harsh way because, at that time, it was the only way I was going to hear him.

God our Father, the Divine Lover, has put us in our place. We are his. He has created us. "For from Him and through Him and to Him are all things." How? Why? Why does he let horrible things happen to us? Because he loves us. We will never be able to understand this completely. For who can know the mind of God? Who can give advice to him? Who can explain his decisions? Who can understand his ways? We cannot. We should not frustrate ourselves in trying. What we can know and experience, though, is his love. Whatever I am, whatever happens to me, whatever I do or become, I am loved by God who has given me life. When we recognize and accept this glorious fact of our existence, we can face anything which may come. Even though we cannot understand or comprehend what exists in the mind of God or what is his plan, there is something we can know. On this truth we can bank our lives: whatever happens, we are loved. When we accept this, we also can say with St. Paul, "To God be the glory forever! Amen."

RICHARD I. PREIS
Trinity Evangelical Lutheran Church
Ann Arbor, Michigan

THE TRANSFORMED LIFE
Fifteenth Sunday after Pentecost
Romans 12:1-8

Life Is a Found Fiver

"I appeal to you . . . present your bodies as a living sacrifice, holy and acceptable to God, which is your spiritual worship. Do not be conformed to this world but be transformed by the renewal of your mind."

Mind . . . and body. Here they are connected by Paul in a call to the brethren to live in Christ. It is a call to begin differently with your body. It is a call for a changed mind, a different way of thinking. Paul's exhortation is to something new and different in body and mind. And without doubt, Paul has called for both together.

At least here, in these verses, Paul does not separate the learning of the mind from the action of the body. Doctrine and life are not separate but of one piece. For Paul, Christians who have heard the gospel with their ears but not with their hands and feet and mouth, have not really heard the gospel.

And it is to that kind of "ears only" congregation that Paul addresses himself. The issue here in these verses is clearly conduct and how it is to be formed to reflect a transformed mind.

There is such a strong feeling of independence among us all. We feel we have our own minds and want to do everything our own way. Individualism; being who you are. Do you not want to decide for yourself?

But you are not your own. You have a Father, and he sent us his Son to influence our minds and bodies. He will ont leave us alone. And we are constrained to answer.

There is something about gifts that forces response. There is a constraint to receiving a gift.

I found a $5 bill last Wednesday. I was in Eau Claire, and as I walked over to an art shop I saw this fiver laying in the gutter. Now this kind of thing never happens to me—yet there it was. And I can tell you it did not lay there long.

As I brushed it off and put it in my pocket, I was already wondering how I might spend it. What a great day it was suddenly. A lot of other little things had gone wrong that day, and what a redeeming find this five dollars was.

And then like the dowdy preacher I am, I got to thinking about the poor sucker that lost that bill. What a rotten day it must have been for him. And I thought of a day in Haverstraw,

New York, six years ago when a $5 bill blew out of my car window. I was able to get over its loss, but I always thought, "I hope the person that finds it needs it and uses it well."

And suddenly I felt constrained. Here I was with a found five dollars in Eau Claire, Wisconsin, and would I use it well? It was in my wallet, already a part of me. Would I use it well?

Is that something like life in relationship with God? Born anew. A new life is ours. A new freedom invigorates life like a found $5 bill. And the question is always there: Today, how shall I spend my life? It is mine. It belongs to me. It has been given to me by God. How shall I spend it? Surely I am free to do as I wish. And the tendency is to blow it, to take a fling with it. To be prodigal and foolish.

But life is a gift, given and received like a $5 bill in the gutter from an unknown source, who wants it back. How shall I spend it? I am constrained by the giver. I owe him something. I owe him at least an attempt to use my life well. I owe him a thought or two about what I will do. I do not mean being sober, or serious, careful, or ponderous and no fun. Probably just the opposite. A sense of celebration. Of using up every moment to the fullest before it is gone forever.

To Receive and to Give

Paul said, "I appeal to you . . . present you bodies as a living sacrifice, holy and acceptable to God." We are called to live a life worthy of what we have received in Christ. Oh, yes—God has given us Jesus as a gift, freely. And purely out of grace. Is there not a responsibility to receiving him in our heart? Are we not constrained by this great gift?

For in this do-your-own-thing world, *we* do not receive Christ for ourselves alone. And though we are among people who live for self alone, *we* do not receive Christ for *our* lives alone. We are not alone and we belong not only to ourselves. We are the church. And the church receives Christ not only for itself, but for the world. We are called not only to receive, but to pass on this gracious gospel. Not only are we receivers; we also turn and give away what we have received.

And so God has placed us here, amid this crooked and perverse generation and in this world of sin and darkness. Why must we endure it? How long O Lord? Is it a test of faith for threescore years and ten? I say "No," but an opportunity since we have received, to be the giver; to bring the light of life into the darkness around us. That is what obedience is about. Jesus was obedient to the Father's will. Because he was a son? To be a good soldier? Nay! For you . . . and for me . . . he was obedient.

Bodily Worship

"Present your bodies as a living sacrifice, holy and acceptable to God, which is your spiritual worship."

Now that idea of bodily worship is strange, indeed, for we look upon our bodies as bad, evil, sinful, lusting, decaying. We are more lenient with our minds, for we see amid the sloth and crust rays of beauty and good intent and admirable thoughts, even holy. But the body—we are embarrassed for ourselves. Paul's own body led him astray, making him do that which he did not want to do. And yet here he is emphatic about connecting the body with worship. The unholy with that which is to be holy.

Strange, we say. And yet Paul speaks of newness and renewal. For our bodies, though dead, are alive. Christ died, yes, and rose again. And by his sacrifice for us, cleanses us from all unrighteousness. Is that cleansing for the mind only? No, the body as well. For Paul reminds us earlier (Rom. 6:6): "we know that our old self was crucified with Christ, so that the sinful body might be destroyed and we might no longer be enslaved to sin."

This gospel is most wonderful, for it places us no more in the category of sin and evil, lust and decay. For in Christ we have died to all of that. That is behind us. Though we sin every day, yet it is behind us. Paul is taking this seriously, if mysteriously. "How can we who died to sin still live in it?" (Rom. 6:2). We are not enslaved to that sin, but freed from it by the blood of Christ.

For before God, the sinfulness of our bodies is dead. Therefore we can offer ourselves holy and righteous and acceptable to God. Paul knew this mystery. And he calls the faithful . . . present your body, offer it up to God, give it over. Sacrifice it in this world. Consecrate yourself in daily worship.

Be Transformed

And then Paul places this kind of life in perspective. "Do not be conformed to this world. Be transformed by the renewal of your mind." We have come back to the other half of the whole—the mind. Body and mind, transformed, and made new.

And we cannot transform ourselves. Our tendency is to conform to the thinking of this world. Yet the new age has dawned upon us in Christ Jesus. "Be transformed," Paul says; let it happen. Let the Spirit of Christ transform you by the renewing of your mind.

A future is now open to us unknown for centuries to all but the prophets. Christ is risen, and he has conquered the world that holds us back. And you and I are made new. New because that which is sinful, and cold and rusty, can be let go. Something better awaits us. We can begin to experience it right now.

We need not be tied to what has been, what once was, even yesterday. Rather we look forward to what we have been called to be—no longer a child of the earth, but a joint heir with Christ. It's like playing golf and counting each and every stroke even though you are the only one counting. It's like burning a beef roast and having someone lean over your shoulder and say, "I love you."

For Christians, living in this new age means seeing life and the world from a different perspective. For now what is real is not that world that lies in control of sin and death and crookedness and power. That world is not real. That world is behind us when we are transformed by faith in Jesus to life in Jesus.

Like a dressmaker's pattern, Jesus' life is laid out for us from one gospel to the next. And we lay that pattern against our own lives, seeing where to cut, where to bind together, what to add, what to waste from our lives. Blessed are the peacemakers. . . . Woe to you hypocrites.

Christ—The Renewing Power

But Christ is not simply the pattern for renewal but the power as well. He reveals our sins—and brings forgiveness. He was goodness—and he sends the Spirit to draw goodness from us. He calls us to new life—and died that we might have it.

Do not be conformed to this world. The new aeon has begun. A new world has emerged from the manger. And it is this world that we must now face. Jesus is the new world. And as we face him our minds can be renewed, for no longer do we belong to our families, or to our belongings, or to our selves. We belong to God.

Open your minds to his renewing. Luther said, "this transformation of our mind is the most useful of all knowledge for Christ's believers. And the clinging to our mind is the most hurtful resistance to the Holy Spirit" (*Lectures on Romans*, 12:2).

Shall we rely on our own thinking and feeling and act only

out of our own experience? Or can we trust God to lead us? To change our thinking? To turn us around?

Peter said, "God forbid it, Lord, that you should suffer and die." Peter was conformed to this world.

Jesus said, "Deny yourself, take up your cross and follow me." That is transforming.

Jesus said, "He who loses his life for my sake, will find it." That's renewal.

Enter what is real. Open that which is closed. Think what you have not thought. Give what you have not dared to give. For the Lord waits on you—to make of you what he would have you be.

CARL R. EVENSON
Trinity Lutheran Church
Boyceville, Wisconsin

AUTHORITY AND POWER
Sixteenth Sunday after Pentecost
Romans 13:1-10

Today we observe church leaders, both clergy and lay, who resist "the authorities" on many counts. During World War II, the names of Dietrich Bonhoeffer, Martin Niemoeller, and Hans Lilje were prominent among those who opposed the Hitler regime. In the civil rights movement, Martin Luther King's name stands out. In Africa, church leaders have been imprisoned or banned for opposing apartheid laws, among them Beyers Naude and Manas Bethelezi. Others have been harassed in a variety of ways. Some have led nationalist movements, such as Bishop Muzorewa and the Rev. Sithole of Zimbabwe. Are these actions condemned by Paul's call to be obedient to the civil authorities? This sermon addresses this question.

The Authority of the Church

In today's Gospel our Lord Jesus Christ authorizes his church to forgive the sins of those who are penitent, but to withhold forgiveness from those who are not. This is not the only time he spoke such words. After his resurrection, he said to his disciples, "Receive the Holy Spirit. If you forgive the sins of any, they are forgiven; if you retain the sins of any, they are retained." Some of our liturgical language calls these passages to memory as for instance when a minister says, "I, by virtue of my office as a called and ordained servant of the word, forgive your sins." There's no doubt about it. The church has the authority to forgive sins and to withhold forgiveness. There are few who would dispute this.

Unauthorized Power

In pre-Reformation days the church not only withheld forgiveness, however, but frequently executed those who were not forgiven. Heretics were burned at the stake. People suspected of opposing the church were tortured. This was an exercise of *power*, but nowhere in the Scriptures do we find that the church was given authority to kill or to torture. On the contrary, when James and John wanted to bid fire to come down to destroy the villages which would not receive Jesus, he rebuked them. Authority is always limited by the word of God. Even in the family setting when the apostles call on children to be obedient to their parents, they warn the parents not to provoke their children to wrath.

Authorized Acts of Government

What has all this to do with the Epistle for this day, a text about civil government? It so happens that the word authority appears in this text a number of times and the examples already cited serve to introduce this word. We explored a few of the things God has authorized—and not authorized—the church to do.

What has God authorized government officials to do? What are their basic responsibilities? St. Paul says that they are to approve what is good and execute God's wrath on the wrongdoer. St. Peter said this also . . . almost in the same language. "Be subject for the Lord's sake . . . to governors as sent by him to punish those who do wrong and to praise those who do right." Those directions are at once so simple that a child can understand them and so profound that statesmen struggle with them.

Our subjection to the governing authorities, our obedience, our respect, our honor, our taxes are all conditioned by those authorities doing what they are authorized by God to do. Once they do what they are not authorized to do, they no longer deserve our subjection, honor, respect, or taxes. This means that the governing authorities must put their minds and energies to formulating just laws which will protect good and punish evil and then enforcing those laws. This is called *law and order* in the best sense of those words.

The Situation in the United States

Generally speaking, Christians in the United States find it possible to be obedient to Paul's directions. There have been isolated instances in our recent history which have posed difficulties, however. One of them was the Indo-China war where a large number of citizens, especially youth, found that for conscience's sake, they could not obey the government. They knew this would not be an easy path to follow, but were willing to face the consequences. In an oversimplification of a complex issue, they felt that the U.S. government was not acting as God's servant to affirm good and oppose evil, but that rather the opposite was true. The nation learned from the Viet Nam experience that when the moral foundation of its government policy is uncertain, its authority will be challenged and its people divided.

Constitutional Provision for Change

Ordinarily in this nation, such dramatic protest as was used in the Viet Nam instance, or before that in the civil rights movement, is not necessary. In this country we have built into our constitution a process for changing unjust laws. While this has been an agonizing experience at times, many laws have been changed in the course of our history in an attempt to create a more just social order. The job is not finished yet. Grievances are aired regularly in the legislative bodies of our nation on every level. Concerned citizens seek to establish "one nation, under God, indivisible with libery and *justice for all.*" God has called the nations—the governments—primarily to justice.

Rome at the Time of Paul

Paul wrote the words of our text at a time when there were flagrant injustices in Rome. The 13th chapter of another book, the Book of Revelation, describes this same government. There it is called an unsavory beast which utters blasphemies against God and makes war on God's people in the name of authority of the state. No one argues that the state has *power* to wield a sword against anyone, but its *authority* to wield it is only for the punishment of evildoers. Ancient Rome had the *power* to kill God's people, but like the pre-Reformation church, it never had the *authority* to do so.

Paul's statement to the Romans, therefore, can be interpreted as revolutionary language. By identifying the activities of a government which operates under God's authority as one which approves what is good and executes wrath on the wrongdoer, he leaves his readers with the question whether a government which approves what is evil and executes wrath on those who do well is really operating under the authority of God. Christians in Rome incurred the government's wrath, not for bad conduct, but for good.

Rome's Pattern Today

There are many places in the world today where Christians and others of moral courage and high ethical standards suffer imprisonment, torture, even death, for nothing more than speaking up for justice. Unjust laws close the kind of routes we know for revising laws and repress all forms of social organization which might sue for reform by peaceful negotiation. While many of those who suffer under such regimes have resisted the conclusion that change can come only by armed struggle, they find little evidence that it comes in any other way. They long for a government which will do what it is authorized to do and not exercise its power for evil.

Love's Concern for the Neighbor

Righteous people not only long for such a government, however, but they are called to bring it into power. The final verses of the text emphasize that love for our neighbors is to be our guiding principle. Love compels us, therefore, to seek our neighbor's good. On a one-to-one basis we can do that in all sorts of ways. Negatively, we refrain from hurting our neighbor by not killing or stealing or committing adultery or coveting, to use the examples of the text. Positively we add the constructive counterparts to those commandments as did Luther. We assist our neighbors when help is needed whether physically or in their family relationships or in respect to their property. That is all well and good, but how do we help our neighbors whom we do not know? Some migrant laborers in fields far away, for instance, or children confined to ghettos, or old people who are sick and have no money to pay for services after their medicare runs out . . . how are we neighborly to them?

Love Works for Justice

It is in cases like these where love fulfills the law by working for justice, by defending human rights and advocating the cause of those who are denied them.

Ezekiel understood this. God's words were not lost on him. When evil and wickedness is in the world, we are called to identify it and to warn those who are involved in it that God's judgment will be exercised against them. Failure to do so will bring God's wrath upon our own heads as well as theirs. Giving such warning is no easy task. It requires great moral courage and inner strength. There are martyrs of the twentieth century whose suffering is widely known. Hans Lilje, former bishop of Hannover, who died in 1977, spoke out against the Nazi regime and was rescued only by the Allied victory on the very day he was to be executed. Bishops and pastors of churches in southern Africa have been expelled, harassed, imprisoned, and mocked because they have confronted the rulers and racists of apartheid lands with their sin. Ministers have been imprisoned in South Korea for holding before the eyes of the people the actions of a regime that often rewarded evildoers and punished those who did well. Dissidents in Eastern Europe are frequently imprisoned, often harassed, denied travel documents and a host of, other civil liberties.

These are but a few examples. Thousands are in jail and millions have died for resisting governments which have institutionalized evil, whether it be racism, anti-Semitism or torture. They suffer for righteousness' sake. They fear the powers of their governments. They fear not because they do evil, but because they do good. They are doing what Ezekiel, Isaiah, Amos and a host of other prophets did in another day. They are attempting to hold the state accountable to the law of God. They are calling on it to do what God has authorized it to do, and in so doing, they are demonstrating love to their neighbors.

The Example and Power of Christ

The greatest example of such love was revealed in the life and work of Jesus Christ. He invested himself fully in a calling to service. We ordinarily think of that service in terms of healing the sick, binding up the brokenhearted, restoring sight to the blind and things of that nature. Jesus identified himself not only with these merciful acts, however, but also with strong acts of justice. He was anointed "to proclaim release to the captives and to set at liberty the oppressed" (Luke 4:18). He has constituted us as his body in the world today and has sent us out even as the Father sent him. By the power of his resurrection, we are enabled to love our neighbors and to resist every evil which would do them harm, and promote every good which will be of service to them. God has given us a government which is to be shaped toward that end, has called us to constructive citizenship in it, and has promised us his Spirit for the love and courage we need to fulfill that calling.

EDWARD C. MAY
USA National Committee—LWF
New York, New York

OUR UNITY IN CHRIST
Seventeenth Sunday after Pentecost
Romans 14:7-9

*In Christ there is no East or West, in Him no South or North
But one great fellowship of love thoughout the whole wide earth.*

*Join hands, then, brothers of the faith, whate'er your race may be.
Who serves my father as a son is surely kin to me.*

"No man is an island." No one is a self-contained unit, existing apart from everyone else. Anyone who thinks that they can achieve happiness by seeking it for themselves alone is in for disappointment and disillusionment. There is no blessing, happiness or fulfillment, which is not to be shared with all sisters and brothers around us. Any who think they can find it for themselves alone will find themselves lonely. Why is this so? The Christian answer, of course, is that God created it that way. The shared life is grounded in the very nature of things.

God Is One

First of all, God is one. That very simple statement of truth is one that most would affirm, but find it difficult to live out in practice. That truth, that God is one, was a truth that was very difficult to come by. The progression of time and revelation in scripture is an unfolding realization of the fact that God is one. God, that ultimate, holy, creator and Lord of my life—is one. Until the people in the Old Testament learned that God is one, they could not go on to learn very much else about him. For instance, one cannot understand that he is a just God, a righteous God, or a loving, merciful God of grace until one understands that he is one. For the Hebrew to finally cry out, "Hear, O Israel: the Lord our God is one Lord; and you shall love the Lord your

God with all your heart, and with all your soul, and with all your might," was a climatic achievement for the people of the Old Covenant. Even at the time of Moses when the commandments were given, the understanding was: "You shall have no other gods before me." Even then it had not fully dawned on them that there are not other gods. And the important insights that follow that important understanding had to wait for later times.

All religions deal with ethics, cultic practice, ritual and fellowship; but central to religion, but especially to Christianity, is the awareness that I, the individual, stand before the one. Rudolf Otto says that we, the finite, limited and incomplete, stand in a tremendously mysterious, overwhelming awesomeness before that holy one and this is the bottom line of religion. Paul Tillich talks about "God the Ground of Our Being." He is the source and ground out of which all being comes. As such, God is the ultimate claim on our life. Teilhard de Chardin talks about God being the fulfillment to which all things are converging until they finally find their unity in the one, God. All religions know something of this one God, although maybe not in the fullness which Christians believe they know it. Others may not know that we can call him Father. Others may not know that the holy and eternal one that stands behind all existence is also a personal, loving, and intimate one whom we call our Father.

Mankind Is One

God is one. And there is an important corollary that follows from it. Not only is God one, mankind is also one. Everywhere I look I see only brothers and sisters, so that all the other distinctions that divide us—Americans from Russians, Republicans from Democrats, men from women, rich from poor, black from white—all those divisions are insignificant compared to one gigantic fact; all mankind is one, one family, because we have a common God, a God who is our Father. Now, all history is unfolding the realization of that truth also. It sounds so simple to us; but even we in our day are still struggling to realize the full understanding of that fact. In our nation, for instance, we have been struggling to achieve the unity of the family. Long ago we fought a civil war over the issue. Back in 1940, Wendell Wilkie was running for president on the Republican ticket. He had just published a book called *One World*. It was an inspiring book, seeking to indicate to the American people what life in a "one world" was like. He indicated that no nation can exist separate from other nations. We will either stand together or we will fall together. We didn't learn the lesson very well then, nor do we know it very well today.

Since God is one, humanity is one also. Therefore, any discrimination, or prejudice, or treating one as less than another, is impossible for the Christian to imagine or acknowledge. Poverty and wealth, likewise, contradicts our understanding of the unity of all things in Christ. When anyone is poor, I am poor. We see some of the consequences in crime and social disorder that results from that kind of division. The unity of mankind is seen in the movements. Martin Luther King was constantly reminding us that there is no liberation of the black man that doesn't result in the liberation of the white man also. Slavery enslaves the slave owner as well as the slaves. Likewise, the movement called Women's Liberation. Regardless of what you think about it, the idea is that not just women are seeking liberation, but men too. For that which enslaves one half of society, always enslaves the other half also. In most nations of the world, the question is being asked: "How do we maintain our unity as well as our freedoms?" The crisis in many nations is being resolved by achieving security and integration through totalitarian control, either fascist or communist totalitarianism. Loss of freedom is too high a price to pay for security and unity. Our task is to achieve unity and security while maintaining freedoms.

Ecologically, we see the same thing. "No man is an island." When you go on a camping trip and pollute the stream, those a thousand miles away will pay the consequences. When you mess up the air over there, I am effected over here. When one nation drops the bomb and it pollutes the atmosphere, nations on the other side of the earth will be effected. When we waste the energy and resources in one nation, other nations will be equally effected. And when we in our generation live ecologically irresponsibly, it will effect every generation in the future. "No man is an island." No nation is an island. There is no such thing as living separated from the rest of life. God is one, and mankind is one.

The Church Is One

The church is one, also. I know it doesn't look and act that way. Look around and the church looks so divided. Even Lutherans are torn apart, and Catholics, Methodists, Pentecostals, Congregationalists, Baptists and Presbyterians. But those divisions are all secondary. The church is one. Martin Marty, in his book *A Short History of Christianity* (p. 9), comments on the creed—"We believe in the one holy, catholic and apostolic church." He says "The church is one, according to its own profession, because it is the one body of which Jesus Christ is the head; holy because God has chosen it for his own and lives in it through his Holy Spirit; catholic because it is all-embracing in intent; apostolic because it bears the imprint of the teaching and discipline of the original witnesses." That is the ideal of what the church is to be, and to heal the disparity from this ideal is the task of the Holy Spirit in and through us. We know that the church isn't holy. How could it be? You are in it! And I am in it! The church isn't holy in the fullness of what God intended, but all history is the church striving to become what God already has made it, holy. Likewise, the church is one. Obviously, it is divided in many, many ways, and yet all of history evidences the movement of the church trying to realize in fact what God has declared already to be, his body, of which he is the head. God is one. Mankind is one, the church is one.

All Life Is One

Modern civilization is struggling to move in two different directions at one time; affirming the uniqueness of individualism and also toward a new integration of life. In part, modern civilization is due to our ability to analyze, to break up things into individual parts, to examine them carefully, to study and therefore to control things. Take the human body for instance, the psychologists analyze it in one way, the psychiatrists another way, the anthropologists, the biologists in still other ways, yet all try to understand and to help the same person. We are experts regarding the parts. We become technologically proficient in our analysis; but the crisis of our day is putting things back together again. Because that person we are examining is not a collection of parts, but a whole person. Likewise, we often suffer when we tinker with the economics of the nation, forgetting that the whole system is interrelated.

Division of labor has been responsible for much of our modern achievement. There was a time when each of us raised our own food, cooked it, made our own clothing, built our own house, and so on. We don't do that any more. Civilization is partly due to separating functions in the division of labor. One is called to be a doctor, another a plumber, or an architect, a mechanic, or an accountant. And through this we have been able to build a richer and more profound life. But can we get it all back together? Can all the parts of life fit together so that it makes sense?

Nietzsche, a philosopher of the last century, put forward the idea that all parts of life moved from an original unity to diversity and individualization; but then must move on toward a new unity. From unity, to individualization, to a higher unity. An example would be our own life cycle. There was a time when each of us had a perfect union with our mother, in the embryo of her body. We were one with another human being, our mother in this case. But we were totally dependent on that mother. There was no personal strength or maturity. It was necessary that that unity be broken, and in birth the separation into distinctive parts took place. I became me, an individual, separate from that of which I had been part. That was necessary for all the good things that life holds, but with it also came loneliness, anxiety, and the hard things about life. Then, through adolescence and young adulthood, the person must move on to independent maturity, taking responsibility for their own identity, for their own life choices. This is necessary and good, but we are all aware of the crisis that presents itself. The fracture in family relationships as that former dependent state is set aside for a new set of relationships, independent of one another, causes many hurts, before a new interdependence is achieved. The need is to achieve a new kind of unification, a new relatedness where individuals stand indpendent of one another and yet inter-dependent, sharing mutually in life together.

We see this struggle in a whole host of ways. We in our society have stressed individualism and it has helped us toward great achievements. But we are suffering from the fracturing of some former unifications of life. And we are struggling to find new relatedness and unifications that we may have healthy and whole lives. Our message today is that Christ came that he might bring all things into relationship. "No man can be an island." No person can exist by himself, to himself, for himself alone. Everything in life has to be linked in some way. The Gospel says that we are linked by life with Christ. And our linkage in Christ will be the unifying force to bring together the wholesome, independent, but inter-dependent new relationships and dynamic unity. "I came that you might have life abundantly."

Teilhard de Chardin said "When Christ, extending the process of his incarnation, descends into the bread at the Eucharist in order to be part of that bread and infuse part of his life into it, his action is not limited to that material morsel which his presence will, for a brief moment, fill, but that act is part of his divinizing of the entire universe. For from the particular cosmic element into which he was entered, the activity of the Word goes forth to subdue and to draw everything into himself," *Hymns of the Universe* (p. 14). "Christ is our unity." His intention is not only to become part of the water in baptism, not only to become part of bread and wine in communion, but the God of all life, of your life and my life, our society's life, that all of it might some how be pulled into "The One."

Chardin says that we sophisticated and scientific people of modern civilization made a drastic mistake after we came to the awareness of the evolutionary process. Oh, he accepts the process; but, he says, we understood that evolution was the constantly unfolding creation for greater diversification and so getting further and further removed from its center and origin. He acknowledges diversification and individuation; but, he insists that whole evolutionary process is also more and more converging to a new unity where all mankind can increasingly merge together in their true identity. "If we are to be fully ourselves we must advance towards a convergence with all other beings, towards a union with what is other than ourselves. The perfection of our own being, the full achievement of what is unique in each one of us, lies not in our individuality but in our personality; and because of the evolutionary structure of the world we can find that personality only in union with others." "For me, my God, all joy and all achievement, the very purpose of my being and all my love of life, all depend on this one basic vision of the union between yourself and the universe" *Hymn of the Universe,* (pp. 111 and 35).

Our unity is in Christ; ours as individuals, nation, humanity, church, and ours in the material and spiritual realms as well. For it is all the realm of the Father, the Creator. Christ is our unity. We know that something is wrong, until it finds finally its center in him. For all life is linked with the Lord. No part of it is a self-contained unit. In life or in death we are in the hands of the Lord. Christ lived and died that he might be Lord both of life and death. The peace of God, which passeth all understanding, keep your hearts and minds in Christ Jesus. Amen.

GERALD O. PEDERSEN
Mount of Olives Lutheran Church
Mission Viejo, California

WHAT A FELLOWSHIP!

Eighteenth Sunday after Pentecost
Philippians 1:3-5, 19-27

I have a favorite aunt who thinks that I am quite a preacher. I attribute her admiration of me to the fact that I am her nephew. Besides the joy that she apparently gets from my sermons, she likes to share good sermons with me, especially those which are delivered by her pastor. One such sermon she shared with me I shall never forget. It was entitled, "Don't Miss the Fellowship."

The Reality of Christian Fellowship

Christian fellowship is very important. The occasion of our text finds St. Paul reflecting upon the fellowship which he had enjoyed with the Christians at Philippi. This fellowship of the gospel is forever before him as a blessed remembrance. Jesus is the center of that fellowship. He is the reality which brings that fellowship into being. It is he who makes it worthwhile. Commitment to him led to a commitment to each other.

I am reminded of the Christian fellowship into which I was born. I remember how I traveled all over the world and never forgot the Christian friends who supported me in their prayers. It was easier for me to face the difficulties of life, even the bitterness of the battlefields in Italy, knowing that there was a fellowship of the gospel back home who lifted my name before the Lord.

Paul is ready, if necessary, to face death, for he knows that because he has been faithful in the declaration of the gospel with his friends at Philippi, that should this be the end of his life, that Christ would at least be magnified. What a fellowship! In terms of that fellowship alone Paul can face the possibility of death with courage. Paul is really faced with a dilemma: "to live is Christ, to die is gain." This is the option of a true child of God. Death for a member of the fellowship is never tragic because death for a member of a fellowship is not final, but always provisional. This is the reason that death is only the last enemy, after that, the resurrection!

Christian Fellowship Is Paradigmatic

Our fellowship in the gospel has its paradigm: You will recall that Jesus was near the end of his life and that he was much aware in those closing days of his life of the existence of a fellowship which had responded to his life and ministry. In his high priestly prayer in the 17th chapter of St. John's Gospel he prays for those whom God has given him. It is an interesting thought. In our text we find St. Paul lifting the fellowship to God which has responded to his ministry. We find St. Paul lifting up the fellowship in prayer which has responded to his gospel.

Jesus knew that he was about to leave this world and that the fellowship would be subject to forces and conditions which would threaten to disperse the fellowship. He knew that alienation of the fellowship would be a constant threat, so he prayed that the fellowship might be one: "That they all may be one, as Thou Father art in me, and I in Thee, that they may be one in us, that the world might believe that Thou hast sent me." Paul is praying the same kind of prayer on behalf of the fellowship that has responded to his preaching. Whether he lives or dies, he wants them to stand fast in the gospel: "That they stand fast in one spirit, with one mind striving together for faith in the gospel."

St. Paul's concern, too, is the fellowship as it stands before the adversary. The adversary desires to sift the fellowship as wheat. And God has promised that not even the gates of hell can prevail against the fellowship. What a fellowship!

Historically our human fellowship has not realized its potential. We have not fully realized that "in Christ there is no east or west, in him no north or south, but one great fellowship of love throughout the whole wide earth. This is far from the experience of many of us and yet we feel that one day we will sing ourselves into a full experience of this fellowship. This is a fellowship of hope. It will not despair but in the language of Jürgen Moltmann, it will stir around in every unfulfilled moment and like Bonhoeffer, it will not become "addicted to the way things are."

The Fellowship and the Pascal Lamb

You will remember another corollary between Jesus' prayer and the concerns of St. Paul as expressed in this letter: Jesus prays that the fellowship will believe that God had sent him. Jesus wants the fellowship to know the full story. He does not want the fellowship to think that he is out on some kind of independent mission, but that all he has said and done has been sanctioned by his father. In fact, the decision has been made way back in the morning of eternity that Jesus should be about this mission. John writes in the 5th Chapter of Revelation, "And I beheld, and lo, in the midst of the throne and the four beasts and in the midst of the elders, stood a lamb as if it had been slain, having seven horns and seven eyes, which were the seven spirits of God sent forth unto all the earth and he came and took the book out of the right hand of him that sat upon the throne. And when he had taken the book, the four beasts and the four and twenty elders fell down ... and they sung a new song, saying, "Thou art worthy to take the book, and to open the seals thereof: For thou wast slain, and hath redeemed us to God by thy blood out of every kindred and tongue and people and nation made us unto our God, kings and priests and we shall reign in all the earth" (KJV).

The Fellowship of Suffering

The fellowship would not be a noteworthy fellowship if its belief in Jesus Christ was only an intellectual exercise or merely the assent to some kind of pious dogma. Paul says to this fellowship at Philippi: "For unto you is given in behalf of Christ, not only to believe on him but also to suffer for his sake." The faith of the fellowship becomes incarnational and as it does, it takes on the capacity to suffer. Historically the fellowship of faith has been a fellowship of suffering. It was true for Israel, bound by its continual bondage and yet learning in all of its suffering that the harder the battle the sweeter would be the victory. The prophets suffered, possibly none like Jeremiah. Hear him in his Lamentations: "O that my head were water, my eyes were a fountain of tears, I would weep both night and day." In modern times none has spoken more lucidly than did Martin Luther King. He finally concluded after he had been to the mountaintop, from which he could view the valley of the shadow that suffering can be redemptive and like Faithful in Pilgrim's Progress, he knew that he could not get to the castle on the other side of the river unless he was able to go through the river.

One of the sustaining realities is that our Christian fellowship looks beyond this vale of tears. We have said that the fellowship of Christ is often a suffering fellowship. We have, however, the promises of God which holds out to us a glorious future, for in Christ we have been made to sit in heavenly places. We are encouraged that nothing can separate us from this fellowship. Heights nor depths, nor principalities, nor powers, things present nor things to come are not able to undo what God has done in us! What a fellowship!

Conclusion

The fellowship is a reality today in spite of the alienation and the forces of perliferation which set man against man. The reality of Christ as the Omega point of our fellowship is undiminished. There is still joy and hope in the fellowship, especially when we are reminded to pray for each other and to hold each other up for the Lord. We are beginning to learn that our unity is not essentially organizational or structural, but it is the life that we have in Jesus Christ. May God give us the courage and commitment to face any adversity and may he grant to our fellowship even the joy to know that we have been counted worthy to suffer with our Lord. What a fellowship!

NELSON W. TROUT
Lutheran Theological Seminary
Columbus, Ohio

YOUR LIFE IN CHRIST
Nineteenth Sunday after Pentecost
Philippians 2:1-5 (6-11)

Do you ever hear voices warning of imminent tragedy, chaos, doom or disaster? I don't mean to be a prophet of gloom, but I hear them. I hear them daily when I pick up the newspaper, listen to the radio or watch the television. From a most recent publication of the Portland *Oregonian* these voices of warning came screaming at me from various press releases:

> "Drought damage look irreversible . . . Irrigated fields may suffer this summer, lawns will almost surely go brown, the lights of our cities may dim next fall."

> "The campaign (bombings) will continue throughout England until the British government announces a withdrawal of its army out of Northern Ireland."

> "Doctors told the police the boy had been the object of gross child abuse and said his chance for survival was limited."

> "If no solution links the island's (Cyprus') communities, there will ultimately be a war."

> "Our family structure is being destroyed by technology, urbanization and mass transit."

The warnings expressed or implied in these press releases pose real threats: drought, bombings, child abuse, war, the destruction of the family structure. Such warnings are repeated daily in every newspaper in the land. But have we become immune to this bombardment of warnings and threats? Or do we feel that most, like Orwell's predictions of 1984, really do not come off? Maybe we're like betting persons feeling the odds are good that any predicted chaos will miss us.

God's Warnings Are Predictions

Pointed warnings are heard in today's Old Testament and Gospel selections. The Lord speaking through the prophet Ezekiel warns an apostate Israel who think God's ways of doing things are wrong:

> "Turn away from all the evil you are doing, and don't let your sin destroy you . . . Turn away from your sins and live" (Ezek. 18:30b, 32b).

Today's Gospel is one of a trilogy of parables in which our Lord for the last time urges repentance from the apostate of his day. He shocks the religious leaders with his words:

> "Truly, I say to you, the tax collectors and the harlots go into the kingdom before you" (Matt. 21:31).

A most drastic warning of our Lord is found in the midst of these three parables:

> "The kingdom of God will be taken away from you and given to a nation producing the fruits of it" (Matt. 21:43).

Such incomparable warnings are heard often on the pages of holy writ. Often heedless, their dire predictions were, are, and will be carried out. And here we see the grave difference between warnings from the mouth of God and those from the mouths of humans. "Press release" warnings sell newspapers but are "iffy" in their predictiveness. People know this and weigh them carefully in light of their contexts and biases. God's warnings are predictions of impending tragedy. No ifs! Why is it, then, that his warnings often go unheeded? Are people so sophisticated that they heed only warnings of an immediate nature? Or is it that there is little in warnings themselves that motivate mindful attention? A small child can receive relentless warnings from a fearful mother not to touch the hot stove. One little touch, however, is worth a thousand warnings!

What Motivates Repentance?

What is it, then, that can motivate people to avoid imminent disaster? The certain outcome of all of God's warnings is spiritual disaster. Yet there is nothing in humans that can stop God's predictions from coming true.

The words "repent!" and "turn," often used in connection with predictions of impending doom in the Scriptures, suggests the direction we ought to take to avoid spiritual disaster. When we look at Paul's words in the Epistle for today, we note that this "turning"—this repentant life—is a heading away from disaster:

> I urge you, then, to make me completely happy by having the same thoughts, sharing the same love, and being one in soul and mind. Don't do anything from selfish ambition or from a cheap desire to boast, but be humble toward one another, always considering others better than yourselves. And look out for one another's interests, not just your own (Phil. 2:2-4 TEV).

"Right on!" we say. "What a way to go!" But if we're honest, we must admit that our lives are not devoid of selfish ambition. We're not really making anyone happy with a disunified Christendom. Humility is hardly a characteristic of the racism and class consciousness so apparent among us. And as for looking out for another's interest, how un-American! Not only have we not made the 180-degree turnabout, I'm afraid we've hardly veered from our course.

Dare we admit this much? Can we look at our lives and be totally honest? If we can, we will know that the way we're heading is the way of God's predictions. And that way is disaster.

It is at this hard spot, where, unable to turn from imminent disaster because of the momentum of selfish ambition and pride, our Lord cries: "Turn!" It becomes a place of much confusion. There are some upon arrival who despair: "What will be, will be!" blaming the organized church or whatever. Others attempt to retrench, deviously covering up idolatrous self-love with form and ritual, with "church-busy-ness," with civil righteousness. Still others, without losing any momentum, simply change idols—legalism, biblicism, exaggerated pietism, godless humanism. None of these is "turning"—not even slowing down.

Repentance: A Change of Attitude—A New Life

Nor can this turning happen without a total change of attitude. One's innermost intentions must take on a new direction. And this direction at first is not a 180-degree turnabout, but a continuation of the disaster road predicted by God's warnings. For unless we go down "the path of obedience all the way to death" we will never know the cost. Not knowing what it cost to bring about the change of heart — the new attitude — would surely cheapen the process into a kind of "have-your-cake-and-eat-it-too" religiosity. It would only be a poor copy of the old original. What God wants when he commands repentance is a new person—all vestiges of the old are to be destroyed. A new attitude. New intentions. A new heart. And, what God demands, he empowers us to acquire. The words: *repent, turn, change,* when God speaks them, are Good News words. They are words wrapped up in his power. They are enabling words.

No Cheap Way Out

God empowers us in our repentance to take on this new attitude. With Christ we now walk the path of obedience to the death of all that is old, all ambitions that are selfish, all cheap desires to boast. We *must* walk that road. It cannot be ignored. But we don't have to bear the brunt. Christ is with us! Christ is for us! It is no longer a disaster road because we walk with him, who of his own free will gave up all he had, and took the nature of a servant. In his servant-role he serves me and he serves you. He serves us his attitude, the attitude of his own humility which fulfilled all God's demands, which paid the total price.

Paul in Romans 6 says it this way:

> By our baptism, then, we were buried with him and shared in his death, in order that, just as Christ was raised from death by the glorious power of the Father, so also we might live a new life (Rom. 6:4 TEV).

It is at Christ's resurrection that our turning takes place. Here we get new life. Baptism is the mark of this resurrection-life. For baptism is the death and burial of the old you and the resurrection of the new you. Now you can make the 180 degree turn. For "your life in Christ makes you strong, and his love comforts you. You have fellowship with the Spirit, and you have kindness and compassion for one another." Each contact with others becomes an opportunity to exhibit your new life in Christ. And every contact represents Christ who is found everywhere, even in the "least important" of his brothers and sisters.

People and their needs, their joys, their complexities, now become your life in Christ. Your ambition will be a selfless one for them. Your boast will be in their achievements. Your interest will be their interests. Your considerations will be their betterment. Your motto will be: "God Is First, Others Are Second, I Am Third." This, of course, is not the American spirit; it surely has little to do with humanistic philosophy, but it is life in Christ. Though we fail often in attaining his perfect attitude, we know where there is always more life and forgiveness. We find it again with Christ on his path of obedience to death. It is a way we must walk with him often.

Your hope and mine will be that all whom we have touched with our new Christ-life may together, in the honor of the name of Jesus, with all beings in heaven, on earth, and in the world below, fall on our knees and openly proclaim that Jesus Christ is Lord, to the glory of God the Father. Soli Deo Gloria.

ROBERT KAMPRATH
Concordia College
Portland, Oregon

EXPERIENCE JOY AND PEACE
Twentieth Sunday after Pentecost
Philippians 4:4-8

Last week I was visiting a woman facing great problems which could drive a person mad. However, she had an inner strength which was able to lift her above the circumstances of her life. I asked her the secret of her joy and peace. She showed me a clipping on which was printed the words of Philippians 4:4-8, our text for today.

Background

What did she find in these words that enabled her to experience joy and peace? What was it that St. Paul was experiencing when he wrote this passage? He was obviously in a good humor. He had a soft spot in his heart for the church at Philippi. This was his first European church, founded about A.D. 51, in the early part of his second missionary journey. Among his converts was Lydia, the seller of purple; later the jailer and Luke, the beloved physician, who wrote the third gospel and served as pastor to the Philippians. As far as we know, the Philippian church was the purest and most faithful of all the New Testament churches.

It was now 10 years later, 61 A.D., Paul was in Rome. It had been three or four years since he had visited Philippi. He had not heard from them for some time and may have been wondering if they had forgotten him or if some false teacher had come along to misguide them, as was the case at Corinth.

After all, Philippi and Corinth had many things in common. Both were part of what we know as Greece. Both were important cities on the great northern highway between the East and West. New ideas and religions would naturally gravitate to these cities.

But Paul's fears were dismissed. A messenger arrived from Philippi with an offering of money for Paul. He was deeply touched and profoundly grateful, for he was in great need. Yet, he was experiencing joy and inner peace through anticipation, supplication and concentration.

These same qualities were absorbed by the woman I visited. I believe that every Christian can have a similar experience.

Anticipation

"Rejoice in the Lord always; again I will say, Rejoice" (Phil. 4:4). Abraham Lincoln once said, "Most people are just about as happy as they make up their minds to be." It's obvious throughout Paul's entire letter to the Philippians that he had made up his mind to be happy. "I thank my God in all my remembrance of you, always in every prayer of mine for you all making my prayer with *joy* (1:3-4). "Yes, and I shall *rejoice*" (1:19). "I shall remain and continue with you all, for your progress and *joy* in the faith" (1:25). "Complete my *joy* by being of the same mind, having the same love, being in full accord" (2:2). "I am *glad* and *rejoice* with you all. Likewise you also should be *glad* and *rejoice* with me" (2:17-18).

"Finally, my brethren, *rejoice* in the Lord" (3:1). "I *rejoice* in the Lord greatly" (4:10). "I have learned, in whatever state I am, to be *content*" (4:11). Paul knew that the source of true joy and peace is the living presence of Jesus in the believer's heart. "I can do all things in him who strengthens me" (4:13).

We need to be reminded of this, for we live in a troubled world. Dr. William Janson, president of the Southeastern Pa. Synod, wrote to his fellow pastors:

"You feel it keenly, don't you? The 'uneasiness' that is abroad, not only in our nation, but in our Church too. You wonder, don't you, what's ahead? Where is this nation going? Where is the Church going?

"We talk of peace and joy but we pray that they may soon be felt in some special way. How long will this uncertainty last? But then think of the birth of God. This was in a stable. The last time I was in a stable I didn't think of peace and joy. Then think of the cross. Where is the peace and joy in that?

"Ah, the mystery of His birth and death. In the midst of the worst of life there is peace and joy. God showed us how in His Son. Take heart, brother. He will be with you until the end of the age!"

Christians know that Christ makes the difference in every situation. The things that are impossible for us are possible with God. If you anticipate failure and sorrow you will experience the blues. However, if you anticipate joy and peace through Christ you will experience his victory and the joy of his salvation.

Lela Gordon Chance grew up on a small farm where horsepower meant horses. He loved the team of horses. When he was nine he asked his father to let him hold the reins. Father agreed. Lela stood between his father's knees as he sat in the springseat. The horses appeared larger than usual as the boy held the reins. Suddenly one of the horses threw his head to one side, irritated by a buzzing fly. Lela felt a sharp tug on his line. He has visions of things getting out of control. He looked excitedly over his shoulder at his father. Then he discovered that Father was smiling. His large hands were on the reins in back of the boy's hands. Lela smiled back and since that day he has always felt an inner joy and peace, for he knows that he has a heavenly Father, whose hands are back of his own, holding the reins.

Supplication

"Have no anxiety about anything, but in everything by prayer and supplication with thanksgiving let your requests be made known to God. And the peace of God which passes all understanding, will keep your hearts and your minds in Christ Jesus" (4:6-7).

These words emphasize Jesus' teachings from the Sermon on the Mount, "Do not be anxious about your life, what you shall eat or what you shall drink, nor about your body, what you shall put on . . . your heavenly Father knows that you need them all. But seek first his kingdom and his righteousness, and all these things shall be yours as well" (Matt. 6:25-33).

Prayer and supplication with thanksgiving means that we learn to "Let go and let God" take over our burdens. A woman was running to catch the bus. The driver saw her and waited until she climbed aboard. As the bus began moving, she stood huffing and puffing to catch her breath. She still clutched the suitcase she had been carrying. At last the bus driver said to her, "Madam, you can put your suitcase down now, the bus will carry it from here."

When we offer our supplications to God we often fail to let go.

We continue to worry about the problem. Our anxiety is a sin because it demonstrates a lack of faith in God. Christ commanded us to pray in faith, believing that mountains can be removed. If we really believe that, we will experience joy and peace each time we pray. We will *know* that God is faithful to his promises!

The trouble with most of us is that we are really seeking first all of these things and then hoping that his kingdom and his righteousness might be ours as well. No wonder we feel anxiety and worry. If we really put God first and were seeking his kingdom, we would know that he hears and answers prayers. There are many ways to pray and many ways that God answers prayers.

An unusual gift was placed on the offering plate one Sunday morning: the wishbone of a large chicken. According to the usher, it had been given by a member of the Jennison family. Some thought that such a practical joke was sacrilegious. The pastor was asked to visit the family for an explanation.

The pastor put the wishbone in his pocket and went to see the Jennisons. He felt an undercurrent of tension, friction and unhappiness in the house.

"A wishbone in the collection plate?" Mrs. Jennison burst out laughing. "Oh, how wonderful! I wish I could take the credit, but I can't. As for my husband, well, he doesn't have enough imagination for that!"

Sure enough, Mr. Jennison denied the irreverent deed. "You don't suppose that Lisa . . ." When the child was confronted with the wishbone, she began to sob, "I wanted God to help with my wish." For a moment nobody spoke. Then the pastor asked, "What wish, Lisa?" The small voice was almost inaudible. "That Daddy and Mommy wouldn't fight. That we'd all be happy, the way we used to be."

The parents sat very still. Their eyes were filled with tears. The pastor went to the child, who looked miserable and lost. He took the wishbone from his pocket. "To get your wish, Lisa, you pull it with somebody." The snap of the wishbone was loud.

"There," said the pastor. "You've got the long end, Lisa. The long end gets the wish. And just to make sure, let's all join hands and ask God to make your wish come true." Father, mother, Lisa and the pastor each gave a short prayer from the depths of each heart. Each confessed putting things and success before God and love for one another. Each one gave thanks to God that they still had faith in God and a deep love for Christ and one another. They asked God to forgive them and strengthen them as they made a new beginning in making a Christian home, where Jesus would always come first; others next and yourself last. Later, they made a banner together:

> J—Jesus
> O—Others
> Y—Yourself

At the bottom of the banner, painted in gold, was another wishbone.

Concentration

The Jennison family experienced joy and peace because they prayed for it and because they worked at it. In most cases, God answers prayers by inspiring us through the Holy Spirit, who works through the Word and Sacraments. The Jennisons began regular family devotions. They read and discussed a chapter from the Bible every night after dinner. Each gave real feelings about the passage. What it meant in each one's experience.

They really put into practice the advice of Paul in 4:8, "Finally, brethren, whatever is true, whatever is honorable, whatever is just, whatever is pure, whatever is lovely, whatever is gracious, if there is any excellence, if there is anything worthy of praise, think about these things."

You have often heard the expression, "You are what you eat." This is true to a certain extent. A good diet helps to build a healthy body. However, it is even more accurate when it comes to the mind and soul. You are what you think. "For as he thinketh in his heart, so is he" (Prov. 23:7).

Most of us spend far more time concentrating on television than we do on God's Word. I'm not talking about the media used, but rather the content. Television in itself is not evil. It can bring us many worthwhile things. But what is the content of the programs we watch? There is so much violence. It can harden us to human suffering. The average child will see 50,000 people killed by the time he reaches 15 years of age.

St. Paul knew that we must concentrate on the things that are true, honorable, just, pure, lovely, and gracious, Have you noticed? All of these refer to God. Take time every day to be alone with God, so that you can feel his peace and joy. Our generation has made war on solitude, meditation and concentration on God and the things of God. We have portable radios to prevent us from being alone. We live our lives in perpetual noise, trying to make a fast dollar. No wonder real joy and peace are so rare.

Today, we have been hearing much more about witches and churches of Satan. It has been said that everything that is Christian is reversed. They use a cross upside down. They recite the Lord's Prayer backwards. I don't know any witches, but I know many people who turn the prayer around and use it backwards. That is, they put their own needs and desires first. Most people think first, "Give us this day our daily bread" before "Hallowed be Thy Name, Thy kingdom come, Thy will be done."

St. Paul felt joy and peace because he learned to concentrate upon God: the Father, Son and Holy Spirit. Nothing else really mattered. Thus he could say, "I have learned in whatever state I am, to be content" (4:11). Follow his example: "And the peace of God, which passes all understanding, will keep your hearts and your minds in Christ Jesus" (4:7).

CARL W. WEBER
St. John's Lutheran Church
Philadelphia, Pennsylvania

THIS IS THE SECRET

Twenty-first Sunday after Pentecost
Philippians 4:10-13, 19-20

Paul had a secret. It was a secret that gave him poise and power in the midst of "any and all circumstances." He was a prisoner in Rome. Years earlier he had spent some time in Philippi where he had established a Christian congregation. The people of Philippi loved Paul very much and so throughout his journeys they had helped him with gifts of money. Now that he was in prison in Rome, they felt constrained to do so again. They sent their gift with Epaphroditus, who delivered it to Paul. That final gift became the occasion for Paul's eloquent expression of gratitude to the Philippians for God's gracious provision through them.

Paul's experience of want and abundance, hunger and plenty during his days as a traveling missionary had taught him how to be content, enabling him to look at material things with a certain detachment. He understood Jesus' words that life does not consist in the abundance of what a man possesses. When he wrote the letter to the Philippians he was an old man who realized the truth that we brought nothing into this world and it is certain we can carry nothing out. We must also remember that Paul was in prison facing a death sentence when he wrote these words. He had literally suffered the loss of all things, as he had given up the possibility of a home and of a living in order to share his life in Christ with others. But Paul had a secret. That seceret was contentment.

In our text there is a three-letter word which recurs three times (KJV) which encapsulates the thinking of Paul about this secret into three great truths. That word is *all*.

ALL Circumstances

"I know how to be abased, and I know how to abound; in any and *all* circumstances I have learned the secret of facing plenty and hunger, abundance and want" (Phil. 4:12).

Paul had learned the secret. In his epistles we see how he had become more and more detached from earthly things. In 2 Corinthians 4:18 he exclaims, "for the things that are seen are transient, but the things that are unseen are eternal." For Paul the eternal values were clear.

In verse twelve we find Paul describing the extremes of life. He mentions abundance and want, hunger and plenty. From these experiences Paul learned contentment. This was his secret. The word for "secret" which Paul uses in the original is a Greek term borrowed from the mystery cults and translates as "I have been initiated." God led him through his many circumstances to be initiated into a life of contentment. Most of us are probably middle-class Americans who have lived in the abundance and affluence of the past two and a half decades. But this has not made us content. Rather because of our affluence we have greater and greater wants which we seek to satisfy by gathering unto ourselves more and more material things. We have reversed Matthew 6:33. "Seek ye first the kingdom of God and his righteousness and all these things shall be added unto you." We are seeking our own "thingdoms" first and God's kingdom last.

Contentment is not our hallmark. Watch Christians at the check-out counter or in a traffic jam. They are not all relaxed, but rushed and discontented over the slightest delay. Discontent is our national disease.

We are like the king who was told that he would be healed from his illness if he could wear the shirt of a contented man. His servants went out to all parts of the country to find such a person and after a long search they found a man who was really happy and contented but he did not have a shirt.

Scripture teaches us that we must learn the secret of contentment in our present circumstances. Many people think that if they move to another house or another state or find another job they will be happy, unaware that their discontented spirit is packed along with the furniture in the moving van. Unless there is a change of heart and mind, our situation will be the same even though we move a dozen times.

One of the symptoms of discontent is complaining. We find people who complain about everything. Such people have a miserable and depressing influence on others. Paul makes it plain in verse 11 of this text that he has not complained. In verse 6 of this chapter he suggests that instead of complaining, we should give God thanks. "In everything by prayer and supplication with thanksgiving let your requests be made known to God." We forget that God has not promised us everything we want. He has promised to meet our needs.

But meeting our needs does not mean that we make God an errand boy, however. Some Christians have the idea that when we are living the Christian life our needs are instantly met by pressing the button of prayer and all difficulties vanish. Instant answers appear and doors suddenly open. God will hear our prayers and is interested in all aspects of our daily life that is true. However, he has given us common sense. Sometimes God allows us to continue in difficult circumstances to learn of his abiding grace and love.

ALL Things

"I can do *all things* in Christ who strengthens me."

In this verse we notice that Paul speaks with a strong affirmation of faith which comes from his deep conviction that God is able. He uses the phrase, "I can." Not everyone has this kind of positive affirmation. Many people find it extremely easy to say, "I cannot." For example, have you heard this or have you said: "I cannot control my anger," "I cannot keep from thinking bad thoughts," "I cannot stand my neighbor," "I cannot help at church," "I cannot teach a class," "I cannot live honestly"? This kind of attitude indicates that we know nothing of what Christ is able to do for us. With our own strength and with our own resources we think we can manage, but we fail. We fail because we do not use the strength of Christ who stands ready at all times to share his strength with us through the Holy Spirit. The secret of this strength is to abide in Christ. Jesus made this amply clear when in John 15:5 he said to his disciples and to us, "I am the vine, you are the branches. He who abides in me, and I in him, he it is that bears much fruit, for *apart from me you can do nothing.*"

The secret of facing difficulties in the strength of Christ can involve dramatic experiences. A thirteen-year-old girl faced an operation on her back for scoliosis. It was terrifying. She almost refused to go to the hospital. But when she got there, she felt good about it. She knew her entire confirmation class was praying for her. The day of surgery, she was able to trust in Christ for his strength.

Someone has criticized you severely. Do you avoid that person or bask in self-pity? If you take to heart the words of Jesus in John 15:12, "This is my commandment, that you love one another," you can find strength to love the most critical person.

Don had to make a choice which cost him his job. He was working as an airline ticket clerk. His job included weighing the baggage of the travelers. Certain passengers insisted that he cheat on the weight of their baggage. He refused to do this and so his immediate supervisor had him fired. Hearings were held, but in the end he lost his job. How did he face that kind of injustice? He knew Paul's secret that in Christ he had the strength for the ordeal. God opened for him another job in which he found much more satisfaction. Have you, my friend, found this strength?

ALL Your Needs

"But my God shall supply *all your need* according to his riches in glory by Christ Jesus" (Phil. 4:19).

Paul is reminding the Philippians that just as they had supplied his need through the gift of money which they had sent him, so God would supply all their needs according to his riches in Christ.

A sociologist reported some years ago that at the beginning of this century the average American wanted 73 different things and considered 19 of them important. A half century later the average American, it was reported, had 496 wants and regarded 96 of them as necessary to his happiness. Imagine how many wants we have today, a quarter of a century later. Imagine our escalating needs. It is sad that when we think of wants, we are not a bit worried about the needs of the hungry and the poor.

How does God supply the needs of people? Often he calls upon you and me to help our needy neighbors to help feed the hungry. At the feeding of the five thousand, Jesus said to his disciples, "Give ye them to eat." That command is challenging us today. Mr. and Mrs. Abner Batalden, who spent many years working for Lutheran World Relief as supervisors at centers in Korea, Viet Nam, India and Bangladesh, have this to say about our responsibility to the hungry of the world. First we should be informed.

We should read everything about hunger and the needs of the world so we might know the facts. Then we should change our own life-styles, including our eating habits. We should live simpler lives, eat good but simple food and seek to save the precious natural resources for future generations. Above all, they urge us to challenge both young and old in our churches to become compassionate with Christ's love for the poor, the needy and the hungry in the world. This is one way God will supply the needs of people throughout the world.

Reflecting further on verse 19 we find Paul speaking very personally about God. He uses the expression, "and my God," indicating that to Paul God was very real and intimate. He was not a remote being far off some place, but a personal friend.

Then Paul speaks very positively about what God will do. "He will supply all our needs" (v. 19). What are our needs? Surely most of us have few material needs. Our greatest needs are those of the mind and spirit. This too God has promised to supply. For example, our minds and hearts may quake with fear. If we apply this verse, we can claim God's promise to take away our fear. Or our hearts may be burdened with guilt and tragedy. God has promised grace to remove the guilt and strength to bear the tragedy. Above all, we have need of a forgiving spirit. What a transformation would take place in congregations if a forgiving spirit would permeate staff and members. We sing every Sunday in the Offertory Prayer, "Renew a right spirit within me." Let it happen. Another need we have is hunger for the Word of God. We do not know the Word nor have a real hunger for it which contributes to our downfall. In the Word of God we can find food for mind and heart and direction to guide us in life's decisions. Surely another great need is for contentment, Paul's great secret.

Perhaps your need is for a Savior? In Isaiah 53:6 we read, "All we like sheep have gone astray; we have turned every one to his own way; and the Lord has laid on him the iniquity of us all" (KJV). In this verse God tells us who we are and what he has done for us. If your need is for a Savior, confess your sins to God and seek his forgiveness through Christ. An evangelist put it this way, "Go in at the first all and come out at the second all." Only thus will the "alls" of Philippians have real meaning.

In conclusion we come to the final verse of the text which is a brief but beautiful doxology. "To our God and Father be glory for ever and ever, Amen." This doxology is Paul uniting with the Philippians in a song of praise for all that God has done for them. Likewise, we ought to praise God for all he has done for us. He has been with us in *all* circumstances. He has given us strength to do *all* things. He has supplied *all* our needs through Christ including Paul's secret, a contented heart.

HARALD D. GRINDAL
Oak Grove Lutheran Church
Minneapolis, Minnesota

GOD MEASURES OUR CHURCH
Twenty-second Sunday after Pentecost
1 Thessalonians 1:1-5a

The words which I have just read to you were written to a church in Greece some 1900 years ago. But suppose the Apostle Paul were writing to this congregation, to you and to me today. What would he say? Would he give thanks to God for us, just as he did for those people in Thessalonica? Would we measure up, so that Paul could praise us for our fine qualities?

Don't assume that the answer is "no." Sometimes we get the notion that all the early Christians were fine people but that the breed has died out today. We are captured by the golden age fallacy, the idea that the past was all good and the present all bad. Let's not jump to any such conclusions. Fortunately Paul used three simple measuring rods for the people in Thessalonica and God would use those same standards for us. So without bias or prejudice let's see how we stack up in God's sight.

Our Work of Faith

It seems very natural to begin with the word "faith." Paul always talked a lot about faith and we hear a great deal about it in the church today. But there is a strange coupling of words here. "Work of Faith" our text says. Work? We usually think of faith as something vague and intangible, or a creed, a doctrinal statement. But Paul says it involves work. He is wise enough to know that our Christianity has its ups and downs. Our lives get shaken by temptations and trials. And if we simply sit back and rely on the faith we had yesterday, we may find that we have lost contact with God.

Our situation can be highlighted by a little ditty that goes something like this:

> It's easy enough to be happy
> When life is a rosy wreath.

> But the man worth while
> Is the man who can smile
> When the dentist is filling his teeth.

With due apologies to all dentists, that little rhyme reminds us that we don't always have a good day, despite what everyone says who greets us. There are difficult days, weeks, months, even years for all of us. We are tempted to doubt, even to despair. The parents who lose a child, the young man or woman who doesn't get an expected promotion, the older person who feels deserted by family and friends, all experience a trial of faith. And so the Christian must grow in faith, must work at it, must seek God's help in this less-than-perfect world.

The American poet Joaquin Miller wrote a poem called "Columbus" that contains a fine statement about the nature of faith. He pictures Columbus persisting in his voyage toward the unknown and finally the mate of the ship asks:

> "Brave Adm'r'l, say but one good word:
> What shall we do when hope is gone?"
> The words leapt like a leaping sword:
> "Sail on! sail on! sail on and on!"

That's faith, faith that can stand even when all hope is gone. And you have to work at that. You have to pray and study God's word and seek his help. If God applied Paul's measuring rod to us, how would we measure up? If Paul wrote this letter to us, would he praise us for our work of faith?

Our Labor of Love

But this is a three-part examination at the second standard which we must meet is our labor of love. Really, Paul, you use strange language. Love isn't supposed to be labor. Love should be joy, pleasure, delight. That's our usual picture of love and most of us have no difficulty finding someone to love. Everyone can love the beautiful girl with the attractive personality and a bank account full of money. No one has much trouble loving the big hulk of masculinity who is at the same time polite and good company. And even if others don't measure up to those standards, we can usually have some love for most of our fellow church members. By and large we are good people, even though every church is like the one whose minister said that he had two hundred souls and a few heels in his membership.

But *Christian* love is different from the usual meaning of that word. It means loving the unlovable, loving your enemies, loving people that you can't even like. Such love involves concern for the beaten man along the road, even though he's a Jew and you are a Samaritan. It is love in action and as Dostoevsky says in *The Brothers Karamazov:* "Love in action is a harsh and dreadful thing compared to love in dreams. For active love is labor and fortitude."

So then love means doing God's business in this world, showing concern and care for the unfortunate, the downtrodden, even for the undeserving and the ungrateful. When we sing, "They will know we are Christians by our love," that's the kind of love we are singing about. It's love that must be worked at, love that tires us, love that makes us go the second mile for others even when we don't want to go the first.

The people in Thessalonica had that kind of love. How about us? If God uses love as his standard for evaluating this congregation, how will we fare? If Paul looked for evidence of our labor of love, what would he find?

Steadfastness of Hope

Never miss the last question in an examination. It may make up for all the rest. Many a student has spent so much time with the first part of a test that he hasn't gotten around to the final question. Well, our third measurement centers around the third member of the triumvirate—hope. Paul commends the people of Thessalonica for the fact that they have not wavered in their Christian hope. They have been steadfast, unchanging, unruffled by any outside circumstances.

Now hope is a beautiful word. Someone has said that the most terrible word in the English language is the word "hopeless" and I think we will all agree to that verdict. Certainly the Bible has a lot to say about hope. But what is our *Christian* hope? Simply stated, it is the assurance that all things are safe in God's hands. Hope always believes that things are going to get better, indeed that eventually they will be just right. So Christian hope means that we believe God has not abandoned this sinful world and that he will eventually triumph over all his enemies. This message is embodied in that great cry in Revelation: "The kingdom of this world has become the kingdom of our Lord and of his Christ."

The events of Good Friday and Easter mirror this whole picture. Good Friday seemed a total catastrophe but the disciples should have had hope. For on Easter God showed that he was still in charge of this world and that even death could not defeat sin. Easter speaks of hope to every believer. Of course this hope also involves the firm assurance that God is still working in his world today. The Christian believes that all things work together for good to those who love the Lord. We know that we cannot always understand God's ways, but we never lose hope. Even when our loved ones die, we know they are going to live again.

Now it's easy for me to stand up here and state this hope. It's easy for you to nod your heads in agreement today. But our text talks about *steadfastness* of hope. Paul is saying that these people in Thessalonica held on to their hope, in dark days as well as in bright ones. We don't know too much about what happened there although in the next chapter of this epistle there is some talk about suffering and persecution. But whatever the difficulties, the people in Thessalonica stood firm in their hope for the future. They did not waver in their faith in Christ and in their belief that the future was safe in God's hands.

Now no one is persecuting us, although there are still many places in the world where Christians are being mistreated because of their faith. But we do live in times that may seem to threaten our hopes. The Christian church today isn't growing in many of the so-called Christian countries. Even in this land membership is declining. Moral standards are low and I don't just mean sexual standards. Politics and business seem corrupt and people seem apathetic about it. Even those in the church who should defend the word of God sometimes seem its worst enemies. It's easy to despair, easy to feel that the world is going to hell in a hand basket. Someone once called Jesus the first and the last Christian and there are times when we are tempted to agree.

But hope must be steadfast if it is to mean anything. It must persist, even when all the evidence seems against it. Hope means that we believe God really is a mighty fortress, a bulwark never failing. Those people at Thessalonica measured up to the hope test too. But how about us? If God reaches down and checks our steadfastness of hope, like a doctor checking our blood pressure, how will we fare? If Paul wrote to us today, would he describe us as having steadfastness of hope?

I won't presume to judge you, but I must confess that I'm not doing too well in this examination. I'm afraid God will give me an F grade in all three parts of the examination. I shall have to send Paul's letter back marked "wrong address." And perhaps you will have to answer in the same way. Oh, we all have worked at our faith somewhat, we have tried to be loving, we have meant to be hopeful every day. But somehow it doesn't seem enough. I suspect that even those Christians at Thessalonica were tempted to say, "Paul, you don't know us as we know ourselves. We're not as good as you think we are."

Chosen by God

But there's something else in this text that changes the whole picture. Paul reminds his readers that they were chosen by God. They had received the gospel with power and the Holy Spirit and with conviction. All these fine qualities that he found among them were the result, not of their being such good people but of God being their God, of Christ being their Savior.

And that makes the difference. You and I do fall short. We may not get any gold stars on our test papers. But God has chosen us. He has given us the gospel and his Holy Spirit to help us through this life. We are to work at our faith. We are to labor in love. We are to persist in our hope. But no matter how many times we fall short, God's gospel lifts us up and carries us through. We are never to be satisfied with our own performance. But neither are we to despair; for the same God who was with the people in Thessalonica is with us today.

A number of years ago I went with a delegation to visit Senator Estes Kefauver of Tennessee. We entered his rather palatial office in Washington and were greeted with some crude pictures and childish scribbles posted around the wall. When we asked the reason for this display, the senator told us they were the work of his children in school. They were obviously not works of art but they were beautiful in the senator's eyes because he saw them through the spectacles of love.

That's the way God sees us. We take to him our little works of faith and labors of love and steadfastness of hope and he accepts them and ennobles them. For God, who measures this church and every church, doesn't use a hard ruler. He is not a stern teacher, ruthlessly putting red marks on a pupil's examination paper. He is a father, who sees us through the spectacles of love and who encourages us to deeper faith, greater love, and abiding hope.

So, Paul, maybe you can't write such a glowing letter to us. Maybe you can't always thank God for our actions. But don't forget. God has chosen us too. And no measurement can take that away from us. We are his and he is ours, forever.

W. A. POOVEY
Wartburg Theological Seminary
Dubuque, Iowa

IT'S THE WOUND!

Twenty-third Sunday after Pentecost
1 Thessalonians 1:5b-10

A Wounding Experience

I recently heard a story about a South Dakota farmer and his hunting dog. Now I don't know too much about hunting dogs, but whatever a hunting dog is supposed to have by way of natural endowments, this dog had. This dog not only had the proper papers, but was visible proof of the papers. He was well bred!

But things weren't all that great between the two hunters, master and dog. Endowed with all the natural instincts, the master hadn't been able to discipline his worthy friend. And needless to say, the dog had not learned it on its own. Unable to control his rambunctious dog from running wild in the field, the two were seldom seen together in the fall when the shotgun was taken from the rack.

But still the dog belonged. He had found a place around the farm. Worthless as a hunter, perhaps, but he could do other things. In haying season, the dog was sent unleashed into the hayfields. He had pheasants flying in every direction, chasing nesting hens lest they become prey for the tractor and the mower. As I recall my days on the tractor in the alfalfa field, I wish I had had a dog like this. Many, many times was that nesting hen struck by the sickle blade of my mower. It was in this way the farmer and his dog became great friends. He may not be of help in the fall hunt, the farmer maintained; but by forcing the hen from her nest, the dog saved many a brood from the oncoming farm machinery.

But accidents happen. One day in his reckless fervor, while working the field ahead of the mower, the dog unexpectedly spun on a dime and crossed the sickle blade. It all happened so quickly there was nothing the farmer could do. And lying whimpering in a pool of blood, the dog reached out to his master for help. But the damage was severe. One foot had been severed. Another was left dangling. And reluctantly and sadly the farmer fetched his shotgun.

But he just couldn't pull the trigger. The pickup ride to the vet's didn't find his trusty friend hanging his head dangerously around the cab of the vehicle gobbling up the fresh air as he so often had done. But instead he lay wrapped in a blanket, scared and still whimpering. But the story had a happy ending. Tearing at his bandages and "hobbling on two" for many weeks, that dog survived to become one of the best hunting dogs in all that county. For you see, he had been wounded. He had to learn a new way; not his way, but his master's way.

My Wounding Experience

You know, I've got a lot in common with that dog. I've got just a little of the undisciplined, rambunctious spirit in me. And sometimes I wonder what my Master thinks. Am I proving to be what my Master wants me to be? Functioning as he intends? Fulfilling the dream he has for me? Which version of the dog am I? Running wild? Or wounded?

Our text for today says, "You know what kind of men we proved to be among you for your sake." The language turns me off, but that's what it says. Paul talks about his having proved himself; not unlike the dog. What about it? This business of proving oneself. How legitimate? How necessary? How important? How Christian? Need I prove myself?

I face the gnawing question: "Have I been wounded?" Maybe it's not been so dramatic that I have a stump to show. Nor even scars from the spikes. Nor tears from the thorns. Nor the sign of the slash from the spear. But still the gnawing question, "Have I been wounded?"

I remember the Apostle Paul asking his friends in Rome: "Do you not know that all of us who have been baptized into Christ Jesus were baptized into his death?" That reminds me of the story of the dog. A part of him had to die before he could become everything his master wanted for him. Thus I ask, "Have I died?" Have I been wounded? Have I died to self? Have I been buried in Christ's death? For in Baptism I am immersed into Christ's struggle, a daily struggle, a daily dying. John the Baptist summed it up when he said, "He must increase; I must decrease."

What Being Wounded Means

What people so often fail to comprehend is that this "dying-process" is very much a part of what it means to be a Christian. And as it sounds, it's sometimes not so easy. But in daily dying to self and letting Christ arise, I begin to experience a joy nowhere else obtainable. To go back to what John the Baptist experienced, he said: "This joy of mine is now full" when reflecting upon the Christ. In the same spirit of things, the apostle Paul would add, "For me to live in Christ; to die is gain." Now for a person to say something like that, he's either on to something pretty big or a blooming idiot.

And so we have in Paul a person whose motivation isn't to prove himself for the sake of proving himself. Rather he is a person who's been made alive through his burial in Christ in Baptism. And being made "alive like he's never been alive before," having died to self, his spirit overflows with joy in the Savior. Thus it's not all that strange that the Thessalonians have acted as they have. They simply could not receive the Gospel without also sharing the Gospel. For you see, they followed in the steps of their teacher. The example had been set. But back again to the question, "Have I been wounded?" Encountering the cross, his and mine, opens vistas only dreamed of, the very kingdom itself. So that no longer running wild, rambunctiously seeking my own ends, I become a part of and merged with the people of the cross. Today I would refer to them as the wounded community in Christ, his church. And Paul's words in our text leap at us and come alive as he describes their nature and ours: "How we have turned to God from idols to serve a living and true God."

The Wounded Ones Speak

How good it feels to be complimented! How good it is to be encouraged! It must have pleased the Thessalonians no end to hear their teacher say to them, "Well done thou good and faithful servants. You have turned from idols to serve a living and true God. You have become an example to all the believers in Macedonia and Achaia, but not only here, it has gone forth everywhere, so that when we come to these communities, we need not say anything!"

How about that? Would Paul have the same to say to us or about us? What's happening with the message of the Savior in my life? In yours? Is it only coming in? And not going out? What are we doing individually with the "Jesus-Son-of-God" story? What are we doing collectively with the "Jesus-Son-of-God" message of life? Is it going forth everywhere?

Disciplined to their task, the sharing of their faith obviously became the priority of their lives. The passage of time really shouldn't make any difference. Nor should geography. Nor should anything under heaven or earth. The gift I have received I am to share. The gift of grace through faith, my living it and telling it, should be the priority of my life. Just a few months ago when they were making the switch from 15¢ candy bars to 20¢ ones, my two kids rather happily came across some 15 centers mixed in with the 20s. And because they happened to be broke that day, they shuffled all the 15 centers to the back of the shelf and then came running looking for me to make out a loan. That's not a stupid thing to do! They were simply trying to preserve their treasure.

Jesus told the same story about a man who when he found a treasure in the field immediately covers it in an attempt to hide it. Why? Because he'd finally discovered what he'd been looking for all his life. The story concludes with the line: "And in his joy he goes and sells all that he has and buys that field."

As I understand it, this is precisely the picture of the Thessalonians. It's the same picture I have of Paul. The treasure, the pearl of great price, the forgiveness the prodigal experienced from his father, the 20 centers available for 15¢, the gift of life itself had been discovered. And when that happens, there's no holding back. Only a fool would do that! There's no hesitancy, only reckless spending. And like their teacher, the thought of proving themselves never entered their minds. But prove themselves they did. For that's what faith causes. That's the nature of faith. For the joy in their discovery spilled all over.

Yes, disciplined to their tasks through the daily experience of "dying to self and being raised in Christ," the sharing of this experience became of uppermost importance in their lives. They could no longer run the cornfields of life, undisciplined and self-willed. For this was not their calling. Nor was theirs even a secondary calling . . . a kind of understanding that calls for us to do the best we can. In other words, to be used in the alfalfa fields in partial justification for our existence.

No, their calling was clear enough all right. Their calling was to be heralds of the gospel, to be bell ringers, to be cymbal clangers, to be door pounders, to be letter writers. The best was given to them. They must give their best in return.

From the Wound Comes Power

How sometimes hard it is for me to remember the Easter in my life. I keep forgetting that when I am weak then I am strong. I keep forgetting that suffering produces endurance, and endurance produces character, and character gives rise to hope, and that hope is Jesus Christ, God's own Son. I want so often to be the take charge guy, the unleashed, rambunctious, spunky Irish Setter. I don't want to sit down. I don't want to be quiet. I don't want to listen. I don't want to follow. I don't want to learn from my Master.

Maybe it's not too late. Maybe we too can become Thessalonians . . . with joy in our hearts receiving the message of salvation in Jesus Christ, and with joy in our hearts spreading this message throughout our world. Not proving our faith in some kind of stuffy, pious, legalistic parade, but plainly and simply letting Christ warm us and others through us.

Could it be that God intends for us to be Thessalonians here in Anchorage? Could it be that he intends for us to minister here, but not only here? Could it be that the world is our mission field? Could it be that now is the time, that this is the place, Jesus the message, and we the messengers? It not only could be. It is.

ALAN L. SOLMONSON
Amazing Grace Lutheran Church
Anchorage, Alaska

RAPTURE OR RESURRECTION?

Twenty-fourth Sunday after Pentecost
1 Thessalonians 4:13-14 (15-18)

"There I was, driving down the freeway, and all of a sudden the place went crazy . . . cars going in all directions . . . and not one of them had a driver. I mean it was wild! I think we've got an invasion from outer space!"

This imaginary incident, taken from Hal Lindsey's popular book, *The Late Great Planet Earth* (p. 136), is an example of what many Christians call "the rapture" of believers. In case you haven't heard about it, this is the theory that sometime before the great Day of Judgment God will suddenly snatch all true believers out of this world and take them directly to heaven. Human society will be left in chaos by the disappearance of all the Christians. Then will come the time of "great tribulation" (severe trouble) of which Jesus spoke (Matt. 24:21), after which will come the resurrection of all the dead and Christ's return to judgment.

Rapture Not Scriptural

There are a number of variations on that description of the so-called rapture, but we are not concerned with details. It is important to know that many serious Bible scholars (including, as far as I know, all Lutheran clergymen) find that idea of a rapture completely out of harmony with Bible teaching about the return of Christ. Our text for today certainly shows that any meeting with Jesus is going to come after the resurrection of all the dead, not before. "The dead in Christ will rise first," it says.

But what is even more important, this text reminds us that our pattern of life as Christians would be quite different if we were really sold on the idea of a rapture, as that term is usually understood. We would be waiting to bail out of the ship instead of working to bring it in safely.

We are coming to the end of the church year (which is always a month before the end of the calendar year), and all the texts assigned to these last weeks remind us of how we ought to live with the end of our earthly life in mind. If we are going to do that, we need to know from the Bible just what is fact and what is fancy about death and resurrection. We can't begin to cover the whole subject today, but we'll let the terms "rapture" and "resurrection" stand for two quite different views of how we should face the future.

Resurrection Faith Is Brave

For one thing, the whole idea of rapture seems to view the end of life on earth as a kind of escape. Maybe that's what makes it so appealing to so many. But that's also why it gives pretty hollow comfort when life really gets rough. Some years ago I tried to comfort a young widow whose husband had died of a heart attack in his early thirties, leaving her with three young children. I used the words of our text to suggest that she should not "grieve as others do who have no hope." I told her she should look forward to seeing her husband in heaven. And I was shocked when she said, "That's no help. I can't wait that long." That was when the Holy Spirit gave me a better insight into what this verse from 1 Thessalonians really means.

I tried to share with that sorrowing mother the thought that the resurrection hope is not just a matter of waiting for heaven. Rather it is learning to understand and believe that because of the resurrection of Jesus and the promise of our own resurrection, life on earth need never be hopeless. There is always a good reason to go on living. We've all got so much to do to get the world ready for our Lord's return. I think God blessed my efforts with that young widow. Her youngest son was drowned a few years later in a tragic accident, and then she said, "I want to thank you for showing me that no matter what happens, I always have a lot to live for." That's resurrection faith.

Rapture Faith Is an Escape

Now whether or not we have ever heard of such a thing as rapture, we can easily be victims of a rapture psychology. That's the desire to escape from the responsibilities of life. From drugs to suicide, from overwork to overdrinking, the world seems full of people today who will try anything to get away from a life that seems hopeless. St. Paul might have liked a rapture too. He said, "My desire is to depart and be with Christ, for that is far better." But then he hastened to add: "But to remain in the flesh is more necessary on your account" (Phil. 1:23-24). No matter what theological or scholarly arguments may be advanced against the idea of a "rapture" (and there are plenty of them), it just looks to me like a "cop out," a way of running (or flying) from the real task of working and struggling and fighting to build God's kingdom.

Sure, there are going to be some rough times before the end of the world. Jesus tells about them in Matthew 24. Or if we aren't permitted to live that long, we must still "through many tribulations . . . enter the kingdom of God" (Acts 14:22). It's going to get worse before it gets better, Jesus says of life. "Such as has not been from the beginning of the world until now" is the way Jesus described some of the troubles ahead of us (Matt. 24:21). And that God's people will not be spared their share of suffering is pretty obvious from the way Jesus goes on to say, "For the sake of the elect those days will be shortened" (v. 22). Life is a battle. That's why all the military terms in our text, like the "cry of command," the "archangel's call," and the "trumpet of God," and even in the Old Testament lesson for today where the "day of the Lord" is called "a day of trumpet blast and battle cry" (Zeph. 1:14-16). As the hymn verse has it: "Sure I must fight if I would reign; increase my courage, Lord. I'll bear the cross, endure the pain, supported by Thy word."

It may sound pious to want to depart and be with the Lord, but somebody has to stick around and finish the work there is to do. I suppose it's human to want to escape, but it is neither saintly nor responsible. A little boy earned his spending money cutting lawns on Saturday morning. When he didn't get up until about ten o'clock, his father asked how he ever hoped to make money that way. To which the wise young businessman replied: "I always wait until people get started with their lawns. Then when they get tired and want to quit, they are glad to pay me to finish the job." We see that in the church all the time—people eager to carry the ball, but even more ready to drop it. That's why the rapture sounds attractive. But I'm afraid we're going to have to wait for resurrection.

Resurrection Faith Is Exciting

I'm sure we'll find it worth waiting for. The picture is a beautiful one. "Caught up together with them in the clouds to meet the Lord in the air!" Billy Graham thinks those clouds are hosts of angels. Maybe so. But however you want to picture it, the most important thing to remember about resurrection is that it comes at exactly the right time. Look at the precision. "The dead shall rise first; then we who are alive, who are left." That's the opposite of rapture. No running away from it all. We're still alive because we have something left to do.

And we'll be given every chance to do it, right down to the last minute. And there will never be a moment when we have "nothing left to live for." Percy Knauth, author of the best seller *A Season in Hell*, says that "people who have faith are way ahead of the game because they have something besides themselves to hang onto." They are like the big Texas millionaire who jumped into a cab, and when the driver asked, "Where to?", the Texan answered, "Just anywhere. I've got business all over." As workers for God, you and I "have business everywhere."

Finality in Resurrection

G. K. Chesterton once made the remark that if it were suddenly announced that the world was coming to an end in five minutes, all the telephone lines on earth would be jammed with people trying to call and tell someone, "I love you." But then it will be too late. We won't be able to get through. Resurrection means we have only so much time—not one minute more or less. We have only so much time, not only to say, "I love you," but to say, "God loves you and died for you in Jesus Christ." Most theories of rapture seem to suggest that those who don't make the "ultimate trip" the first time will still have another chance after all the years of trouble are over. That's not the way our text sounds. That's not the way it sounds in that Gospel story about the wise and foolish maidens. "The door was shut," was the way Jesus put it (Matt. 25:10). That's pretty final. "So shall we *always* be with the Lord." That's it. We wouldn't want to return.

Comfort in Resurrection

"Comfort one another with these words"? Yes, that's just what St. Paul says, but how can there be comfort in a rigid deadline? If you're all checked in and waiting at the gate, it's reassuring to know that your plane is right on time. But if you're still trying desperately to find a parking place near the terminal, you can go mad hoping that somehow the plane will be a little late. Jesus won't be late. Whether he comes for you and me by the sleep of death or the shout of the angel; whether we are buried in the grave or caught up in the clouds, God doesn't wait. "Watch, therefore!" But watch and be glad, because "your redemption is drawing near" (Luke 21:28). You won't have to wait one second longer than necessary. "The great day of the Lord is near; near and hastening fast" (Zeph. 1:14).

Real Rapture in Heaven

Rapture or resurrection? The difference even affects our hope of heaven. Too easily we think of heaven as a do-nothing experience. "Don't mourn for me now; don't mourn for me ever. I'm going to do nothing forever and ever." Listen to the way St. John's Revelation described it: "Therefore are they before the throne of God and serve him day and night in his temple" (Rev. 7:15). That hardly sounds like doing nothing—not even strumming a harp or singing in a choir. Serving God day and night sounds like work, and long hours at that.

A great Christian who had given his whole life in the Lord's service was asked if he was looking forward to the eternal rest of heaven. "Who said anything about rest?" he asked. "When I get on the other side, the first question I ask will be: 'Master, what's my next task?'" That's rapture in a different sense. That's the breathtaking joy of being forever with the Lord to serve him day and night in his temple.

PAUL G. HANSEN
Our Saviour's Lutheran Church
Fresno, California

THE TENSION OF NOW

Twenty-fifth Sunday after Pentecost
1 Thessalonians 5:1-11

Rocking in his chair and leaning with elbows on his knees, an elderly gentleman asked me, "What's the world coming to? How are we going to make it?" Shaking his head, he continued, "Best I can tell from the paper and television, it's all about to end. It makes you think about what the Bible says. I just don't know what's going to happen."

With his past dimming and his future becoming cloudy, this octogenarian feels the tension of now. Daily his paper and television show him a now when the cost of living, crime rate, and pace and brutality of life are all escalating. News of droughts, floods, earthquakes, strange diseases, plus fractured national and domestic relationships seems to be one big sign pointing to some yet more catastrophic event.

Could it all be the shadow of the Last Day approaching? The thought has occurred to the old gentleman.

The Apostle Paul's letter to the Thessalonians means more to me as I remember my friend's tension of now. The Thessalonians, an infant church, were feeling the tension of their now. Paul writes that he learned of their concerns from Timothy. A portion of Paul's letter is in our second lesson for today. One should read the entire letter to get the full tone of the apostle's reply.

Paul's Thessalonian friends were concerned over the delay in the coming of "the day of the Lord." Paul was concerned, too, but he had explained it before and the Thessalonians knew its date was the Lord's business—not theirs. They still wondered, though, and their wondering tightened the tension of their now.

Paul writes not so much to lessen the tension, but to encourage his friends in Christ to live in it hopefully. Paul's encouragement is for us, too. Can it break through the tension of our now? This is what my aging friend wants to know. He knows as well as we that the tension has not lessened.

Traps of Now

The final fullness of the day of the Lord is still in the wings of his time. It could occur before this sermon is finished! Who knows? None of my desk or pocket calendars has it dated. Yet, obsession with calculating that day's date, as Paul knows so well, erects a barrier to his words of encouragement. The temptation to calculate is still with us. Ours is a calculator age. Tons of tracts, books, tapes—all offer to help us in our calculating the Lord's time. As a result, thousands of people have chosen an eschatological posture geared toward one date—their date—for the day of the Lord in which their eyes are fixed, calendars are marked, and lives are led. Pat Boone expresses the attitude in these words:

> My guess is that there isn't a thoughtful Christian alive who doesn't believe we are living at the end of the age. I don't know how that makes you feel, but it gets me pretty excited. Just think about actually seeing, as the apostle Paul wrote it, the Lord Himself descending from heaven with a shout! Wow! And the signs that it's about to happen are everywhere.

Perhaps; but Paul seems to speak from a slightly different perspective. Where he stands "times and seasons" are not the concern but where Jesus' words are remembered: "the kingdom of God is not coming with signs to be observed" (Luke 17:20); "of that day or that hour no one knows, not even the angels in heaven, nor the Son, but only the Father" (Mark 14:32).

Paul wants to prevent the Thessalonians from falling into the calculation trap. We, too, are served well by his reminder.

The Apostle also wants to prevent his readers from falling into the trap of frantic preparation. Not too unlike ourselves, some of the Thessalonians may have gotten excited about last things only when they saw the shadows approaching. In that case, instead of living hopefully, we are caught in the trap of frantic preparation. This second barrier to Paul's words of encouragement is illustrated well in Henri Cartier-Bresson's photograph of a December 1948 Shanghai scene.

The photographer captures the panic of several Shanghai citizens in a queue outside a government bank. Knowing the event to come, they hang on to one another. Shoving, climbing, reaching, crushing, they frantically push to exchange their paper money for gold before the Communists take over. This is certainly not a picture of hopeful living.

Paul's advice encourages us to see that we can live hopefully now. There is no real reason that we should fall into the trap of the calculating game or that of frantic preparation if we share with the Thessalonians the birthright of being people of light!

Neither is there any reason that the Day of the Lord should find us trapped in perpetuating and participating in the kind of darkness of which my friend sees so much. We must beware, however, for even Job in his tension was accused of stripping the naked of their clothing, not giving water to the weary, withholding bread from the hungry, sending widows away empty handed, and crushing the arms of the fatherless while the powerful and the "in crowd" possess and inhabit the land.

Because this kind of darkness in its 20th century forms make now so tense for my friend, he asks what this world is coming to.

"Now is the hardest place to live," writes Dennis Reiman in *Living in the Between Time*. He continues, "My mind, my emotions, my soul itself rock with the continual demands, questions, decisions, pains, hopes, fears, that are in me and around me. Now is the hardest place to live."

I can remember well the difficulty my seminary class's interpersonal relationship group had in dealing with the "here and now" of our lives. The past always seemed more tangible and the future more exciting. Most of us would have readily agreed with Reiman's reflections.

Encouragement for Now

Paul must have sensed something of the same struggle within the church of Thessalonica. So Paul's subtle reminder for the generations seems to say, "children of God, there is no need for you to be caught in the pictures and traps of idle calculation, frantic preparation, and dark desperation. Have you forgotten your Baptism? You are children of light! Living in the tension of now, between promise and fulfillment, shouldn't rob you of hope, lull you to sleep or catch you unaware. You are children of light! Living in the tension of now, between promise and fulfillment, should challenge you with encouragement, awaken you to service, and keep you always steadfast and in God's care."

Paul's right, you know. We are filled with the life and light which John reminds us "enlightens everyman." Living hopefully finds us not trapped by our now but living in response to our birth in Baptism. In *God Is Up to Something,* David Redding reflects:

> When one thinks about the prospects for good ever being able to triumph in general over the forces of evil, it all appears as hopeless as the headlines, but this kind of abstraction is an evil distraction from our specific duty. We are to leave to God the saving of the world, and you and I are to concentrate on the God-given job to which each has been assigned.

Paul, too, seems intent that we remember our God-given jobs in the tension of now, building up one another, as he does in his letter to the Thessalonians. This task is a proper response to what God has already done for us "through our Lord Jesus Christ, who died for us so that whether we wake or sleep we might live with him." From our task of building we are clothed in God's gifts of hope, faith, and love. God would have us wear these in our tension of now with a sense of readiness and vigilance as we continue to support and build up one another in love and with hope through the water of our Baptism. Herb Brokering says in *The Wet Walk:*

> Here I am; here, Lord. . . . The mark of your created water is on me and them. We are saved from the deep, from floods,

from death. The promise of your Word is on us. We own the cross and glory of Christ. Your water and word are a Ya on us. Your Ya does not quit. Our walk is wet. The wind of your Spirit is stirring. Keep us saints; keep us saved. God *if* in your Word and water you saved us, *then*, we will walk wet and in wonder.

St. Peter declares:

You are a chosen race, a royal priesthood, a holy nation, God's own people, that you may declare the wonderful deeds of him who called you out of darkness into his marvelous light (1 Peter 2:9).

St. Paul calls us people of light.

A church drama group has taught me that the kind of light one stands in can make a world of difference in the effect of a scene. Our standing in and being filled with the light of Christ when there is so much darkness makes a world of difference for us and the lives we touch.

As I try to touch the life of my aging friend perhaps he can live a little more hopefully with the tension of now. The next time I see him I think I'll read today's second lesson and then share with him part of Bernard of Cluny's hymn "Brief Life Here Is Our Portion":

> And now we fight the battle,
> But then shall wear the crown
> Of full and everlasting
> And passionless renown.
>
> And now we watch and struggle,
> And now we live in hope,
> And Sion, in her anguish,
> With Babylon must cope;
>
> But he whom now we trust in
> Shall then be seen and known,
> And they that know and see him
> Shall have him for their own.
>
> The morning shall awaken,
> The shadows shall decay,
> And each true-hearted servant
> Shall shine as doth the day.

There, God, our King and portion,
In fullness of his grace,
We then shall see forever,
And worship face to face.

ROBERT H. SHOFFNER
Holy Trinity Lutheran Church
Hickory, North Carolina

GOD'S NEW WAY

Twenty-sixth Sunday after Pentecost
1 Thessalonians 2:8-13

God Wants to Get Through to Us

There is always the danger that words and personalities get in the way between God and people. Even as I speak, some of you may think it preachy—just words, words, and more words. Some of you may remember a particular failure of mine in my relationship with you and that may block God's good news coming to you through me. Or some may stand in such awe of "my pastor" that they cannot see or hear beyond my person the message of God's grace and forgiveness. There is always the danger that words and personalities get in the way of God's message of his life and peace which he wishes to share with all people. It's always been that way—it's that way now.

God's intent from the very beginning was to deal with that problem. He wanted his promises taken seriously by people who lived way-back-when. The Bible characters who are praised are people who trusted God completely and lived by his promises.

Covenant to Come Through Priests

To help the whole nation of Israel to live by God's promises, God chose one of the tribes to be devoted to that task. The Levites were given the responsibility of sharing God's life and peace with all the people. An agreement, covenant, was made that this tribe of priests devote themselves to the tasks of all that need be done for God to present his grace and mercy to the whole nation of Israel.

Now, a quick flashback to the time of Malachi. Our Old Testament lesson for today reveals that there were some serious problems among those priests. They did not listen, seemed not to care, did not "lay it to heart," instructed people any way they wanted to, and they were even selective in who was to receive God's gifts. Their instruction was with their mouths and lips, but their hearts were disconnected from the words. If God's compassion came through their words, the rest of their bodies were too distant from the mouths which spoke of love. They showed partiality, they perverted God's goodness so drastically that Malachi had to give them a message of judgment and condemnation from God. God wanted life and peace to be shared with his people. The people received much less. God wanted to share himself with the people, they received priests instead who were far from godly. God wanted life and peace to be shared, the priests shared death and conflict.

Another flashback to the time of Jesus shows that things were not much better then. Jesus is talking about the religious leaders of his day and he warns people, "Don't do what they do, listen to what they say,"—they want to get the places of honor and the praise of people for themselves. People need not do the burdens the religious place upon the hearts and minds of people because they do things to be seen, they do things to get the places of honor, they like to be called "Rabbi" and be greeted and bowed to in the streets. God's plan for his peace and life to be shared with people seems to be going little better in Jesus' time than at the time of Malachi.

God's New Way to Get Through

Matthew reveals something new and different—A new way of doing things to get through to people. Jesus' words are: "One is to be called rabbi, one is to be called Father, One is to be called master." Before it was God coming through priests to get to people—now it is God coming through Jesus! Jesus places himself in the center as the Rabbi, the Father, the Master, eliminating the position of priests between God and people. The real, authentic One is now in relationship with people. In effect Jesus says, "Now you are in direct relationship with God. I have come from the Father to show the real way. Now you are responsible to God—directly through me."

It is as if Jesus eliminates the distinction between clergy and lay people. He makes it possible for people to relate to God through Himself: "Pray to God like this. . . ." "Haven't you read what Scriptures say? . . ." "Follow My example . . ." "The relationship to God is through Me. . . ." All such words of Jesus may not sound strange to us, but it was very different and strange for the people of Jesus' day. It was another of those "strange" teachings from this "strange" "deranged" man that convinced the religious leaders that Jesus had to go. Jesus' talk of one rabbi, one Father, one master was God's solution to the centuries-old problem of wayward priests.

As Rabbi—

As any real Rabbi would, Jesus teaches and acts out a life of pointing to the mercies of the God who sent him. He teaches what God wanted taught. He teaches God's truth, and people who hear proclaim "He is something else!" People recognized the difference—there was an authentic ring to all he taught—as one with authority.

As Father—

As any real Father would, there is the care and concern for his family and even beyond the family. He shares himself and gathers people 'round to share the most important things in life. The healing power is given to those who are sick, blind and deaf and is powerful enough to bring people back to life. As a father gives us life, Jesus is and shares the power of life, God's life, with people.

As Master—

As any real Master would, this one humbles himself to wash the feet of the disciples. As he does it, he teaches and he cares—he wants everyone to know that to be a Master means to be a servant also—strange words which are acted out again and again as The Master becomes the slave to death.

> Jesus is for the religious leaders, for all people then, and for us, the One who makes our real and authentic relationship with God possible. He takes anything that smacks of conflict and death and changes it to God's life and peace. He absorbs all the conflict and death in himself so that the very life and peace of God may belong to us.

Jesus' Way Is St. Paul's Way

It is not at all strange then to learn how St. Paul relates to the Thessalonians as he shares the Gospel of life and peace with them. St. Paul puts into practice the "new way" Jesus had taught and practiced. Paul seems to be very much aware of past clergy failures and he is intent on living out God's life and peace with the Thessalonians. He had been with them preaching the Good News. Words, words, and more words to be sure, but *he also shared his very own life.* By this sharing, the Thessalonians see and experience the mercy and grace of God in a real person and they are attracted to it. There is a congregation of people in relationship with God through a person sharing himself with them!

No Hindrances—

As St. Paul writes to them, he is very careful to point out that there was nothing done by him or his fellow ministers that stood as a block or hindrance to their receiving God's Good News. He is almost boastful of the fact: "Here I am, people. Look at me and how I have done nothing to stand in the way between you and God. Through me you have received God's life and peace."

For St. Paul the "new way" was the language of relationship in addition to the language of words. For St. Paul the "new way" was to take God's promises, place them in his own flesh, and very unlike the priests of previous years, live out the life and peace of God with people. The people received it, not just as hearing the Gospel, but as St. Paul *being the Gospel* with and for them." "—We were ready to share with you not only the Gospel of God but also our own selves." That is how Jesus did it. That is godly.

Jesus' Way Is Our Way

Having received God's life and peace, it is our responsibility to share it with others. God continues to share himself through you —the life and peace God gives us in Jesus is the same we give to others by giving our own selves to others. In addition to teaching and words, it means being the Gospel in relationship with others.

I remember very clearly an author's words which have impressed me, written in 1953: "There is abundant evidence that the church in carrying on its teaching function has put too much faith in the use of words and too little in the language of relationship" (Reuel Howe, *Man's Need and God's Action* p. 73). Isn't it true that we have trusted too much the use of words and have often failed to trust or understand the communication of God's love through relationship. The words of Malachi and Jesus which condemn religious leaders need to be heard and "laid to heart" by all of us. We find it very difficult to grasp the true meaning of the language of relationship as it is lived out by Jesus. We want that relationship between ourselves and Jesus, but the problem is to be in relationship with others so that we are sharing the Gospel with and through our own beings.

To empower us the very life and peace of God is ours. "You do not have it within yourselves to practice the language of relationship, but I will help you with my life," is God's offer. "And

I do not want your weaknesses and failures to stand in the way of your relationship with others. I will remove sin through my Son." God gives us his life and peace to make the language of relationship possible for us.

He does more. We as faithful stewards receive the body and blood of Jesus in the holy Sacrament. It is a concrete and clear feeling/smelling/tasting message from God to us, that we are relationship to God, and that these same human senses we use to receive God's goodnesses are the same human senses we may use in our language of relationship with others. This bread and wine enables us to be nourished so that lips, mouths, brains, and bodies function as a unit to bring God's life and peace to others who are in relationship to us. God's way is always new!

Like St. Paul, we share ourselves, we are the Gospel for other people. It happens through our direct relationship with Jesus from the time we were baptized into his name, marked with the sign of the cross, taken in with God's complete acceptance and belongingness. It happens as we learned through words in our childhood and youth, heard people instruct and confess, imitated the godliness of some and avoided the imitation of those less than godly. It happened by others telling and showing us how to be people of God. It was certainly someone, or more than one, who shared self with us to such a great degree that we now view that person as leading us to God. It is the language of relationship that did it for us—now we are that person for our children, husband, wife, relative, friend, co-worker or wherever we are with people.

God's New Way

As your pastor, I would greatly appreciate more people coming to me and saying, "Pastor, what can I do about my relationship with . . . ?" Instead of that, I often hear second- or third-hand what so-and-so has said or done to so-and-so and that "Mary Lou has made Ruby angry" and pastor should do something about the situation—as if the words from a pastor will solve the problem. I am willing and have accepted the responsibility to live out the language of Christ in my relationship with others—your responsibility is no less than that. I am willing and do listen to the burdens of others and to be in a relationship with them—your responsibility is no less than that. I am willing and do hear people admit their failures and guilt and I always assure them of God's forgiveness, life and peace—your responsibility is no less than that.

God's new way is the language of relationship—we share our

very own selves with others. You cannot do it with everyone in this congregation, or city or state, but you can do it with some, as did our Lord. When each of us promises to adopt God's new way, we will be on our way as a loving, life-giving, and peace-sharing congregation. We become the Levites of the 20th century to show God's life and peace to the people of this community and where we work and live and play.

God's new way begins now. It continues in us until the struggles of relationships are finished—until our death. The time is coming when we will know the perfect relationship—we shall see God and we shall be like God—perfect in relationship.

Until that perfect time comes we struggle. Every false and strained relationship which we may cause at any time, directly or indirectly for another person, has the potential of being a blockade between God and that person—a hindrance to God's life and peace coming to people. However, there is also the godly potential of a taste of relationships that give satisfaction, joy, life and peace—a taste of God himself!

We struggle to remove the hindrances from our lives and personalities and live in the certainty of God's forgiveness and grace. We vow to be faithful stewards of our lives to share God's life and peace with people. . . . To make the language of relationship between ourselves and others as blessed as it is between Jesus and us.

KARL THIELE
Bay Shore Lutheran Church
Miami, Florida

THE KINGLY RULE OF CHRIST

Last Sunday after Pentecost—Christ the King
1 Corinthians 15:20-28

I have traveled across the desert from Las Vegas to Los Angeles a number of times. About 200 miles of hot, barren, windy, gravelly, lizard-infested land is along that freeway. When I have made this trip, I think of people who rode in the covered wagons, or on horseback, or even walked, before this era of cars, air conditioning, rest stops and cool restaurants.

During the pioneer days in the 110-degree heat, it was a life and death struggle. Who was the victor? Was the traveler going to survive, or were the elements going to win? The struggle in so much of life seems like those pioneer struggles. And yet the greatest struggle for survival has already been fought and there is a victor! It is the struggle over death. And the victor is Christ the King. But the victory is not easily discernible to many people today.

Life is a long, often tedious, journey. And we need Christ to help us discover goals for our life. What does Christ the King mean for ethical decisions? How does Christ the King struggle with me as I decide whether I did the right thing for myself and my children when I divorced my mate? Is Christ the King aware of that struggle? Is Christ the King bringing his forgiveness to me?

Paul the apostle wrote, "Christ has been raised from death as the guarantee that those who sleep in death will also be raised. For just as death came by means of a man, in the same way the rising from death comes by means of a man. . . . For Christ must rule until God defeats all enemies and put them under his feet. The last enemy to be defeated will be death" (TEV).

Death in Us

There are all sorts of deaths in your life and in mine. The death of dreams: the dream of being a good parent, the dream of my own business, the dream of my family, my job and being a person who is loved. And it is by man that these deaths have come. We are the killers in this battleground. We have turned a God-centered universe into a man-centered universe. We believe we are the generals. And so we are the enemy that is to be defeated.

We are so much like the characters in Charles Dickens' book, *Dombey and Son*. Those three words in that title conveyed the one idea of Mr. Dombey's life. The earth was made for Dombey and Son to trade in. The sun and moon were made to give them light. Rivers and seas were formed to float their ships. Winds blew for or against their enterprises. Stars and planets circled in their orbits to preserve a system of which they were the center. A.D. did not mean *Anno Domini* (in the year of our Lord); it stood for Anno Dombey.

When we see ourselves as the center of the universe, there is little possibility of conceiving of Christ as our Lord. But once we die to ourselves, then the possibility of resurrection to new life is real. Only in our hurting are we healed. And only in the abdication of our lordship, is Christ Lord of our lives. We must realize that Christ the King can do what he sets out to do. His kingdom can be resisted but it cannot be overcome. Jesus never switched his major in his junior year. Instead he moved through his mission with purpose, direction and certainty.

We, too, have a mission—A mission we do not always comprehend. We are soldiers for the King of kings in the battlefield of history. We are the army of Jesus; questioning defense spending; questioning whether Lockheed kickbacks to politicians are more morally tolerable than sexual indiscretions by politicians; questioning whether people or institutions are more important; questioning whether it is more human to maintain one's image than to show oneself as a vulnerable human being.

There have been times when I have died to my success, my job, my role as pastor, and have become a person who can cry and feel hurt, who is lonely in the midst of people, who trembles at the thought of facing a situation of conflict with a person. These are the times I have been healed. When I have openly confessed my life and laid my hurts bare, then I have been healed through the power and grace of Jesus Christ, as his people live his Word.

Life for Us

No matter where you are struggling in the battleground of life, remember that Christ is the King. He helps us in all situations; he fights at our side. He calls us his children so we can declare him as our Lord. But the decisive battle has already been won because of the victory of Christ the King over death. That victory is what makes our battles endurable. It gives us strength and encouragement. For Christ was the first to live beyond death, and he shows us that this is what God has in store for us. For we are his people, the Baptized people in his name. The resurrection is real. I trust that it is real. I believe that it is real. And that makes my momentary fears of death fade away.

Death is not the end, because Christ is the King! He is the King over death. He is the King of the universe. He has defeated the last enemy. And he has done it all for us! Thanks be to God!

RAYMOND D. CHRISTENSON
Community Lutheran Church
Las Vegas, Nevada

THANKS — AND NO THANKS

A Day of Thanksgiving

1 Timothy 2:1-4

Today is Thanksgiving. Thanksgiving is a typical American festival. It has historical and religious roots, it has traditions and myths, it has family customs, community attitudes, and many memories—most of them pleasant. These roots and traditions have evolved during our 200-year history. They began by exalting God, but now many holiday practices almost obscure God's part in our day-by-day blessings. Many people refer to this holiday not as Thanksgiving but as "Turkey Day." The cry in mid-century was, "Put Christ back into Christmas." The cry today perhaps ought to be, "Put thanks back into Thanksgiving."

A New Humanism

We are about to enter a humanistic period. The last one we went through was in the '30s. Hitler's Third Reich and Roosevelt's New Deal were both grounded in the theory that society was improvable because people were improvable. With new socialistic attitudes, the Western world began to nurse itself back to economic health after the depression.

It was only economic health. Our world was spiritually and morally sick; its cancers became apparent in World War II crimes and atrocities, and sent us spinning into a postwar period of penitence and spiritual reevaluation. Many people looked in the mirror and saw what Luther called "lost and condemned creatures." People were reminded that they could only be bought and freed with the blood of Jesus.

Humanism is not new. There is latent humanism in Paul's letter to Timothy. Paul calls for a better world, here and now. What keeps his challenge from being like the 1930's humanism is that Paul invites Timothy to *expect* God to make the changes in response to prayer. Paul admonishes Timothy to use prayer for human improvement. The result to be expected when people live under God's rule is a peaceful life, Godly and respectful.

Paul says God likes it when we live peaceable lives. Perhaps the mention of God's desire that all people be saved is connected with a quiet and peaceable life. Did Paul believe that a peaceful society was the best seedbed for spreading the faith? Do you believe it?

If that were true, then the American 1950s were God's prime time. As a result of postwar penitence, Americans joined the church in great flocks. They were responding to their loss of humanistic hope and their shock over a world war. The spiritual search was on.

But the real church may never have been weaker in recent history. There is always danger in measuring the strength of an organization in numbers. The church was probably strongest when it had 11 members with tongues of fire over their heads. The breakdown of our society has roots deep in the established church, in the booming institutional church of the 1950s.

Containing communism, for instance, became a hallmark of the mid-century church. Communism was the enemy and whatever measures were necessary to contain it had to be OK. With communism as enemy number one, we could forget about our traditional enemies: sin, death, and the power of Satan. But Viet Nam was not OK. Neither were some of the washtub economic and political and moral attitudes winked at by the thriving church. A church, a generation nurtured on humanism left our whole nation shaken to the core.

Prophets: An Endangered Species?

What has this to do with Thanksgiving week? Why muck up our nice family feelings, our cozy thankfulness with politics and history? Because politics, history, and religion are the stuff of thanksgiving in any year. God is still in his heaven and all is not right with the world. Politicians, historians, and men and women of religion, today's prophets, *care* that all is not right with the world. A national holiday is an ideal time for Christians to look at their nation, to look at their church with the prophetic eye, with the keen eye of an Isaiah or an Amos. With such eyes we should look at our age—and then with a sharp tongue cut it up for easy chewing.

There were prophets and martyrs in Hitler's Germany who cried "look," who cried "turn back"—but too few were willing to look and to turn back. By the time the numbers grew, it was too late, there was no turning back. As Hitler and his Nazi party made their bid for the world, comfortable Christians drank their tea and read in the book, "What does it profit a man . . ." We dare not come to that point a second time. We dare not let our prophets become an endangered species.

We may not be anywhere near the situation in Hitler's prewar Germany, but similar pressures are building in our society. A gulf has been building between the commoners and kings. The prophets of the church, the prophets on the campus, the prophets of the printed page are telling us that the commoners are experiencing poverty and unemployment while the kings eat caviar. You couple that with forecasts of a dry season coming on—and visions of dust bowls dance like sugar plums around the Thanksgiving turkey. We may be in for it—like the lines from Robert Frost's "Once by the Pacific":

> It looked as if a night of dark intent
> Was coming, and not only a night, an age.
> Someone had better be prepared for rage.

Being prepared for rage is being ready for struggle and persecution. Peaceable times are not the best for the Christian gospel. The 11 disciples were the strong beginning of the church, and the church's next strong time was under Roman persecution. Christians who faced lions because of their faith were strong Christians. Medieval martyrs were strong. Luther was strong. Conscientious Christians in Nazi Germany were strong. Many Christians in Russia, Eastern Europe, and Red China are strong. Persecution made and makes all of these Christians strong. Like a Darwinian purge, persecution weeds out the faithless and leaves the fittest. The Arabs and Egyptians learned that when they waged war on the people of Israel who had survived 10 years of European hell. Persecution strengthens.

If the Going Gets Tough

As we face this Thanksgiving, perhaps we are looking ahead to tougher times, to times when commoner and king will not be so widely separated. If we were not so middle class in our values, we could kneel and pray for persecution, for trial, for tougher times. The gospel of Jesus thrives on tough going. It may be that because God desires all men to be saved and come to the knowledge of the truth, he will lay his testing hand upon our nation—perhaps upon our world. God help us if we, the most blessed and the least thankful of all people, are not prepared.

"Shall we receive good at the hand of God, and shall we not receive evil?" Job said. "The Lord gives," said Job, "and the Lord takes away. Blessed be the name of the Lord."

> ... a night of dark intent
> Is coming, and not only a night, an age.
> Someone had better be prepared for rage.

STEVE SWANSON
Dennison Parish
Dennison, Minnesota